Microsoft®

WORKS FOR
WINDOWS 95

Step by Step

Other titles in the *Step by Step* series:

Microsoft®

WORKS FOR
WINDOWS 95

Step by Step

COMPUTERPREP
A Drake International Company

Microsoft Press

PUBLISHED BY
Microsoft Press
A Division of Microsoft Corporation
One Microsoft Way
Redmond, Washington 98052-6399

Library of Congress Cataloging-in-Publication Data
Microsoft Works for Windows 95 step by step / ComputerPREP, Inc.
      p.   cm.
   Includes index.
   ISBN 1-55615-881-5
    1. Microsoft Works for Windows.   2. Microsoft Windows 95.
  I. ComputerPREP, Inc.
  QA76.76.I57M523 1995
  650'.0285'5369--dc20   95-33019
                                         CIP

Printed and bound in the United States of America.

1 2 3 4 5 6 7 8 9 QMQM 9 8 7 6 5

Distributed to the book trade in Canada by Macmillan of Canada, a division of Canada
Publishing Corporation.

A CIP catalogue record for this book is available from the British Library.

Microsoft Press books are available through booksellers and distributors worldwide. For further
information about international editions, contact your local Microsoft Corporation office. Or
contact Microsoft Press International directly at fax (206) 936-7329.

For ComputerPREP, Inc.
Project Manager: Stephanie Karabets
Project Editor: Victoria Fodale
Associate Editors: Mary Millhollon Taylor and Phil Shanks
Production and Graphics Assistants: Teri Bagley and Jeff Castrina
Writer: James S. Downes

For Microsoft Press
Acquisitions Editor: Casey D. Doyle
Project Editor: Laura Sackerman

ComputerPREP, Inc. & Microsoft Press

Microsoft Works for Windows 95 Step by Step has been created by the professional trainers and writers at ComputerPREP, Inc., to the exacting standards you've come to expect from Microsoft Press. Together, we are pleased to present this self-paced training guide, which you can use individually or as part of a class.

ComputerPREP produces a variety of software training courseware for corporations, educational institutions, learning centers, and government agencies. ComputerPREP's three-phased training approach utilizes each student's previous knowledge to set learning expectations, introduces new software functions in easily understandable steps, and then helps apply evolved skills to real-world scenarios. *Microsoft Works for Windows 95 Step by Step* incorporates ComputerPREP's years of training experience to ensure that you'll receive the maximum return on your training time. You'll focus on the skills that increase productivity the most while working at your own pace and convenience.

Microsoft Press is the independent—and independent-minded—book publishing division of Microsoft Corporation. The leading publisher of information on Microsoft software, Microsoft Press is dedicated to providing the highest quality end-user training, reference, and technical books that make using Microsoft software easier, more enjoyable, and more productive.

Contents at a Glance

Table of Contents

Table of Contents

Table of Contents

*Quick*Look Guide

Using WordArt, see
"One Step Further: Using WordArt,"
page 88 (Lesson 4)

Inserting graphics in documents, see "Adding Graphics to a Document," page 83 (Lesson 4)

Inserting database fields for form letters, see "Creating Form Letters," page 96 (Lesson 5)

Creating bulleted lists, see "Add bullets," page 72 (Lesson 4)

Creating and formatting tables, see "Insert a Table," page 74 (Lesson 4)

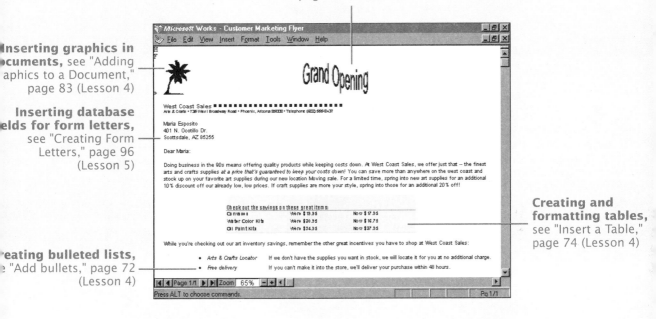

Emphasizing text, see "Changing the font size and font style of text entries," page 184 (Lesson 7)

Using EasyCalc to create formulas, see "Use EasyCalc," page 174 (Lesson 7)

Using shading for emphasis, see "Add shading," page 187 (Lesson 7)

Using different number formats, see "Change number formats," page 181 (Lesson 7)

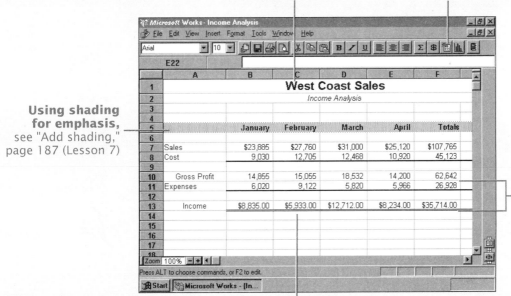

Using borders for definition, see "Add borders," page 186 (Lesson 7)

Making charts more informative, see "Add data labels," page 206 (Lesson 8)

Inserting charts into documents, see "Inserting a Chart Into Another Document," page 216 (Lesson 8)

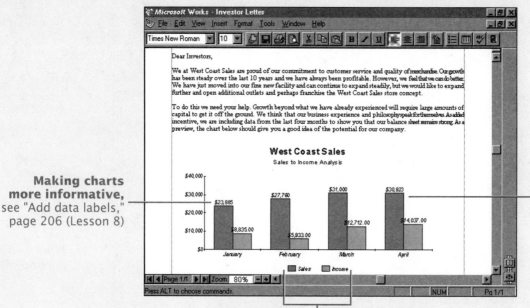

Formatting legends, see "Add a legend label," page 205 (Lesson 8)

Creating drawings with Microsoft Draw, see "Adding a Drawing Object to Your Database Form," page 246 (Lesson 10)

Creating stylish labels, see "Add shading," page 245 (Lesson 10)

Adding new database fields, see "Insert a field," page 43 (Lesson 3)

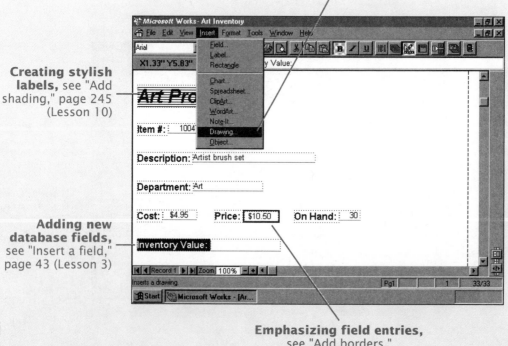

Emphasizing field entries, see "Add borders," page 244 (Lesson 10)

About This Book

In "About This Book" you will learn:

- How to best work through the lessons in this book, based on your experience.
- How to use this book as a classroom aid.
- What the terms and notational conventions used in this book mean.
- Where to find additional information about how to use Microsoft Works.

Microsoft Works for Windows 95 is an integrated software package for the Windows 95 operating system. It includes word processor, spreadsheet, database, and communications tools. You can use these tools independently or together to create flexible, professional-looking documents. Works also includes accessories such as a drawing application (Microsoft Draw), a graphics application (Clip Art), and an application for creating text objects with special effects (WordArt).

Microsoft Works for Windows 95 Step by Step shows you how to use the most popular features of Works in the easiest and most efficient methods. You can use the book as a self-paced tutorial or as a classroom teaching aid.

The disk located inside the back cover of this book contains practice files you will use to complete hands-on exercises in each lesson. The "Getting Ready" section of this book has instructions for copying these files to your computer's hard disk.

Finding Your Best Starting Point

This book is designed primarily for new users of Microsoft Works for Windows 95. It is divided into four parts, each containing exercises that you can work through independently of the other parts.

■ Part 1 provides a quick tour of the Word Processor, Spreadsheet, and Database. You learn how to create new documents and open existing documents in each of the three tools. You also learn basic skills for each tool, such as copying and moving data, adding text and numbers, and deleting entries.

■ Part 2 focuses on the Word Processor and how you can use it to create common business documents. You learn how to create, format, and enhance documents; how to create form letters; and how to use TaskWizards to create matching labels and envelopes. You also learn how to easily update a document by linking spreadsheet data to a Word Processor document.

■ Part 3 shows you how to illustrate and communicate information using the Spreadsheet and Communications tools. You learn how to create and modify spreadsheets and charts, how to use and customize templates created from TaskWizards, and how to use the Communications tool to connect to bulletin boards, online information services, and other computers using a modem. You also find out how to send and receive information and how to record and play back scripts.

■ Part 4 shows you how to track and manipulate information with the Database. You learn how to modify, enhance, and extract specific information from databases; how to add database information to a Word Processor document; how to convert database information into a spreadsheet; and how to create and modify database reports.

The lessons in the book progress in complexity. Part 1 presents basic concepts to help you become comfortable with using the tools. The lessons in the remaining parts cover more complex concepts and methods for using the tools to their full potential.

At the end of each lesson is a lesson summary. If some of the topics listed in the summary are unfamiliar, you can work through the sections of the lesson that pertain to those topics. If many of the topics are unfamiliar, you can work through the entire lesson.

If you are new to Microsoft Works for Windows 95, or to computers in general, you should start with Lesson 1 and progress through the lessons sequentially. If you are familiar with Works, or if you want to learn about a particular Works tool, you can start with the part of the book that covers that tool first.

The following table can help you choose an appropriate starting point.

If you are	Follow these steps
New to using a computer or to using Microsoft Windows 95	Read the "Getting Ready" section of this book and follow the instructions for copying the practice files to your computer's hard disk. Pay special attention to the sections "If You Are New to Microsoft Windows 95" and "If You Are New to Using a Mouse." Next, work through the parts of the book and the lessons sequentially.
Familiar with using Microsoft Windows 95, but new to using Microsoft Works for Windows 95	Read the "Getting Ready" section of this book and copy the practice files to your computer's hard disk. Next, work through the parts of the book in any order, but work through the lessons in each part in numerical order.
Familiar with using word processor, spreadsheet, database, or communications applications	Follow the instructions in the "Getting Ready" section of this book to copy the practice files to your computer's hard disk. Next, find the part of the book that covers the tool you want to learn about, and then work through the lessons in that part in any order.
Experienced with Microsoft Works for Windows 95	Read the "Getting Ready" section of this book and copy the practice files to your computer's hard disk. Work through the parts and lessons of the book in any order.

Using This Book as a Classroom Aid

If you are an instructor, you can use *Microsoft Works for Windows 95 Step by Step* as a classroom aid while teaching your course. You might want to use selected lessons as a supplement to your own curriculum or you can use this book as a complete training manual.

If you choose to teach all of the lessons in this book, you should allocate two days of classroom time to present the lessons, answer questions, and incorporate any customized exercises.

Conventions Used In This Book

To ensure that your learning is optimized, it is important that you understand the terms and conventions used in this book before you begin any of the lessons.

Procedural Conventions

- Each exercise is presented as a series of consecutively numbered steps, beginning with the number 1. An arrowhead bullet ➤ indicates that an exercise contains only one step.

- The word "click" is used when you are to execute a command from a menu or a dialog box; highlight folders, filenames, or text blocks; and select options in a dialog box.

Notational Conventions

- Text that you need to type appears in bold type. No ending punctuation is included unless it is part of the text you are typing. For example, "Type **Thanks in advance for your cooperation.**"

- Important terms appear in italic type when they are first defined; for example, "A *header* is information that prints at the top of every page."

Keyboard Conventions

- Names of keyboard keys that you are to press appear in small capital letters; for example, "Press TAB."

- When a plus sign (+) appears between two or more key names, press the keys at the same time. For example, "Press SHIFT+TAB means that you press the TAB key while holding down the SHIFT key.

Other Features of This Book

- Text in the left margin provides additional information about the task you are learning or directs you to related information in other sections of the book.

- The One Step Further exercise at the end of each lesson presents additional techniques or options related to the skills you learned in the lesson.

- The Lesson Summary at the end of each lesson lists the skills you have learned and briefly reviews how to accomplish key tasks.

- The Review & Practice exercise at the end of each part of the book reinforce the skills presented in that part. Each exercise ends with a reference table that shows you which lesson you can refer to for information about the skills reviewed in that exercise.

Paste

- Pictures of toolbar buttons that you are instructed to click during a lesson exercise appear in the left page margin, as the Paste button does here. Each tool in Works contains a toolbar with buttons you can click to perform tasks.

- The Appendix, "Matching the Exercises," shows you the Works options and settings used in this book. If your screens do not match the illustrations shown in the lesson exercises, or if your exercise results are different than those presented in the book, you can refer to this appendix to see if your settings or options need to be changed.

Cross References to the Online Help System

Each lesson ends with a table that lists the major topics presented and cross references to those topics in the Works online Help system. Some margin notes in the lessons may also direct you to the Help system. In the Help system, you will find information about all the Works features, various ways you can use those features, and sometimes on-screen demonstrations as well. You will get a more in-depth look at the Help system in the "Getting Ready" section of this book.

Getting Ready

In "Getting Ready" you will learn how to:

- Install the practice files on your hard disk.
- Start Microsoft Windows 95.
- Start Microsoft Works.
- Explore the window, menu, and dialog box components of Windows 95.
- Use the online Help system in Works.

This section tells you how to install the practice files that are included with this book. It also presents the basic skills required to start using Works and an overview of Windows 95 concepts.

If Windows 95 and Works are not both installed on your computer, you'll need to install them before you begin the lessons in this book. To install Windows 95, refer to your Windows 95 documentation. To install Works, refer to your Works documentation.

 IMPORTANT Do not break the seal on the practice disk envelope in the back of this book until you verify that you have the correct version of the software. This book was written for Microsoft Works 4, which runs on the Windows 95 operating system. Check the software documentation or product packaging to determine which software you are using.

Installing the Practice Files

If you've never used a mouse, read the section "If You Are New to Using a Mouse" before you install the practice files.

All the practice files you'll use with this book are contained on a disk named "Practice Files for Microsoft Works for Windows 95 Step by Step," located inside the back cover. You will use the practice files to perform the tasks you learn in each lesson. For example, the lesson that teaches you how to enter numbers into a spreadsheet instructs you to open one of the practice files—a partially completed spreadsheet—and enter numbers into it. Before you can complete the exercises in the book, you'll need to copy the practice files to your hard disk.

Copy the practice files to your hard disk

1   Turn on your computer if it isn't already on.

Windows 95 starts and the desktop appears.

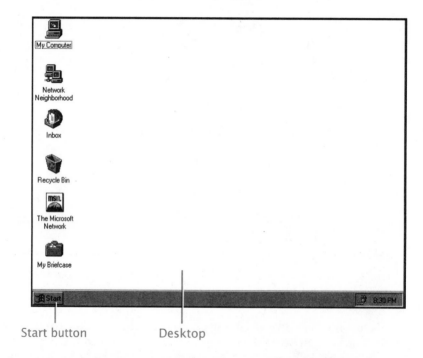

Start button   Desktop

2   Remove the practice files disk from the package inside the back cover of this book, and insert the disk into drive A or drive B of your computer.

3   Click the Start button at the bottom of your screen.

4   On the Start menu, click Run.

...and then
click Run

Click the
Start button...

5 In the Run dialog box, type **a:setup** (or **b:setup** if the practice files disk is in drive B), and then click the OK button. Do not type any spaces in the command.

6 Follow the directions that appear on your screen.

The setup program window appears, displaying recommended options. To achieve the best results when using the practice files, accept the recommended options.

7 After the files are copied, remove the practice files disk from your computer and replace it in the envelope on the inside cover of the book.

The setup program on the practice files disk has copied the files to your hard disk and placed them in a folder named Works SBS Practice. You will open the Works SBS Practice folder whenever you open a practice file. When it is time to use a practice file in a lesson, the book will list instructions for how to open the file.

Lesson Background

The exercises in this book are based on the following scenario: You are the owner of a small arts and crafts supply company named West Coast Sales. In the past two years your store has been very successful, and you are now preparing to move to a new, larger location. You are also preparing to offer new services to your clients, such as a volume discount program, a way to order by phone or fax, and arts and crafts classes in your store. As you prepare for the move, you will use Works to create advertising flyers, form letters to customers, and financial analyses for your bank and for prospective investors. You'll also use Works to keep a database of client names and addresses and an easily updated inventory database.

Starting Microsoft Windows 95 and Microsoft Works

The following procedures show you how to start Windows 95, if it isn't already running, and how to start Works. Depending on how your computer is set up, your screen may look different than the screens shown in the following illustrations. For more information about Windows 95, see your Microsoft Windows 95 documentation.

Start Windows 95

To start Windows 95, you simply need to turn on your computer.

> If your computer isn't already on, turn it on now. If you usually enter a user name or password, you will be prompted to type it. If you see the Welcome dialog box, click the Close button or press ENTER.

The Windows 95 desktop should now appear.

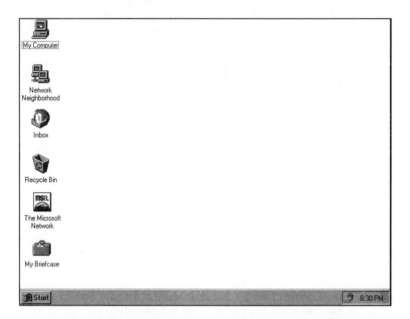

The desktop is a central location from which you can start any Windows 95-based applications loaded on your computer. At the bottom of the desktop is the *taskbar*, which you can click to open menus to select programs you want to start. Depending on how applications are loaded onto your computer, the desktop may also contain icons called *shortcuts*, which you can double-click with the mouse to start applications. You will learn more about the taskbar and how to use the mouse in the sections "If You Are New to Microsoft Windows 95" and "If You Are New to Using A Mouse," which appear later in this section.

Start Works

1 Click the Start button, point to Programs, point to Microsoft Works 4.0, and then click Microsoft Works 4.0.

The Works Task Launcher dialog box appears.

Shortcut to
Microsoft
Works 4.0

 NOTE If the Shortcut to Microsoft Works 4.0 icon is on your desktop, you can double-click it to start Works.

The Works Task Launcher dialog box is a central location from which you can start TaskWizards, which are automated processes for creating various types of documents. From the Works Task Launcher dialog box you can also open existing documents and any of the Works tools.

If You Are New to Microsoft Windows 95

Windows 95 is an operating environment in which you can run multiple applications simultaneously and share text, data, and graphics between applications. This information sharing is possible because Windows 95 provides a common interface for different application programs so they can operate in the same way.

You should become familiar with the basic elements of Windows 95 before starting the exercises presented in this book. Once you understand these elements, you will find it easy to understand and use any Windows 95-based application.

Using Window Components

Although all Windows 95-based applications do not look exactly the same, they do share some common characteristics. After you open an application, you work in individual work areas called *windows*. You can change the size and location of any window, and you can have multiple windows open at the same time and move or copy information between them. Most Windows 95-based applications share the common window components shown in the next illustration.

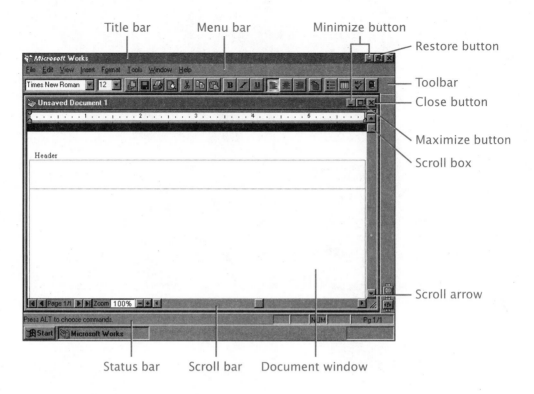

You can use the mouse to move, size, scroll through, and close a window.

To	Do this
Scroll through a window	Click a scroll bar or drag a scroll box.
Change the size of a window	Drag any edge of the window
Enlarge a window to fill the entire screen	Click the window's Maximize button
Reduce a window to a taskbar button	Click the window's Minimize button.
Restore a window to its previous size	Click the window's Restore button.
Move a window	Drag the window's title bar.
Close a window	Click the window's Close button.

Using the Taskbar

In addition to using the taskbar to start applications, you can use it to switch between open applications. Each open application is represented by a button on the taskbar. To display the application you want to use, click its taskbar button.

Using Menus

Microsoft Works commands appear within menus that you access from the *menu bar*, which is located above the toolbar. You can use the mouse or the keyboard to choose commands from the menu bar. To choose a command using the mouse, you click a menu name on the menu bar. When the corresponding menu opens, you click the command you want to execute.

The following illustration shows the File menu opened from the menu bar.

Shortcut key combination

To the right of some command names you'll see *shortcut key combinations*, which indicate the keys you can press to execute commands without using the menu system. Shortcut key combinations can save you time and are useful when you are typing large amounts of text and don't want to move your hands from the keyboard.

If you're not using a mouse, you can use the keyboard to choose menu commands. Every menu name has a keyboard equivalent that you can use by holding down ALT and pressing the key that corresponds to the underlined character in the menu name. After a menu is open, you can execute a command from the keyboard by pressing the key that corresponds to the underlined character in the command name. For example, to execute the File Save command using the keyboard, you hold down ALT and press F on the keyboard. After the File menu opens, you press S to choose the Save command.

Not all commands are appropriate for the operations you are performing. For example, the Paste command on the Edit menu will not be available until you use either the Cut or Copy command. Commands that are not accessible for the current situation appear dimmed on the menu.

A check mark displayed to the left of a command indicates that the command is active. For example, the check mark to the left of the Ruler command in the following illustration means that the ruler is currently displayed on your screen. If you don't want the ruler to appear on screen, you can click the Ruler command to remove the check mark and the ruler will no longer appear on the screen.

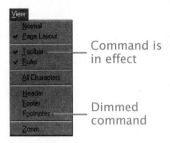

Command is
in effect

Dimmed
command

If you want to close a menu without choosing a command, you can click the menu name or press ESC.

Using Dialog Boxes

Many menu commands are followed by an ellipsis (...), which indicates that a *dialog box* appears when you click that command. A dialog box appears because additional information is necessary to execute the chosen command or because there are multiple options available to you. To supply needed information, you may have to type text or numbers or make selections from groups of options.

You can change existing information or click different options before you execute the command. When you have correctly specified the options you want, you execute the command by clicking the OK button or pressing ENTER. Occasionally you click a different button to execute a command. If you want to close a dialog box without executing a command, you click the Cancel button or press ESC.

Controls are the components of a dialog box that you use to supply the information needed to execute a command. All dialog boxes contain at least one of the controls shown in the following illustration.

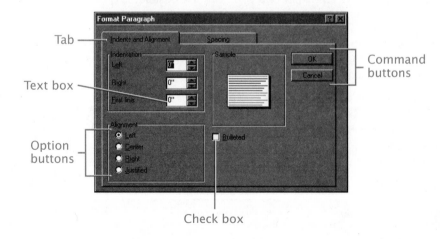

Tab

Text box

Option
buttons

Command
buttons

Check box

Tabs   You click tabs to view additional sections of a dialog box.

Option buttons   You click an option button to select a single option from a set of two or more options. A black dot appears in the center of an option button when it is selected. Only one option button in a section of a dialog box can be selected at one time.

Check boxes   You click a check box to turn an option on or off. When you turn on a check box option, a check mark appears in the box.

List boxes   A list box (see below) shows the choices that are available for an option. If you can't see all the items in the list, you can use the scroll bar in the list box or you can click the down arrow button to view the rest of the list.

Command buttons   You click a command button to complete an operation or to display additional options. A command button name followed by an ellipsis indicates that more options are available in other dialog boxes. If a command button appears dimmed, it is not accessible for the current situation.

Text boxes   You type text or numbers in a text box. Sometimes text is displayed in a text box when a dialog box appears. You can accept the information that is already there or type new text.

The following illustration shows a dialog box with an open list box.

List box

Selecting Dialog Box Options

You don't have to move through dialog box options in any particular order or direction. You can use the mouse to click any dialog box item. If you are not using a mouse, you can press TAB to move from option to option, or you can hold down ALT and press the key corresponding to the underlined letter in an option name.

You can use the following mouse actions to select dialog box options.

To	Do this
Select an option button	Click the option button.
Deselect an option button	Click another option button.
Turn a check box option on or off	Click the check box.
Open a list box	Click the arrow to the right of the list box.
Select an item in a list	Click the item.
Move to a text box	Click the text box
Select text in a text box	Double-click to select a word or drag with the mouse to select a group of words.
Scroll through a list	Click the scroll bars or scroll boxes.
Select a tab	Click the tab.

Using Toolbars

Toolbars contain buttons that provide shortcuts for executing commands. For example, instead of clicking Print on the File menu to print a document, you can click the Print button on the toolbar.

In Works, there is a toolbar for each productivity tool. The toolbar is located below the menu bar. The Word Processor toolbar is shown in the following illustration.

These list boxes and buttons
appear on all Works toolbars

This button
also appears

When you position the mouse pointer over a toolbar button, a descriptive label appears that identifies the function of the button. Toolbars provide the quickest method for accomplishing most Works operations, so you'll be using toolbars frequently as you complete the exercises in this book.

If You Are New to Using a Mouse

Many features of Works and other Windows 95-based applications, such as menu bars, toolbars, and dialog boxes, are designed primarily for mouse use. You can perform most tasks in Works using the keyboard; however, using the mouse to accomplish these tasks is often easier and faster than using the keyboard.

Mouse Pointers

When you use a mouse, you move an on-screen symbol called a *pointer*. The pointer indicates the location in your document at which the next action will occur. To move the pointer, you slide the mouse across a flat surface or a mouse pad in the direction you want the pointer to move. Should you run out of room to move the mouse, you can pick it up and put it down again. As long as you don't click a mouse button, lifting and repositioning the mouse will not affect your document in any way.

As you perform different actions and drag the pointer across different parts of a Works document window, the shape of the pointer changes. As you become familiar with Works, you will recognize each of the pointer shapes as an indicator of what action you can execute at that point. As you work through the exercises in this book, you'll use the following pointers.

This pointer	Appears when you point to
⌖	A title bar to move a window, the menu bar or the toolbar to click a command or button, or a scroll bar to scroll through a document.
I	Text in a text document, a cell, or the entry bar in a spreadsheet or database document. If you click text, a blinking vertical bar called the *insertion point* appears.
✛	A spreadsheet cell or database field.
DRAG MOVE COPY	Highlighted text. If you drag the highlighted text, the Drag pointer changes to the Move pointer. If you hold down CTRL while dragging highlighted text, the Drag pointer changes to the Copy pointer.
ZOOM	Text in the Print Preview window. Use this pointer to magnify the view of your document.
ADJUST ADJUST	A column heading or row heading boundary in a spreadsheet or database document to change the column width or row height.
👆	A Help topic term that you can click to display another topic.

Using the Mouse

There are five basic mouse actions that you will use as you work through this book.

Point   Position the mouse pointer over an item.

Click   Point to an item and quickly press and release the left mouse button. You click to move around a document or to select an item on the screen.

Double-click   Point to an item and press and release the left mouse button twice in rapid succession. Double-clicking is a shortcut for many Works tasks.

Click with the right mouse button   Point to a highlighted area in a document and press and release the right mouse button. Clicking with the right mouse button is a shortcut for many Works tasks.

Drag   Hold down the left mouse button while you move the mouse. You can drag to highlight text in a document or to highlight a range of spreadsheet cells or database fields.

Using Help

If you forget how to complete a task or want to find information about a task that is new to you, you can refer to Works' extensive online Help system. You can find Help information related to the tool you are currently using or you can search for specific information.

Use Help menus

Help menus list common topics for which you might want Help information. You click topics to display other related topics or Help procedures.

1   If Works isn't running, start it now.

2   Click the Cancel button in the Works Task Launcher dialog box.

The dialog box closes and a Help menu appears on the right side of the screen.

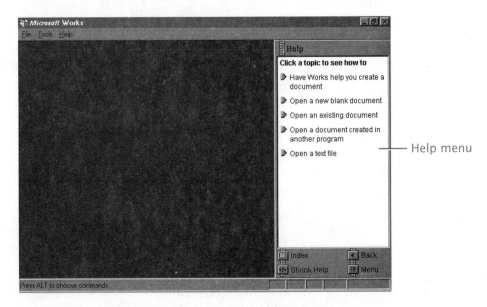

Help menu

NOTE If the Help menu does not appear, you can click the Shrink Help button in the bottom right corner of the screen to display it. If the Shrink Help button is not visible, click Contents on the Help menu, and then click the Close button.

3 Click the topic "Open an existing blank document."

A numbered procedure appears on the Step-by-Step tab in the Help menu window.

Below the procedure are buttons you can click to show an alternative way to complete the task or to print the Help procedure.

For some Help topics, the More Info tab also contains a Show Me button, which you can click to see an on screen demonstration.

4 Click the More Info tab.

This tab contains an Overview button you can click to see an overview of the Help topic. It also contains tips about related tasks and a button you can click to print the Help topic overview.

5 Click the Menu button to return to the original Help menu window.

 NOTE When you open a document or create a new document, Works displays a Help menu window related to the Works tool you are using.

Use the Help index

If the topic you want is not listed in the Help menu window, you can display an index of Help topics.

1 Click the Index button in the Help menu window.

The Index tab of the Help Topics dialog box appears.

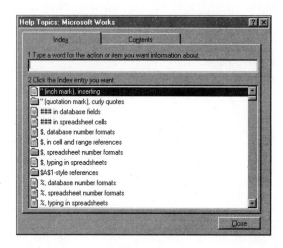

2 In the text box at the top of the dialog box, type **clip**

The Help topic "ClipArt Gallery: adding pictures to documents" is now highlighted in the Click The Index Entry You Want list box. The list box automatically scrolls to the topic that most closely matches what you type.

3 Click the highlighted Help topic.

Two related subtopics appear below the highlighted topic.

4 Click To Add A Picture From The ClipArt Gallery To A Document.

The Help procedure appears in the Help window on the right side of the screen.

Notice the terms in the Help window that appear with a dotted underline. When you click a term with a dotted underline, a definition for that term appears in a small pop-up window.

5 Click the term "Switch."

A pop-up window appears with the definition of the term "switch."

6 Click the mouse button to close the pop-up window.

Use Help Contents

The Contents tab of the Help Topics dialog box shows Help topics grouped according to the Works tool with which they are associated.

1   Click the Contents tab in the Help Topics dialog box to display the Help contents.

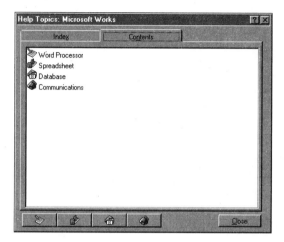

2   Click the topic "Word Processor."

A list of Help topics related to the Word Processor appears.

3   Click the topic "Word Processor Basics," click the topic "Toolbar and Ruler," and then click "To use the toolbar."

The Help procedure appears in the Help window.

4   Click the Close button in the Help Topics dialog box to close it.

NOTE   You can shrink the Help window almost entirely out of view by clicking the Shrink Help button, or you can hide the Help system altogether by clicking Hide Help on the Help menu. If you hide Help, you can display it again by clicking Show Help on the Help menu. Lesson 1 of this book begins with Help displayed.

Quitting Microsoft Works

To quit Works, complete the following step.

Quit Microsoft Works

➤ Click the Close button in the Microsoft Works title bar. If the Save dialog box appears, click the No button.

Quitting Microsoft Windows 95

If you would like to quit Windows, complete the following steps.

Quit Microsoft Windows 95

1 Click the Start button on the taskbar, and then click Shut Down.

The Shut Down Windows dialog box appears.

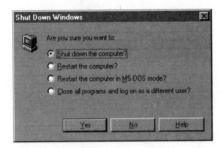

2 Click Shut Down the Computer? if the option isn't already selected, and then click the Yes button.

A warning screen appears, advising you to wait while the computer shuts down.

3 When the message "It's now safe to turn off your computer" appears, you can turn off your computer.

Part 1

A Quick Tour of the Works Tools

Using Word Processor Documents

Estimated time
30 min.

In this lesson you will learn how to:

- Start the Word Processor.
- Save a document.
- Open a document.
- Use Easy Text.
- Delete, copy, and move text.

Using the Word Processor is similar to using a typewriter, but as you type, your work appears on a screen instead of printing on a sheet of paper. This way you can view and make changes to your work before you print it. You can also save your document and continue to work on it later.

West Coast Sales is moving to a new location. To help you organize your move, you will use the Word Processor to create two letters. In this lesson, you'll learn the basics of creating and editing documents.

Getting Started

You can use the Word Processor to create letters to business associates, memos to fellow employees, advertising for customers, and so forth.

In the next exercises, you'll start the Word Processor and then create and save a letter.

 NOTE For information about using a mouse, see "If You Are New to Using a Mouse" in the "Getting Ready" section of this book.

Start the Word Processor

1   If Works isn't running, click the Start button on the taskbar to show a list of options, and then point to Programs.

When you point to Programs, another list of options appears.

If this is the first time you have started Works since installing it, a message box will appear asking if you want to see a demonstration of how to get started with Works. Click the OK button to see a demonstration, or click the Cancel button to go directly to the Works Task Launcher dialog box.

2   Point to Microsoft Works 4.0, move the pointer to the new list of options that appears, and then click Microsoft Works 4.0.

Works starts and then displays the Works Task Launcher dialog box.

Click here to access the Works Tools

Shortcut to Microsoft Works 4.0

 TIP If you chose to add a shortcut to your desktop when you installed Works, you can double-click the Shortcut to Microsoft Works 4.0 icon on your desktop to start Works.

The Works Task Launcher dialog box contains three tabs from which you can access different options for using Works.

The TaskWizards tab lists *TaskWizards,* a Works feature you can use to create several types of forms and documents quickly and efficiently. The Existing Documents tab displays the names of your most recently opened documents. The Works Tools tab provides a starting point for each of the Works tools. This is the tab you'll use to start the Word Processor.

3 Click the Works Tools tab.

Buttons for each of the Works applications appear.

4 Click the Word Processor button.

The Word Processor starts and a new document window opens.

Word Processor

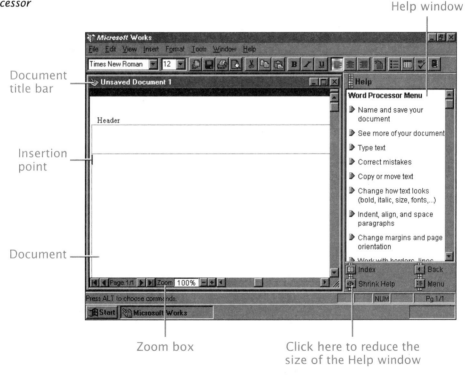

Help window

Document title bar

Insertion point

Document

Zoom box

Click here to reduce the size of the Help window

NOTE You can open additional new document windows by clicking the New command on the File menu after you start the Word Processor from the Works Task Launcher.

When you open a document, the *Help window,* which contains online information about the Works tool in use, appears to the right of the document. You can resize the Help window to take up less space in the Works window.

Shrink Help

5 At the bottom of the Help window, click the Shrink Help button.

The Help window shrinks, providing more room for you to view your document. The window will remain this size until you change it again. Clicking the Shrink Help button again will redisplay the Help window.

For information about using the Works Help system, see "Using Help" in the "Getting Ready" section of this book.

TIP If you want to keep the Help window open and be able to see more of a document, you can click the Zoom button at the bottom of the document window to display a list of percentages that affect how much of a document will appear in the window. You can click Whole Page to see the entire document in the window or click Margin Width to see all the text that appears between the left and right margins.

Type in the Word Processor

Now that you have opened a new document, you can begin to type text for your letter.

1 Type **Dear Joe:**

A blinking vertical line, called an *insertion point,* appears and marks where characters will appear on the screen as you type.

2 Press ENTER to insert a blank line.

3 Press ENTER again to begin a new paragraph.

4 Type **The display cases we ordered for the new store are ready. I've arranged to have them installed on Thursday. Would you please show the installers where to put them?**

As you type, you don't have to be concerned about how much text will fit on each line because Works figures out what will fit between the document margins and automatically moves text to the next line. This feature is called *word wrap.*

TIP If you make a mistake while typing, you can press BACKSPACE to delete characters to the left of the insertion point or press DELETE to delete characters to the right of the insertion point. After you delete your mistake, you can continue typing.

5 Press ENTER twice to end the paragraph and insert a blank line.

6 Type **Thanks for your help!**

Your document should now match the following illustration.

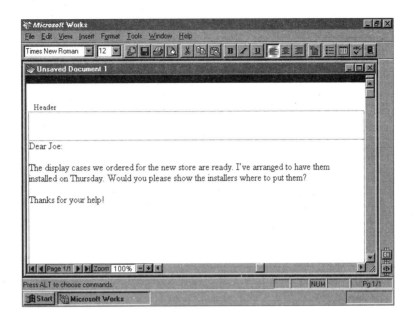

Save a document

As you create or change a document, your work is held in the computer's temporary memory until you save it. To ensure that you don't lose data, you should save your document frequently. If you are saving a document for the first time, you must give the document a name.

1 On the File menu, click Save As.

The Save As dialog box appears.

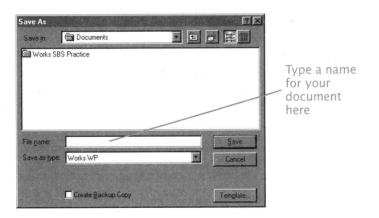

Type a name for your document here

The folder name that appears in the Save In list box specifies the folder in which your document will be saved. The area below the Save In list box shows documents and other folders that have already been saved in the folder specified in the Save In list box. You can save your document in a different folder by clicking the drop-down arrow next to the Save In list box and selecting another folder name or by double-clicking a folder that appears in the area below the Save In list box. For now, you'll save your document in the folder currently specified, Documents.

You can enter a name in the File Name text box. Filenames can be as many as 250 characters long, and they can contain spaces. Take advantage of this flexibility by assigning descriptive names that make your files easy to identify.

2   Type **Installation Letter** in the File Name text box and then press ENTER.

The document is saved with the name Installation Letter. The name of the document appears in the document title bar.

When you are finished with a document, you should close it.

Close

3   In the document title bar, click the Close button to close Installation Letter.

The Works Task Launcher dialog box appears on your screen. This dialog box appears whenever you close a document, providing a convenient location from which you can open other documents and use TaskWizards or other Works tools.

Changing Information

When you use the Word Processor to create a document, you can make changes to the document quickly and easily. You can add a few words or several paragraphs, replace existing text with new text, delete text you no longer need, or copy and move text to a new location.

Making changes to document text is called *editing*. With the Word Processor, you can see all of your editing on the screen before you print your document so you don't waste time and paper. In the next exercises, you will use some of the editing features of the Word Processor to make changes to an existing letter to one of your suppliers.

Open an existing document

Before you can make changes, you'll need to open the document. When you installed the practice files for this book in the "Getting Ready" section, the files were copied to your hard disk and stored in the Works SBS Practice folder. To locate and use the files, you must make the Works SBS Practice folder the current folder.

1   In the Works Task Launcher dialog box, click the Existing Documents tab.

The Existing Documents tab displays a list of the documents you've worked with most recently, as shown in the following illustration.

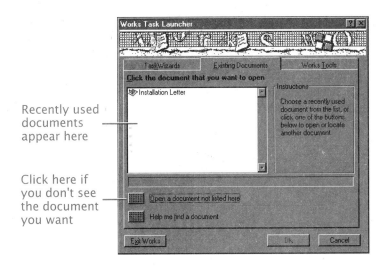

Recently used documents appear here

Click here if you don't see the document you want

NOTE Depending on the documents you have worked with previously, the list of recently used documents that appears on your screen may differ from what appears in the preceding illustration.

If the document you want to open is not listed, you can display a list of all the files available in the current folder or any other folder you choose by clicking the Open A Document Not Listed Here button in the lower left corner of the dialog box.

2 Click Open A Document Not Listed Here.

The Open dialog box appears.

Double-click a folder icon to open a different folder...

...or double-click a filename to open a file

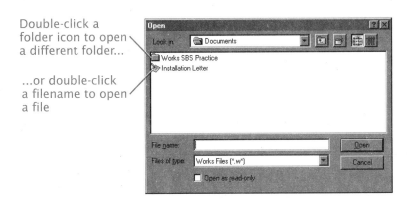

The Documents folder is the default Works folder. To select a different folder, you double-click the corresponding folder icon. When a folder is selected, its name appears in the Look In text box.

3 Double-click the Works SBS Practice folder icon to open the folder in which the practice files are stored.

Now that you have selected the Works SBS Practice folder, a list of available files in that folder appears, as shown in the following illustration.

Available files —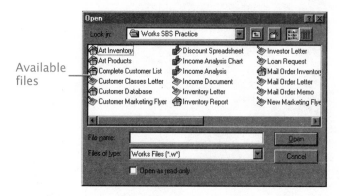

4 Click the right scroll arrow in the Open dialog box until Supplier Letter is visible, and then double-click Supplier Letter.

The file opens.

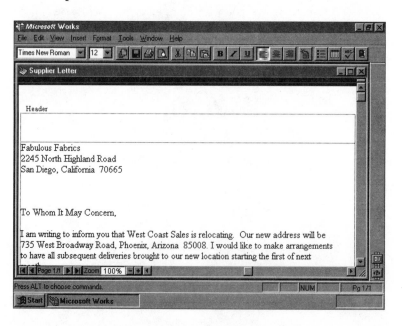

Maximize

5 Click the Maximize button in the document title bar to make the document fill the Word Processor window.

Insert a blank line and a paragraph

1 Click after the period at the end of the third paragraph.

2 Press ENTER twice to insert a blank line and begin a new paragraph.

3 Type **Thank you in advance for your cooperation.**

Replace text

1 In the first paragraph, double-click the word *subsequent* near the middle of the third sentence.

When you double-click a word the word is highlighted. You highlight text when you want to make changes to it. Highlighted text appears in white against a dark background, as shown in the following illustration.

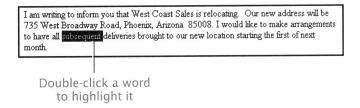

Double-click a word
to highlight it

2 Type **future** to replace the highlighted word, and then press SPACEBAR.

Use Easy Text

If you use certain phrases, sentences, or paragraphs frequently, you can type them once, save them as *Easy Text*, and then use them again without retyping. Easy Text saves you time by automating the entry of long text such as disclaimers, addresses, or standard company information.

1 In the first paragraph, click to the left of the word *West* near the end of the first sentence.

2 Hold down the mouse button, drag to the right of the word *Sales* in the same sentence, and then release the mouse button.

When you drag across a block of text, the text is highlighted, as shown in the following illustration.

Drag with the mouse to
highlight a block of text

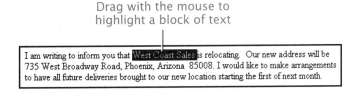

3 On the Insert menu, point to Easy Text, and then click New Easy Text. The New Easy Text dialog box appears.

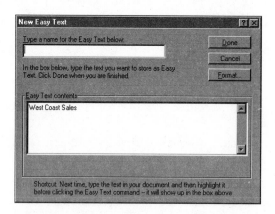

You can use the selected text, add additional text, delete text, or type new text to create Easy Text in the dialog box.

4 Type **wcs** to name the Easy Text, and then click the Done button to add the text as an Easy Text entry.

5 Click to the right of the word *current* in the first sentence in the third paragraph.

6 Press SPACEBAR to add a space after the word *current*.

7 On the Insert menu, point to Easy Text, and then click wcs.

The Easy Text entry, *West Coast Sales*, is inserted at the location of the insertion point, as shown in the following illustration.

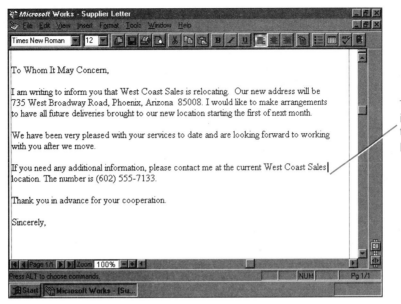

The Easy Text is inserted at the insertion point

NOTE You can also insert Easy Text by typing an Easy Text entry and then pressing F3.

8 Press BACKSPACE to delete the extra space after the Easy Text entry.

Delete text

1 In the first paragraph, click to the left of the word *to* near the beginning of the third sentence.

2 Hold down the mouse button, drag to the right of the word *arrangements* in the same sentence, and then release the mouse button.

3 Press DELETE to delete the highlighted text.

Undo a change

You can correct typing errors by pressing BACKSPACE and typing new information. But what if you accidentally delete an entire sentence or paragraph? You don't need to retype all the deleted text. You can reverse the deletion by clicking the Undo Editing command on the Edit menu.

If you undo a change and then decide you want to keep it after all, you can reverse the undo operation by clicking Redo Editing on the Edit menu.

 On the Edit menu, click Undo Editing.

The block of text you previously deleted is restored to the document. You can use the Undo feature to reverse most typing, editing, and formatting changes; however, you cannot undo an operation such as saving or closing a document.

 NOTE You can undo only the last change you made. If you cannot undo a change, the Undo command will appear in dimmed text as *Cannot Undo*.

Copy Text

You can avoid retyping text by copying existing text in a document.

1   In the third sentence in the first paragraph, highlight the words *to our new location.*

Copy

2   Click the Copy button on the toolbar.

The highlighted text is copied and retained in the computer's memory until you copy or paste other text.

3   Click to the right of the word *move* at the end of the second paragraph.

4   Press SPACEBAR.

Paste

5   Click the Paste button on the toolbar.

Works pastes the text into the document at the insertion point.

6   Press BACKSPACE to delete the extra space to the left of the period.

Your document should now match the following illustration.

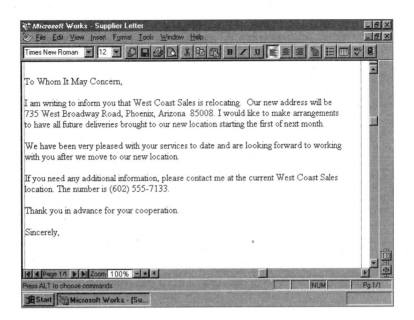

Move text

Instead of deleting text and retyping it in another location, you can move the text from one location to another.

1 Highlight the paragraph that begins *We have been very pleased...* and the blank line beneath it.

2 Click the Cut button on the toolbar.

Cut

The highlighted text is cut from the document.

3 Click to the left of the paragraph that begins *Thank you in advance....*

4 Click the Paste button on the toolbar.

Paste

The text is pasted into the new location. Your screen should match the following illustration.

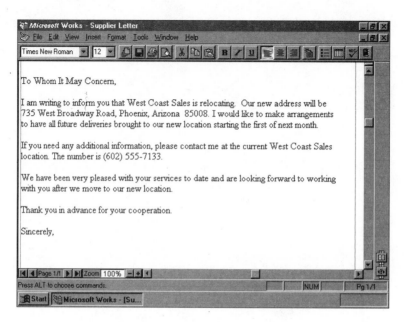

Save

5   Click the Save button on the toolbar to save your changes.

The document is saved with its current name, Supplier Letter.

One Step Further: Using Drag-and-Drop

Before you move on to the next lesson, you can try another editing feature. Instead of using the Cut and Paste buttons on the toolbar to move text, you can use another method, called *drag-and-drop*, in which you highlight text and drag it with the mouse to another location.

Use drag-and-drop

1   Highlight the paragraph that begins *We have been very pleased...* and the blank line beneath it.

2   Position the pointer on the highlighted text.

The pointer changes to the Drag pointer.

DRAG

3   Drag the pointer to the beginning of the paragraph that begins *If you need any...,* and then release the mouse button.

The highlighted text is moved to the new location. Notice that as you drag the highlighted text, the Drag pointer changes to the Move pointer.

MOVE

COPY

 NOTE You can use drag-and-drop to copy text by holding down CTRL as you drag the highlighted text. The pointer changes to the Copy pointer.

Save

4   Click the Save button on the toolbar to save your work.

If you want to continue to the next lesson

Close

➤   Click the Close button in the Supplier Letter document menu bar.

If you want to quit Works for now

Close

1   Click the Close button in the Supplier Letter document menu bar.
2   In the Works Task Launcher dialog box, click the Exit Works button.

Lesson Summary

To	Do this	Button
Start the Word Processor	Click the Word Processor button in the Works Tools tab of the Works Task Launcher dialog box.	
Open an existing document	Double-click the document name in the Existing Documents tab of the Works Task Launcher dialog box. If the document is not listed, click Open A Document Not Listed Here, and then double-click the name of the document you want to open.	
Save an existing document	Click the Save button on the toolbar.	
Save a new document or save a document with a different name	On the File menu, click Save As, type a name for the document, and then press ENTER.	
Insert a new paragraph or a blank line.	Click where you want the new paragraph or line, and then press ENTER.	
Replace text	Highlight the existing text, and then type the replacement text.	
Delete text	Highlight the text, and then press DELETE.	

To	Do this	Button
Move text	Highlight the text you want to move, and then click the Cut button on the toolbar. Position the insertion point where you want to move the text, and then click the Paste button on the toolbar.	
Copy text	Highlight the text you want to copy, and then click the Copy button on the toolbar. Position the pointer where you want to copy the text, and then click the Paste button on the toolbar.	
Move text using drag-and-drop	Highlight the text, and then drag the highlighted text to a new location.	
Copy text using drag-and-drop	Highlight the text, hold down CTRL, and then drag the highlighted text to a new location.	

For online information about	Display the Help window, and then
Saving a new document	Click "Name and save your document," and then click "To name and save your document the first time"
Saving an existing document	Click "Name and save your document," and then click "To save your document as you work"
Highlighting text	Click "Copy or move text," click "To copy text," and then click the word "Highlight"
Inserting text	Click "Type text," and then click "To type text"
Replacing text	Click "Correct mistakes," and then click "To replace highlighted text"
Deleting text	Click "Correct mistakes," and then click "To delete a block of text"
Moving text	Click "Copy or move text," and then click "To move text"
Copying text	Click "Copy or move text," and then click "To copy text"

Preview of the Next Lesson

In this lesson, you created a letter, and you opened and edited another letter. In the next lesson, you'll learn the basics of creating and editing spreadsheets. You'll enter text, numbers, and a series. You'll also replace, edit, clear, copy, and move cell entries.

Using Spreadsheets

In this lesson you will learn how to:

Estimated time
20 min.

- Start the Spreadsheet.
- Open an existing spreadsheet.
- Enter data in cells.
- Save a spreadsheet.
- Edit cell entries.
- Copy and move cell entries.

With the Spreadsheet, you can manage a budget, develop a bookkeeping system and maintain records, or create complex business forecasts and projections. You can use the Spreadsheet to make simple or complex calculations. In addition to making calculations, you can use Spreadsheet editing and formatting features to easily revise data and create professional looking, easy to read documents.

West Coast Sales recently started a discount program for large volume purchases. To determine if the program is effective, you'll use the Spreadsheet to keep track of the sales figures for some of your most popular items, based on purchases made with and without the discount.

In this lesson, you'll learn the basics of creating and editing spreadsheets.

Getting Started

A spreadsheet is a grid of columns and rows, similar to a ledger sheet used by an accountant. A spreadsheet contains 256 columns, labeled with letters, and 16,384 rows, labeled with numbers. The area formed by the intersection of a column and a row is called a *cell*. Each cell has a unique *cell reference*, which consists of the *column label* and *row number*. For example, the reference for the cell at the intersection of column A and row 1 is A1.

You create a spreadsheet by entering data in cells. A rectangular border in the spreadsheet, called the *highlight*, shows you the cell in which the next entry you type will be stored. The cell reference of the highlighted cell appears to the left of the *entry bar*, which is an area in which you can type or edit information to be entered in a cell. The components of a spreadsheet window are shown in the following illustration.

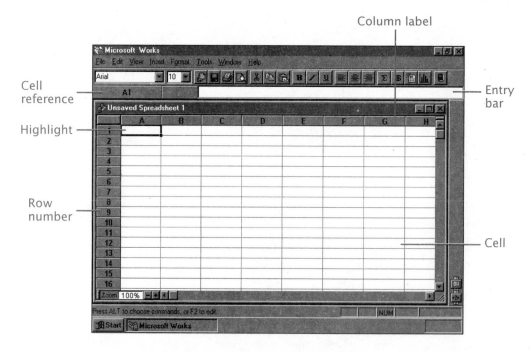

In the next exercises, you'll enter data in a spreadsheet that you will use to determine if your volume discount program is effective. You'll start the Spreadsheet, open an existing spreadsheet, enter data, and save the spreadsheet.

Start the Spreadsheet

Spreadsheet

1   Click the Works Tools tab in the Works Task Launcher dialog box.

2   Click the Spreadsheet button.

The Spreadsheet starts and opens a new spreadsheet window. Once the spreadsheet window is open, you can start entering information to create a new spreadsheet document. For the following exercises, you'll use a partially completed spreadsheet. As you work with this spreadsheet, you'll learn skills you can use to create a spreadsheet from scratch.

NOTE   You can open additional new spreadsheet windows by clicking New on the File menu after you start the Spreadsheet from the Works Task Launcher.

Open an existing spreadsheet

Before you can open your existing spreadsheet, you need to make sure that Works SBS Practice is the current folder.

1   On the File menu, click Open.

The Open dialog box appears.

2   If Works SBS Practice isn't the current folder, make it current by double-clicking the Works SBS Practice folder icon.

3   In the list of files, double-click Discount Spreadsheet.

The file opens.

Maximize

4   Click the Maximize button in the Discount Spreadsheet title bar so the spreadsheet fills the entire spreadsheet window.

Enter text

You use text in a spreadsheet to create titles and descriptive labels for the data in rows and columns. To enter text in a spreadsheet, you move the highlight to a cell using the mouse or using the arrow keys on the keyboard, type the data, and then press ENTER or an arrow key to complete the entry.

1   Click cell C2.

The highlight moves to cell C2.

2   Type **Discount Program Figures**, and then press ENTER.

The text appears in cell C2 and in the entry bar. The quotation mark (") that appears to the left of the text in the entry bar denotes the entry as a text entry.

3   Click cell A7.

The highlight moves to cell A7.

4   Type **Enamel colors**, and then press the DOWN ARROW key.

The text appears in cell A7, and the highlight moves down to cell A8.

5   Type **Silk flowers**, and then press ENTER.

Your screen should now match the following illustration.

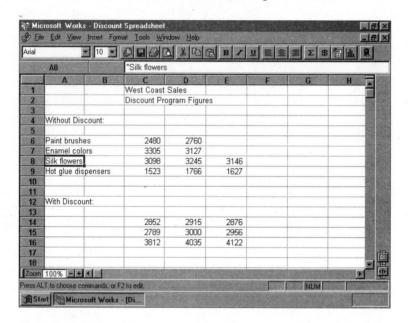

Enter numbers

You use numbers in a spreadsheet to make calculations. Numeric entries can be whole numbers (such as 1 or 256), decimals (such as 0.5 or 8.27), fractions (such as 1 1/2), dates (such as 12/25/96), or times (such as 10:32 AM). The sales data for January and February has already been entered in columns C and D. You will enter missing data for March in column E.

1   Click cell E6.

2   Type **2512**, and then press the DOWN ARROW key.

3   Type **2942**, and then press ENTER.

Enter a series

To clarify the entries in your spreadsheet, you will label each column of data with the corresponding month. You can create a series of numbers or dates that automatically increases or decreases by a specified increment by using the Fill Series command on the Edit menu.

1   Move the highlight to cell C5.

2   Type **jan**, and then press ENTER.

January appears in cell C5. This entry is the starting value for a series of dates. You can use it to fill the adjoining cells with an increasing or decreasing series of dates.

   NOTE   You can also enter the name of a month as a text entry, which is simply text and cannot be used to enter a series. To do this, you must precede the entry with a quotation mark (for example, "January).

---

3   Position the pointer over cell C5.

4   Hold down the mouse button, drag the pointer to cell E5, and then release the mouse button.

Dragging across a range of cells highlights those cells. You've just highlighted the range C5 through E5. You highlight a range when you want to apply a command or an action to two or more adjacent cells. Your screen should now match the following illustration.

Highlighted range

	A	B	C	D	E	F	G	H
1			West Coast Sales					
2			Discount Program Figures					
3								
4	Without Discount:							
5			January					
6	Paint brushes		2480	2760	2512			
7	Enamel colors		3305	3127	2942			
8	Silk flowers		3098	3245	3146			
9	Hot glue dispensers		1523	1766	1627			
10								

5   On the Edit menu, click Fill Series.

The Fill Series dialog box appears.

6   In the Units section, click Month, as shown in the following illustration.

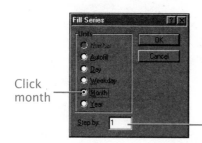

Click month — This number specifies
the increment of the series

7 Click the OK button.

The highlighted cells are filled with a series of dates that increment by one month.

 TIP To enter a decreasing series, change the Step By entry in the Fill Series dialog box to a negative number.

Your spreadsheet should now match the following illustration.

	A	B	C	D	E	F	G	H
1			West Coast Sales					
2			Discount Program Figures					
3								
4	Without Discount:							
5			January	February	March			
6	Paint brushes		2480	2760	2512			
7	Enamel colors		3305	3127	2942			
8	Silk flowers		3098	3245	3146			
9	Hot glue dispensers		1523	1766	1627			
10								

 TIP You can also enter a series by highlighting the cell that contains the starting value and moving the pointer to the lower right corner of the cell until it appears as the Fill pointer, and then dragging accross the cells in which you want to enter the series.

FILL

Save the spreadsheet

As you create or change a spreadsheet, your work is held in the computer's temporary memory until you save it. To ensure that you don't lose data, you should save your spreadsheet frequently. If you are saving an existing spreadsheet, you can save it with its current name or give it a different name.

1 On the File menu, click Save As.

The Save As dialog box appears with the current filename highlighted in the File Name text box.

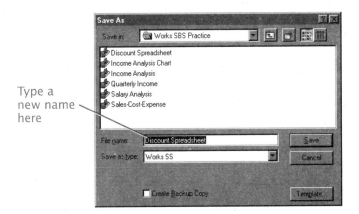

Type a new name here

2   Type **Discount Sales Figures** in the File Name text box, and then press ENTER.

The spreadsheet is saved with the name Discount Sales Figures, as indicated in the spreadsheet title bar. The original file, Discount Spreadsheet, is left in its original form.

Save

TIP   To save a spreadsheet with its current name, click the Save button on the toolbar.

Changing Information

As you review the data in your spreadsheet, you realize that some of the information is incorrect and that some of the sales figures are unnecessary.

The Spreadsheet has many editing features you can use to make changes quickly and easily. You can replace all or part of a cell entry with new data, clear data from a cell or range, and copy or move data from one cell to another.

In the next exercises, you'll edit your spreadsheet to reflect the correct figures, remove unnecessary information, and copy and move cell entries.

Replace a cell entry

You need to replace the January sales figure for hot glue dispensers.

1   Move the highlight to cell C9.

2   Type **1492**, and then press ENTER.

The new entry, 1492, replaces the content of cell C9.

Edit a cell entry

The March sales figure for silk flowers is also incorrect; however, you need to change only one digit in the number. Instead of replacing the entire entry, you can use Edit mode to change only the incorrect digit.

1   Move the highlight to cell E8.

2   Click to the right of the number in the entry bar.

     Clicking the entry bar turns on Edit mode. The insertion point and the contents of the cell now appear in the entry bar, and the word *EDIT* appears in the status bar.

3   Press the LEFT ARROW key two times.

     The insertion point moves two characters to the left in the entry bar.

4   Press DELETE to delete the character to the right of the insertion point.

NOTE   You can press BACKSPACE if you want to delete the character to the left of the insertion point.

5   Type 5, and then press ENTER.

     The edited entry, 3156, now appears in cell E8. Your spreadsheet should now match the following illustration.

	A	B	C	D	E	F	G	H
1			West Coast Sales					
2			Discount Program Figures					
3								
4	Without Discount:							
5			January	February	March			
6	Paint brushes		2480	2760	2512			
7	Enamel colors		3305	3127	2942			
8	Silk flowers		3098	3245	3156			
9	Hot glue dispensers		1492	1766	1627			
10								

Clear cell entries

You decide you don't need to show the sales figures for hot glue dispensers since they are not among your most popular items. You can delete this information by clearing the cell entries.

1   Drag the pointer across cells A9 through E9 to highlight the cells.

2   Press DELETE to clear the entries from the cells.

Copy cell entries

The portion of your spreadsheet that contains the discount sales figures doesn't have any labels to identify the items sold. Instead of typing the labels, you can save time by copying the labels in cells A6 through A8.

1   Drag the pointer across cells A6 through A8 to highlight the cells.

2   Click the Copy button on the toolbar.

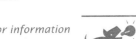

Copy

     The labels are copied to a temporary storage area in the computer's memory.

3   Move the highlight to cell A14.

4   Click the Paste button on the toolbar.

Paste

     The labels are pasted into cells A14 through A16.

For information about how to use drag-and-drop, see the One Step Further exercise, "Using Drag-and-Drop," in Lesson 1.

> **TIP**   You can use drag-and-drop to copy cell entries the same way you can use it to copy text in a Word Processor document.

Move cell entries

To make reading your spreadsheet easier, you can move the discount sales figures up a couple of rows.

DRAG

1   Highlight cells A12 through E16.

2   Position the pointer on a border of the highlighted range so that it appears as the Drag pointer.

3   Drag the highlighted cells until the top left cell in the range moves to cell A10, and then release the mouse button.

     The data moves to cells A10 through E14.

4   Press CTRL+HOME to move the highlight to cell A1.

Your spreadsheet should now match the following illustration.

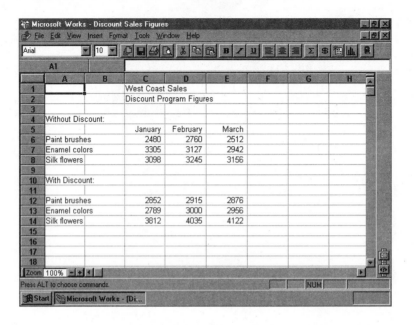

Cut   Paste

NOTE   You can also use the Cut and Paste buttons on the toolbar to move cell entries.

One Step Further: Finding and Replacing Cell Entries

Before you move on to the next lesson, you can try another editing feature. You decide that Enamel paints is a more descriptive label than Enamel colors. You decide to replace *colors* with *paints* throughout the spreadsheet. You can use the find and replace feature to quickly accomplish this task.

Find and replace cell entries

1   Click any cell in the spreadsheet.

If you highlight a range of cells, Works will find and replace data within the highlighted range only. If you highlight only one cell rather than a range, Works will find and replace cell entries throughout the entire spreadsheet.

2   On the Edit menu, click Replace.

The Replace dialog box appears.

3   Type **colors** in the Find What text box, press TAB to move to the Replace With text box, and then type **paints**

The Replace dialog box should now look like the following illustration.

4   Click the Replace All button.

Works replaces all instances of *colors* with *paints*.

5   Click the Save button on the toolbar to save your work.

Save

If you want to continue to the next lesson

1   Click the Close button in the Discount Sales Figures menu bar.

2   Click the Close button in the Unsaved Spreadsheet 1 menu bar.

Close

If you want to quit Works for now

1   Click the Close button in the Discount Sales Figures menu bar.

2   Click the Close button in the Unsaved Spreadsheet 1 menu bar.

3   In the Works Task Launcher dialog box, click the Exit Works button.

Close

Lesson Summary

To	Do this	Button
Start the Spreadsheet	Click the Spreadsheet button in the Works Tools tab of the Works Task Launcher dialog box.	
Open an existing spreadsheet	On the File menu, click Open, and then double-click the name of the file you want to open.	
Highlight a range of cells	Drag the pointer across the cells.	
Enter data in a cell	Move the highlight to the cell, type the data, and then press ENTER or an arrow key.	

To	Do this	Button
Enter a series	Enter the starting value in a cell, highlight the starting cell and the adjacent cells you want to fill with the series, and then click Fill Series on the Edit menu. Select a Units option, and then click the OK button.	
	or	
	Highlight the cell containing the starting value, and then move the pointer to the lower right corner of the cell so the pointer changes to the Fill pointer. Drag with the mouse to highlight the cells you want to fill with the series.	
Save a spreadsheet	Click the Save button on the toolbar.	🖫
Replace a cell entry	Move the highlight to the cell, type the new entry, and then press ENTER.	
Edit a cell entry	Move the highlight to the cell, click the entry bar, change the entry in the entry bar, and then press ENTER.	
Clear cell entries	Highlight the cells you want to clear, and then press DELETE.	
Find and replace cell entries	Click Replace on the Edit menu. Type the entry you want to find, press TAB, type the replacement entry, and then click the Replace All button.	
Copy cell entries	Highlight the cell entries you want to copy, click the Copy button on the toolbar, highlight the destination cells, and then click the Paste button on the toolbar.	📋 📋
	or	
	Highlight the entries you want to copy, and then position the pointer on a border of the highlighted cells. Hold down CTRL and drag the highlighted cells to a new location.	

To	Do this	Button
Move cell entries	Highlight the cell entries you want to move, click the Cut button on the toolbar, highlight the destination cells, and then click the Paste button on the toolbar. *or* Highlight the entries you want to move, and then position the pointer on a border of the highlighted cells. Drag the highlighted cells to a new location.	✂ 📋

For online information about	Display the Help window, and then
Entering data	Click "Type and correct entries," and then click "To type text or numbers"
Saving a spreadsheet	Click "Name and save your spreadsheet or chart," and then click "To save your spreadsheet as you work"
Editing a spreadsheet	Click "Type and correct entries," and then click either "To type over an entry with new information" or "To change part of an entry"
Copying cell data	Click "Copy or move entries," and then click "To copy an entry within the same spreadsheet"
Moving cell data	Click "Copy or move entries," and then click "To move an entry within the same spreadsheet"

Preview of the Next Lesson

In this lesson, you opened your discount spreadsheet, entered data, and changed some cell entries. In the next lesson, you'll learn the basics of creating and editing a database.

Using Databases

Estimated time
40 min.

In this lesson you will learn how to:

- Create a database.
- Save a database.
- Open an existing database.
- Enter and edit records and field entries.
- Delete records and undo changes.
- Use a TaskWizard to create a database.

A *database* is an organized collection of information. With the Database, you can store large amounts of information, and then view and print the information to produce reports, forms, mailing lists, and so forth. You can use the Database to create and organize information such as the names and addresses of customers and the types, quantities, and prices of products in your inventory.

Information in a database is divided into fields and records. *Fields* are categories of information. Each column in a database is a field. *Records* are collections of related information about a person, place, item, or event. Each row in a database is a record. The following illustration shows the components of a database.

Field

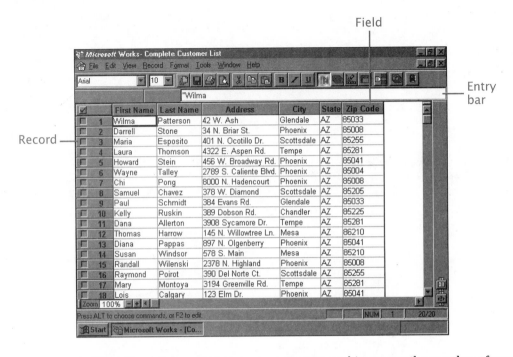

Entry bar

Record

As West Coast Sales acquires more customers and increases the number of products it sells, you'll use the Database to keep a list of customers and to keep track of your inventory.

In this lesson, you'll learn the basics of creating and editing a database.

Getting Started

You create a database by defining fields and then entering record information. Before you begin creating a database, you should think about the information you want the database to contain and how you want to categorize that information. For example, if you want to create a database that will store customer names and addresses, you'll probably want to define fields for each customer's first and last name, street address, city, state, and zip code.

In the next exercises, you'll create a database for storing customer names and addresses, and then you'll enter records into the database.

Create a database

When you create a database, you first need to define the fields. After you define the database fields, Works creates the database, and then you're all set to start entering information.

1 In the Works Task Launcher dialog box, click the Works Tools tab.

Database

2 Click the Database button to start the Database.

The Create Database dialog box appears.

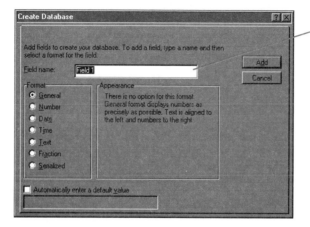

Type here to name each database field

If this is the first time you have created a database, the First-Time Help dialog box appears. Click Don't Display This Message In The Future, and then click the OK button.

You use the Create Database dialog box to name the fields that will make up your database and to define the format of each field. You will use the General format for the fields in this database.

3 Type **First Name** in the Field Name text box to name the first database field.

4 Click the Add button.

Works adds the First Name field to the database. Notice that *Field 2* now appears in the Field Name text box, prompting you to type a name for the second database field. Field 2 will be the Last Name field.

Make sure each field has a unique name to distinguish it from the other fields in the database.

 TIP You can also press ENTER to add a field to a database.

---

5 Type **Last Name** to name the second database field, and then press ENTER.

Works adds the Last Name field to the database.

6 Add four more fields named *Address, City, State,* and *Zip Code,* pressing ENTER after each entry.

7 Click the Done button.

The Create Database dialog box closes and the database appears, as shown in the following illustration.

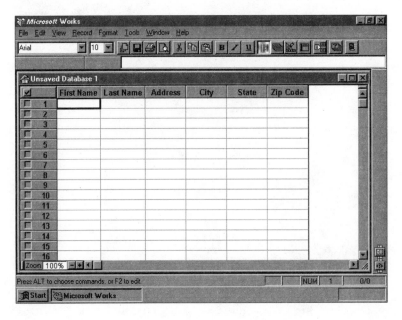

When you create a database, it appears in *List View*, which displays your database as a grid of columns and rows like a spreadsheet. The labels across the top of the database window show the names of the fields. The numbers at the left of the window identify each record. In List View you can view several records at once. Right now there are no records in the database. You will need to add them.

Enter Records

You enter records by typing information into a field and then pressing TAB to move to the next field.

You can press SHIFT+TAB to move the highlight to the previous field.

1 Type **Wilma**, and then press TAB.

The first field entry is entered, and the highlight moves to the Last Name field.

2 Type **Patterson**, and then press TAB to move to the Address field.

3 Type the remaining field entries shown below, pressing TAB after each entry.

Field	Entry
Address	**42 W. Ash**
City	**Glendale**
State	**AZ**
Zip Code	**85033**

When you press TAB after entering the last field entry, the highlight moves down to a new blank record for the next entry. You can also add records in *Form View*, which displays your database one record at a time.

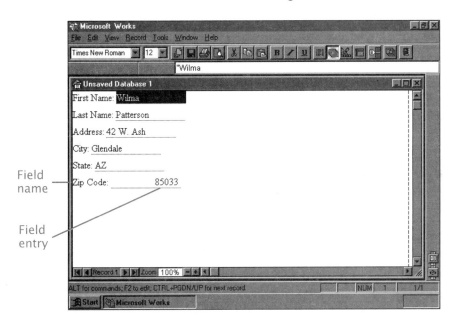

Form View

4 Click the Form View button on the toolbar to switch to Form View.

Your screen should match the following illustration.

In Form View, fields display on a database form, which is similar to how you would see information on a printed data entry form.

Notice that the record you just added in List View now appears in Form View. Changing the view doesn't affect the contents of your database; it affects only the way in which the contents display.

Last Record

5 In the bottom left corner of the database window, click the Last Record button to display a blank record.

6 Type **Darrell**, and then press TAB.

The first field entry is entered, and the highlight moves to the Last Name field.

7 Type **Stone**, and then press TAB to move to the Address field.

8 Type the remaining field entries shown below, pressing TAB after each entry.

Field	Entry
Address	**34 N. Briar St.**
City	**Phoenix**
State	**AZ**
Zip Code	**85008**

When you press TAB after the last field entry, a new blank record displays so that you can enter information for another new record.

Save the database

As you create or change a database, your work is held in the computer's temporary memory until you save it. To ensure that you don't lose data, you should save your database frequently. If you are saving a database for the first time, you should give the database a name.

1 On the File menu, click Save As.

The Save As dialog box appears.

2 If Works SBS Practice isn't the current folder, make it current by double-clicking the Works SBS Practice folder icon.

3 Type **Customer List** in the File Name text box, and then click the Save button.

The database is saved with the name Customer List. The name of the database appears in the database title bar.

Close

4 Click the Close button in the Customer List title bar.

The Works Task Launcher dialog box appears.

Changing Information

If you make mistakes when entering data or if customer information needs to be updated, you can edit your database. The Database has many editing features you can use to make changes quickly and easily. You can replace all or part of a field entry with new data. You can also delete records you no longer need.

In the next exercises, you'll open a completed version of your customer list database, and then edit the database to reflect changes in customer information.

Open an existing database

1 In the Works Task Launcher dialog box, click the Existing Documents tab.

The Existing Documents tab displays a list of the most recently opened documents.

2 Click Open A Document Not Listed Here.

The Open dialog box appears.

3 In the list of files, double-click Complete Customer List.

The file opens.

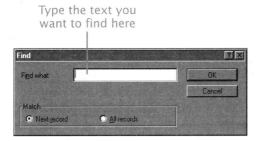

Maximize

4 Click the Maximize button in the Complete Customer List title bar to make the document fill the entire window.

Replace a field entry

As customer information changes, you can use the Find feature to quickly locate a field entry in one of your database records and then update your data.

For example, the last name of one of your customers, Helena Vaughn, has changed. You need to find her record and enter her new last name.

1 On the Edit menu, click Find.

The Find dialog box appears.

Type the text you
want to find here

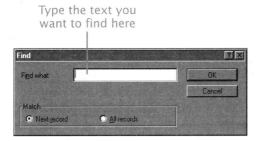

2 Type **Vaughn** in the Find What text box.

This specifies the name you want to find.

3 In the Match section, click All Records.

This specifies that Works should search all records for the text you typed in the Find What text box. The Find dialog box should look like the following illustration.

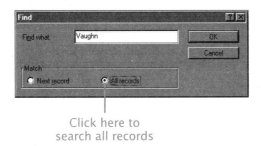

Click here to
search all records

4   Click the OK button.

Notice that only record 19 appears in the database window, and the highlight appears in the Last Name field, as shown in the following illustration.

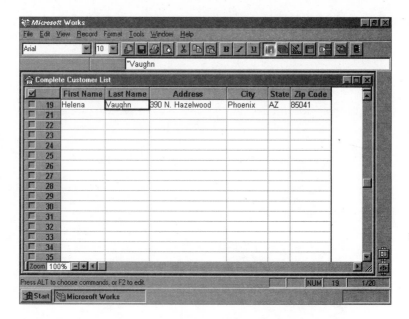

5   Type **Clark**, and then press ENTER to replace the field entry.

Edit a field entry

It has come to your attention that you entered an incorrect zip code for Thomas Harrow's address. You can correct errors in data without retyping the entry by using the Edit feature. Since you need to change only one digit in the zip code, you choose to use the Edit feature instead of replacing the entire entry.

1   On the Edit menu, click Find.

2   Type **Harrow** in the Find What text box.

3   In the Match section, click All Records, and then click the OK button.

Notice that only record 12 appears in the database window.

4   Highlight the Zip Code field in record 12.

5   Click in the entry bar to the right of the zip code.

Clicking the entry bar turns on Edit mode. An insertion point and the contents of the field now appear in the entry bar, as shown in the following illustration.

Field contents   Insertion point

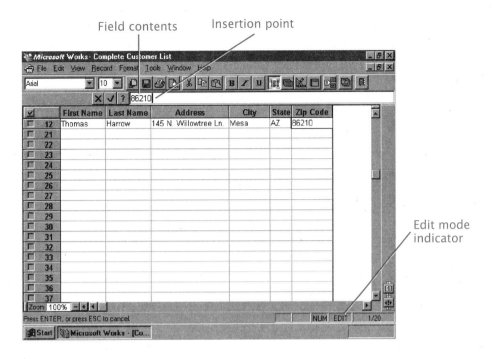

Edit mode
indicator

Notice that *EDIT* appears in the status bar.

6   Press the LEFT ARROW key three times.

The insertion point moves three characters to the left in the entry bar.

7   Press BACKSPACE to delete the character to the left of the insertion point.

NOTE   You can press DELETE to delete the character to the right of the insertion point.

---

8   Type **5**, and then press ENTER.

The edited entry now appears in the Zip Code field, as shown in the following illustration.

41

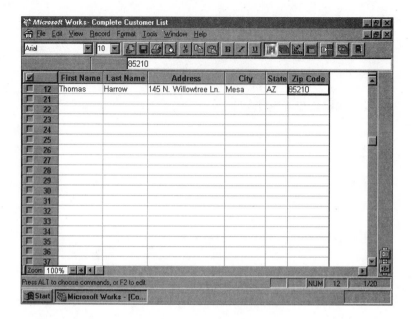

Delete a record

One of your customers has moved out of state. Since he will no longer be a West Coast Sales customer, you will remove his record from the customer list database. The easiest way to delete a record in List View is to highlight the entire record and then delete it.

1 On the Record menu, point to Show, and then click 1 All Records.

   All records now display in the database window.

2 Scroll up through your database, and then click record number 9 to highlight the entire record, as shown in the following illustration.

Click here to highlight the entire record

3 On the Record menu, click Delete Record.

   The record is deleted, and all subsequent records are renumbered.

TIP You can also delete a record in Form View by displaying the record you want to delete and then clicking Delete Record on the Record menu.

Undo a change

The Undo feature will reverse only the last action performed.

You realize you have deleted the wrong record. You can use the Undo feature to restore the record.

1 On the Edit menu, click Undo Delete Record.

The Undo command reverses the last action and restores the deleted record.

2 Delete record 8.

3 Click the Save button on the toolbar to save your work.

Save

Insert a field

You decide to include the telephone number in each customer record. Before you can show this information, you need to insert a field in the database form.

In order to add a field, you must be in Form Design or List View. Form Design is similar to Form View; however, in Form Design you can change the appearance of the form.

Form Design

1 Click the Form Design button on the toolbar.

The database appears in Form Design, as shown in the following illustration.

X and Y coordinates

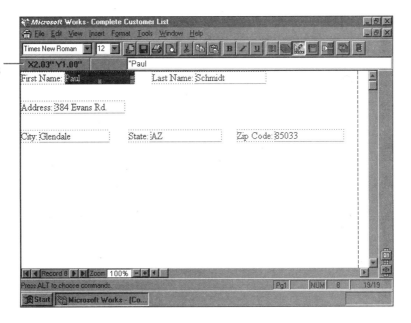

43

Notice the X and Y coordinates on the left side of the entry bar. You can use these coordinates to position the insertion point before inserting the field. That way, you can align the fields with each other by matching their X and Y coordinates.

2   Click in the blank area beneath the City: field name.

3   Using the arrow keys, position the insertion point at X1.25" Y2.50".

The coordinate X1.25" matches the horizontal position of the City field. The coordinate Y2.50" determines the vertical position of the new field.

4   Type **Phone:**

Field names can have as many as 15 characters. In Form Design, field names must be followed by a colon (:) or the field will not be created.

Your database form should now match the following illustration.

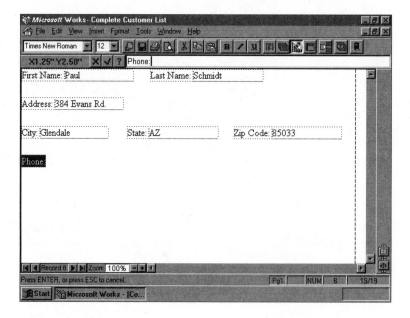

5   Press ENTER.

The Insert Field dialog box appears.

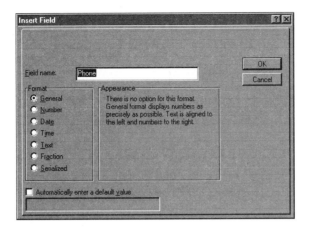

You use the Insert Field dialog box to specify the field format.

6 Click the OK button to accept the General format.

The field is added to the database.

Form View

7 Click the Form View button on the toolbar to switch to Form View.

Your database form should now match the following illustration.

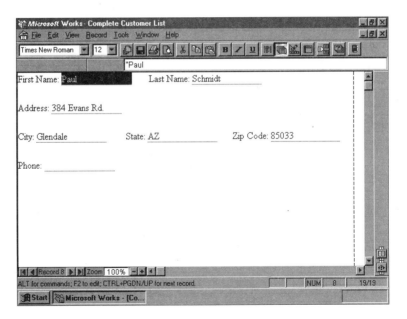

8 Click the Save button on the toolbar to save your work.

Save

9 Click the Close button in the Complete Customer List menu bar.

Close

45

One Step Further: Using a TaskWizard

Because databases can store large amounts of information that can be manipulated in a variety of ways, they can sometimes be a bit complex to plan and create. If you create a database from scratch, you need to think about the information you want the database to contain and how you want to categorize that information. If you are new to creating and using databases, or if you don't feel comfortable creating a database from scratch, you can use a TaskWizard, which makes creating a database as easy as answering a few questions.

A *TaskWizard* is an automated process that you can use to create professional-looking documents and forms. When you use a TaskWizard, a series of dialog boxes appears with questions about the task you want to complete. All you need to do is answer the questions, and the TaskWizard will complete the task according to your specifications. The Address Book TaskWizard is ideal for creating a customer information database similar to the one you created earlier in this lesson.

Start the TaskWizard

1 In the Works Task Launcher dialog box, click the TaskWizards tab if it isn't the displayed tab.

2 Double-click the Address Book TaskWizard.

The following dialog box appears.

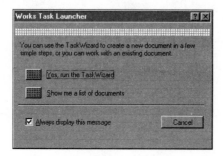

3 Click Yes, Run The TaskWizard.

The first Address Book TaskWizard dialog box appears, as shown in the following illustration.

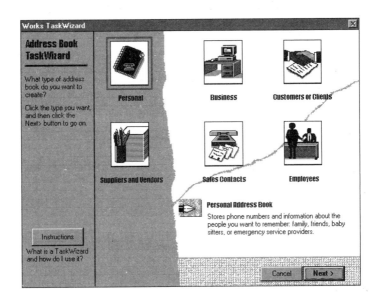

You can choose from six different types of address books. When you click an address book type, a short description appears near the bottom of the TaskWizard window.

4   Click the Customers Or Clients address book type, and then click the Next button.

The address book type is selected and the second Address Book TaskWizard dialog box appears.

This dialog box lists the fields that will be automatically included in the address book database. After you complete the TaskWizard, you can delete any fields that you don't need.

5   Click the Next button to display the third Address Book TaskWizard dialog box.

You will learn how to reorganize the contents of a database in Lesson 10.

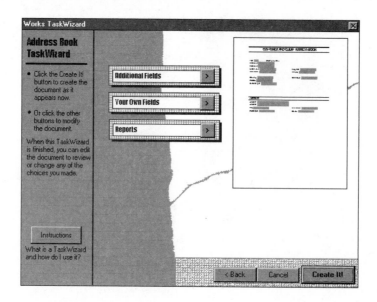

Using this dialog box, you can add more fields already defined by Works, create and add your own fields, or specify different ways to organize your address book. For now, you will not add any fields or reorganize the address book.

6   Click the Create It! button.

A check list appears so you can verify your choices before the address book database is created.

7   Click the Create Document button to complete the TaskWizard.

The address book appears in a database window, as shown in the following illustration.

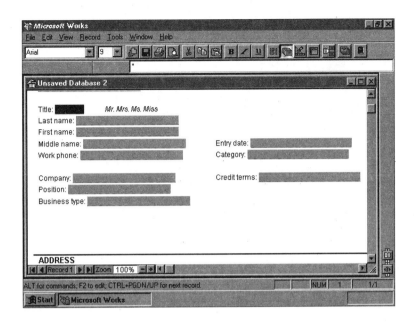

The address book database appears in Form View. For the Title field, Works provides sample text to show the titles you can use in the field.

8 Maximize the document.

9 Scroll down to view all the fields in the database and then scroll back up to the top of the database.

Delete database fields

In addition to name and address fields, the address book database contains fields for other types of information, such as credit terms and the business for which a customer or client works. If there are fields in the database that you don't think you'll use, you can easily delete them.

Form Design

1 Click the Form Design button on the toolbar to switch to Form Design.

2 Position the pointer to the left of and slightly above the Middle Name field, click the mouse button, and then drag down and to the right to highlight the Middle Name through Business Type fields, as shown in the next illustration.

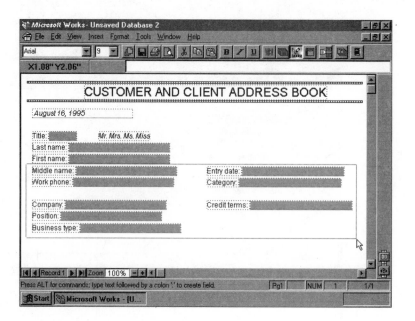

3 Release the mouse button.

The fields are now selected.

4 Press DELETE.

A message box appears asking you to confirm that you want to delete the fields.

5 Click the OK button to delete the fields.

Move database fields

Now that you have deleted the fields you don't need, you can move the address fields up so you can see them along with the Last Name and First Name fields. You move database fields by selecting them and dragging them to a new location.

1 Scroll down, and then drag with the mouse to select the ADDRESS label and all the address fields.

2 Drag the selected fields to the coordinates X1.10" Y2.26".

3 Click outside the selected fields to deselect them, and then scroll up to the top of the document.

Now you can see all the fields at once, and you can enter information into the database.

4 Save the database with the name Address Book.

If you want to continue to the next lesson

▶ Click the Close button in the Address Book menu bar.

⊠
Close

If you want to quit Works for now

⊠
Close

1 Click the Close button in the Address Book menu bar.
2 In the Works Task Launcher dialog box, click the Exit Works button.

Lesson Summary

To	Do this	Button
Create a new database	In the Works Task Launcher dialog box, click the Works Tools tab, and then click the Database button.	⊞
Enter a record	Display a blank record, highlight the first field, and then type each field entry, pressing TAB to move between entries.	
Save a database	Click the Save button on the toolbar.	◻
Open an existing database	In the Works Task Launcher dialog box, click the Existing Documents tab, click Open A Document Not Listed Here, and then double-click the name of the database you want to open.	
Replace a field entry	Highlight the field containing the entry, type a new entry, and then press ENTER.	
Edit a field entry	Highlight the field containing the entry, click in the entry bar, change the entry in the entry bar, and then press ENTER.	
Delete a record	Highlight the record in List View, and then click Delete Record on the Record menu.	
Undo a change	On the Edit menu, click Undo.	
Insert a field	Click the Form Design button on the toolbar, position the insertion point, and then type a field name followed by a colon (:). Press ENTER, set the field format, and then click the OK button.	▦

To	Do this	Button
Use a TaskWizard	In the Works Task Launcher dialog box, click the TaskWizards tab, double-click the TaskWizard you want to use, click Yes, Run The TaskWizard, and then follow the instructions that appear in the TaskWizard.	
Delete a database field	Select the field you want to delete, press DELETE, and then click the OK button in the message box that appears.	
Move a database field	Select the field you want to move, and then drag it to a new location.	

For online information about	Display the Help window, and then
Entering database information	Click "Type and correct information," and then click "To type text or numbers"
Editing database information	Click "Type and correct information," and then click "To replace text or numbers"
Adding a database field	Click "Add columns (fields) and rows (records)," and then click "To add a category of information (field) to a form"

Preview of the Next Lessons

In this lesson, you learned the basics of creating and editing a database. In Part 2 of this book, you'll learn how to enhance the appearance of your Word Processor documents; create form letters, labels, and envelopes; link a spreadsheet to a Word Processor document; and create and use a template.

Review & Practice

In the lessons in Part 1, "A Quick Tour of the Works Tools," you learned how to create and edit Word Processor documents, spreadsheets, and databases. If you want to practice these skills and test your understanding before you proceed to the lessons in Part 2, you can work through the Review & Practice section following this lesson.

Review & Practice

Estimated time
30 min.

You will review and practice how to:

- Open and edit a document.
- Open and edit a spreadsheet.
- Open and edit a database.

In this Review & Practice, you'll have the opportunity to fine tune the skills you learned in the lessons in Part 1 of this book. You'll use what you have learned about opening and editing documents, spreadsheets, and databases to advertise your new store location; track your sales, costs, and expenses; and manage your product inventory.

Scenario

As the date for West Coast Sales' relocation approaches, you'll use the Works Word Processor, Spreadsheet, and Database to complete several tasks. To inform your customers about the move, you'll create a letter to promote the new location. To make sure your sales, cost, and expense figures are current, you'll update financial data. Finally, to make sure your inventory database is accurate, you'll update product information.

Step 1:   Open and Type in a Document

1   Open New Store Letter from the Works SBS Practice folder.

2   Position the insertion point to the left of the colon (:) in the first line of text in the letter, and then type **Friend**

3   Insert a new paragraph between the first and second paragraphs.

4   Type **Helpful, friendly service.**

5   Insert a blank line below the new paragraph.

For more information on	See
Opening a document	Lesson 1
Typing text in a document	Lesson 1

Step 2:   Replace Text and Use Easy Text

1   Replace the text *(your name)* at the bottom of the letter with your name.

2   Highlight the text *West Coast Sales* in the first paragraph.

3   Display the New Easy Text dialog box.

4   Name the Easy Text *Sales.*

5   Place the Sales Easy Text entry below your name at the bottom of the letter.

For more information on	See
Replacing text	Lesson 1
Using Easy Text	Lesson 1

Step 3:   Deleting and Moving Text

1   Delete the paragraph that begins *We look forward...* and the blank line below it.

2   Use drag-and-drop to move the paragraph that begins *Helpful, friendly...* to below the paragraph that begins *A money-back guarantee....*

Your document should now match the following illustration.

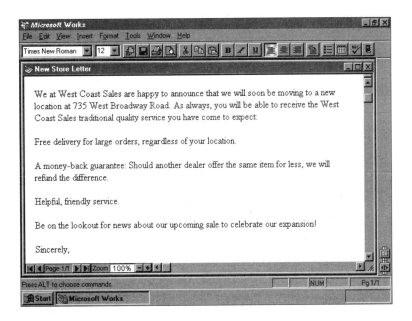

3 Save and then close New Store Letter.

For more information on	See
Deleting text	Lesson 1
Moving text	Lesson 1

Step 4: Add Data to a Spreadsheet

1 Open Sales-Cost-Expense.

2 Enter the text and numbers shown in the following table:

Cell	Entry
A7	**Sales**
A8	**Cost**
A9	**Expenses**
B14	**3245**

For more information on	See
Opening an existing spreadsheet	Lesson 2
Entering data in a spreadsheet	Lesson 2

Step 5: Edit a Spreadsheet

1 Highlight the range A7 through A9.

2 Copy the highlighted range to cells A14 through A16.

3 Replace the entry in cell D7 with *2647*.

4 Move to cell C9, click the entry bar to turn on Edit mode, and then change *407* to *417*.

5 Move the entry in cell A10 to cell A11.

6 Use the Replace dialog box to replace *Qtr* with *Quarter* throughout the spreadsheet.

Your spreadsheet should now match the following illustration.

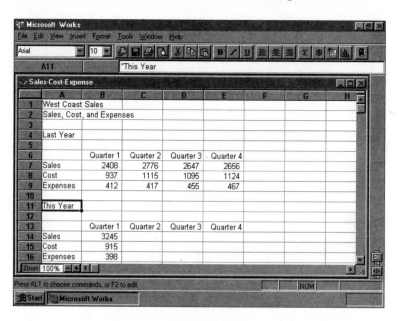

7 Save and then close Sales-Cost-Expense.

For more information on	See
Copying and replacing cell entries	Lesson 2
Editing cell entries	Lesson 2
Moving cell entries	Lesson 2
Saving a spreadsheet	Lesson 2

Step 6: Add Records to a Database

1 Open Art Products.

2 Maximize the database window.

3 Add the record shown in the following table:

Field	Entry
Item #	**1007993**
Description	**Paint thinner 2 oz.**
Cost	**0.75**
Price	**1.55**
On Hand	**21**

4 Change to Form View, and then add the record shown in the following table:

Field	Entry
Item #	**2005975**
Description	**Enamel paint 10 color assortment**
Cost	**2.99**
Price	**6.55**
On Hand	**50**

5 Switch to List View, and then scroll down to the two records you added.
Your screen should now match the following illustration.

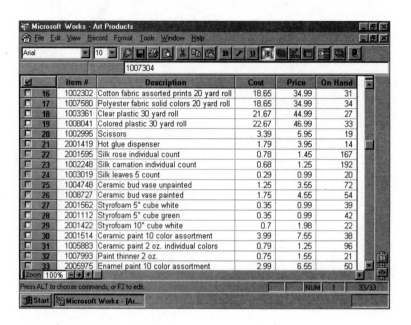

For more information on	See
Opening a database	Lesson 3
Adding records	Lesson 3

Step 7: Edit a Database

1 Use the Find dialog box to display the record for Scissors.

2 Change the On Hand field entry to 15.

3 Delete record number 24.

4 Undo the deletion.

Your screen should now match the following illustration.

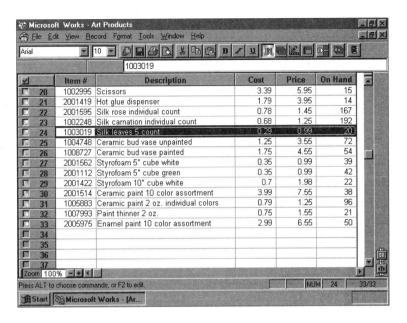

5 Save and then close Art Products.

For more information on	See
Finding records	Lesson 3
Changing records	Lesson 3
Deleting records	Lesson 3

If you want to continue to the next lesson

➤ Be sure the Works Task Launcher dialog box is open.

If you want to quit Works for now

➤ Click the Exit Works button in the Works Task Launcher dialog box.

Creating Business Documents

Part 2

Enhancing the Appearance of Documents

Estimated time
50 min.

In this lesson you will learn how to:

- Change margins and page orientation.
- Change line and paragraph spacing.
- Insert and adjust tabs.
- Insert, resize, and format tables.
- Work with fonts.
- Add graphics to documents.
- Print documents.

You are working on a promotional flyer that advertises West Coast Sales' new location and incentives for selected customers. The flyer is well organized and tells your customers what you want them to know. But it could look better—perhaps a bit flashier. Also, some of the information is more important than other information, so you want to emphasize certain points. You can enhance the appearance of your documents by using the Word Processor's formatting features.

Formatting is the process of changing a document to improve its appearance. You can use features such as bold or a larger text size to emphasize words or phrases, tabs to align text, and indents to draw attention to key paragraphs.

In this lesson, you'll learn how to use the formatting features of the Word Processor to make your document easy to read. You'll also learn how to add bullets, insert and format tables, and add graphics to your document. Finally, you'll print your document.

Making Your Document Easy to Read

You can use the Word Processor's formatting features to specify margin settings, page orientation, and the amount of space between the lines and paragraphs in your document. You can also change the paragraph alignment to draw attention to certain paragraphs.

In the following exercises, you'll change the margin settings and page orientation, change line and paragraph spacing, and set paragraph alignment.

Open the document

1 Open New Marketing Flyer in the Works SBS Practice folder.

2 Maximize the document.

Change margins

Currently, the bottom, left, and right margins of the flyer are fairly large, resulting in a large amount of blank space between the text and the edges of the document. You can reduce the amount of blank space by changing the margins.

1 On the File menu, click Page Setup.

   The Page Setup dialog box appears with margin options.

2 Click the Margins tab, if it isn't the displayed tab, double-click the Bottom Margin text box, and then type .7.

3 Press TAB to move to the Left Margin text box, type .75, and then press TAB to move to the Right Margin text box.

4 Type .75 and then press TAB.

   The bottom margin is now .70 inch and the left and right margins are now .75 inch. The Sample section of the dialog box illustrates the new margin settings.

You can click the Reset button in the Page Setup dialog box to change the margins back to the original settings.

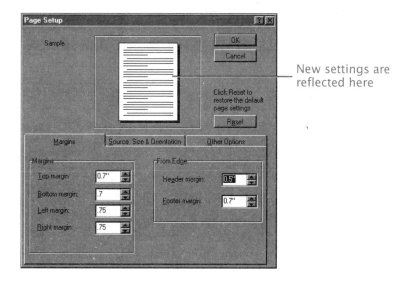

New settings are reflected here

 NOTE You can also change margin settings by clicking the up or down arrows to the right of each margin text box.

5 Press ENTER.

The margins change to reflect the new settings.

Change page orientation

1 On the File menu, click Page Setup.

2 Click the Source, Size & Orientation tab.

The current orientation is *portrait* (vertical), as shown in the Sample section of the dialog box.

3 In the Orientation section, click Landscape.

The orientation is now set to *landscape* (horizontal). The Sample section illustrates the new orientation.

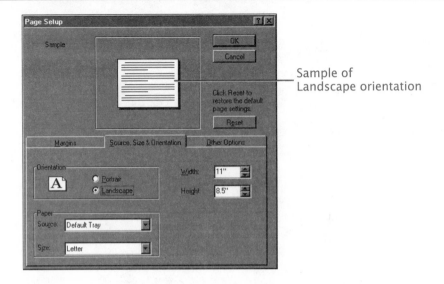

Sample of
Landscape orientation

4 Click the OK button.

The page orientation has changed to landscape. You can preview your document to see how it looks with landscape orientation.

5 Click the Print Preview button on the toolbar.

Your document now appears in the Print Preview window, as shown in the following illustration.

Print Preview

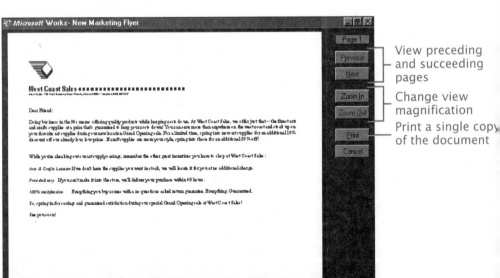

View preceding and succeeding pages

Change view magnification

Print a single copy of the document

If you have trouble reading the text in the Print Preview window, you can magnify the view.

You can click a specific area of a document to magnify the view of that area.

6 Click the Zoom In button twice to magnify the view.

7 Click the Zoom Out button twice to shrink the view back to normal magnification.

NOTE In a multiple page document, you can click the Previous and Next buttons to preview other pages.

8 When you're finished previewing the flyer, click the Cancel button to close the Print Preview window.

Change line spacing

You can make your document easier to read by changing the *line spacing*, which is the amount of space between lines of text.

1 Starting with the paragraph that begins *Doing business in the 90s...*, highlight all paragraphs down to the end of the document.

NOTE You can change the line spacing of a single paragraph by clicking anywhere within the paragraph.

2 On the Format menu, click Paragraph.

The Format Paragraph dialog box appears.

3 Click the Spacing tab.

4 In the Line Spacing text box, type **1.4**.

The Format Paragraph dialog box should now match the following illustration.

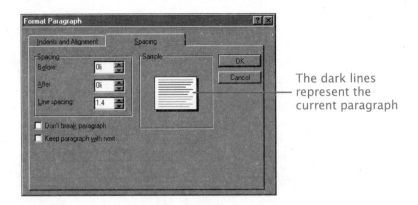

The dark lines represent the current paragraph

5 Press ENTER, click anywhere in the document to deselect the paragraphs, and then click the up scroll arrow until you can see the first paragraph.

The new line spacing is applied to the paragraphs, as shown in the following illustration.

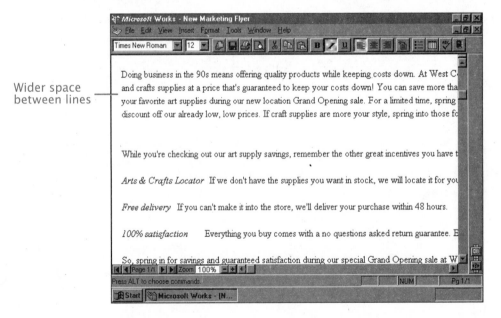

Wider space between lines

Change paragraph spacing

By changing *paragraph spacing*, which is the amount of space between paragraphs, you can create distinctions between blocks of text. Although you can press ENTER to insert blank lines in a document, the spacing feature lets you add spaces of varying sizes.

1   Click the blank line below the paragraph that begins *Arts & Crafts Locator....*

Since this paragraph and the two that follow it are related, they might look better with less space between them.

2   Press DELETE to delete the blank line.

3   Delete the blank line below the paragraph that begins *Free delivery....*

4   Highlight the three paragraphs (*Arts & Crafts Locator...*, *Free delivery...*, *100% satisfaction...*), as shown in the following illustration.

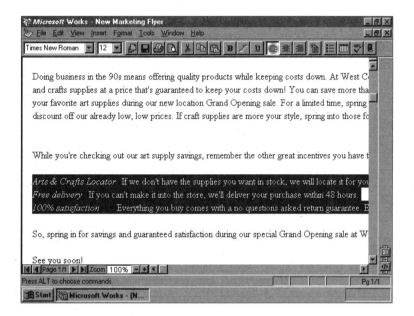

TIP   You can highlight sequential paragraphs without dragging the mouse. To highlight paragraphs this way, move the pointer into the left document margin, next to the first paragraph you want to highlight, so the pointer changes to a right-pointing diagonal arrow. Click the mouse button to highlight the first paragraph, press and hold SHIFT, click on the left document margin next to the last paragraph you want to highlight, and then release SHIFT.

5   On the Format menu, click Paragraph.

You use the Before and After options to add extra space before or after paragraphs or both. You can specify paragraph spacing as a whole number or as a decimal.

6   Double-click the After text box.

7   Type **.45**, and then press ENTER.

69

TIP Add space after paragraphs rather than before them so the extra spacing doesn't appear at the top of a subsequent page.

8 Click and hold on the left scroll arrow at the bottom of the document window to scroll left, and then click the blank line below the paragraphs to deselect them.

Set the alignment for multiple paragraphs

Paragraph alignment determines how paragraphs are positioned between the left and right margins of a document. To apply the same alignment to two or more paragraphs at the same time, you must highlight the paragraphs first.

1 Starting with the paragraph that begins *Doing business in the 90s...*, highlight all paragraphs down to the end of the document.

 NOTE If you want to set the alignment for only a single paragraph, click anywhere within the paragraph.

2 On the Format menu, click Paragraph.

3 Click the Indents And Alignment tab.

Indent and alignment options appear in the Format Paragraph dialog box.

4 In the Alignment section, click Justified.

The Sample section of the dialog box now shows justified alignment.

5 Click the OK button.

With *justified alignment*, paragraphs align evenly between the left and right margins.

Print Preview

6 Click the Print Preview button on the toolbar.

See how justified alignment changes the look of your document.

7 Click the Cancel button to close the Print Preview window.

8 Save your work.

Emphasizing Information

The appearance and organization of information in your document can improve its effectiveness. You can use indents, bullets, and tabs to emphasize information in your document. You can also use the Table feature to organize information in a document.

In the next exercises, you'll indent and add bullets to emphasize paragraphs and insert and adjust tabs to align paragraph text. You'll also add a table to your flyer.

Indent paragraphs

1 Highlight the paragraph that begins *Arts & Crafts Locator...* and the two paragraphs beneath it.

2 If the ruler is not displayed in the Word Processor window, click Ruler on the View menu.

The ruler contains indent markers you can drag to indent the current paragraph.

First line indent marker

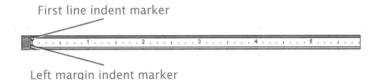

Left margin indent marker

When you drag the left margin indent marker, the first line indent marker will move with it. If you set a first line indent, you can drag the first line indent marker independently.

3 Drag the left margin indent marker to the 1-inch mark on the ruler, and then click anywhere outside of the highlighted paragraphs.

If this is the first time you have used the ruler to create an indent, the First-Time Help dialog box appears. Click Don't Display This Message In The Future, and then click the OK button.

4 Scroll to the left to view the indented paragraphs, shown in the following illustration.

The paragraphs are indented one inch from the left margin

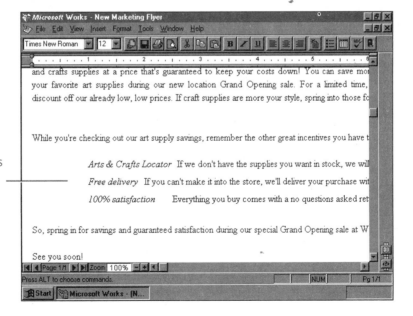

Add bullets

1 Highlight the paragraph that begins *Arts & Crafts Locator...* and the two paragraphs beneath it.

Bullets

2 Click the Bullets button on the toolbar, and then click anywhere in the document.

Works inserts bullets to the left of the highlighted paragraphs.

3 Scroll to the left to view the bullets, shown in the following illustration.

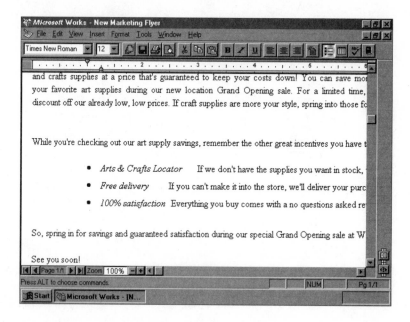

Bullets

TIP To turn off bullets, highlight the bulleted text, and then click the Bullets button on the toolbar.

Insert tabs

When you press TAB, the insertion point moves from its current location to the next tab stop. Existing text and text that you type aligns at the tab stop, based on the style of tab. You can choose from the tab styles shown in the following illustration.

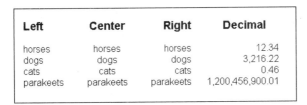

Left	Center	Right	Decimal
horses	horses	horses	12.34
dogs	dogs	dogs	3,216.22
cats	cats	cats	0.46
parakeets	parakeets	parakeets	1,200,456,900.01

In a new document, tabs for all paragraphs are left-aligned and preset every .5 inch. If you want tabs at different locations, you must set the tabs manually.

1 Highlight the paragraph that begins *Arts & Crafts Locator...* and the two paragraphs beneath it.

2 Click below the 3.5-inch mark on the ruler.

A tab marker is inserted on the ruler and the information in the paragraphs aligns at the position of the tab marker, as shown in the following illustration.

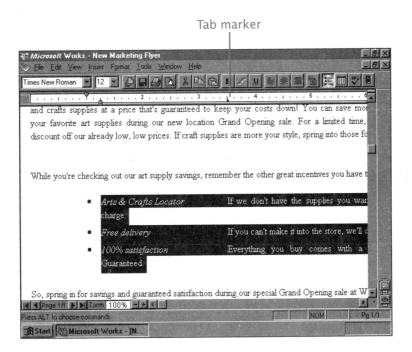

Tab marker

Adjust tabs

The information in your document could be easier to read if the columns of text were closer together. You can adjust tabs to realign columns of text.

1 If necessary, highlight the paragraph that begins *Arts & Crafts Locator...* and the two paragraphs beneath it.

2 Drag the tab marker at the 3.5-inch mark to the 3-inch mark on the ruler, and then scroll left.

The space between the two columns of text is reduced, as shown in the following illustration.

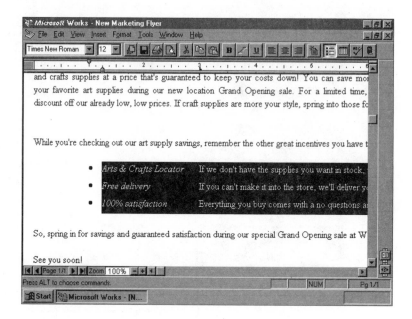

Insert a table

Tables are formatted blocks of text, organized in cells like a spreadsheet. You can use tables to organize tabular information.

1 Position the insertion point on the first blank line beneath the paragraph that begins *Doing business in the 90s...*, and then press ENTER.

2 In the toolbar, click the Insert Table button.

Insert Table

The Insert Table dialog box appears.

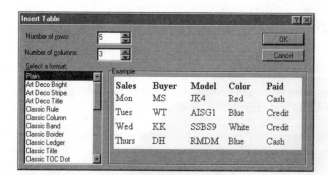

If you installed Bookshelf '95 when you installed Works, the Insert Table button will not appear on your toolbar. You can open the Insert Table dialog box by clicking Table on the Insert menu.

3 Click the down arrow button in the Number Of Rows text box to change the number of rows to 4.

4 Click the OK button.

The table is inserted into the document, as shown in the following illustration.

Table →

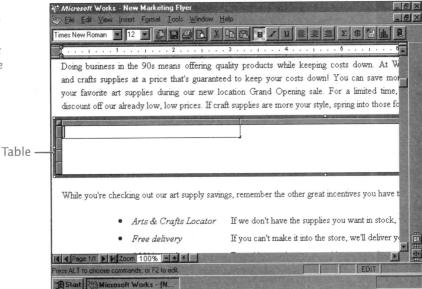

Tables, like pictures and spreadsheets, are objects, which can be moved, copied, and sized in a document.

Resize the table

When you add a table, it automatically extends from the left margin to the right margin. If the table is too wide, you can resize it.

1 Click the table selector to highlight all the columns in the table, as shown in the following illustration.

Column selectors

Table selector

Row selectors

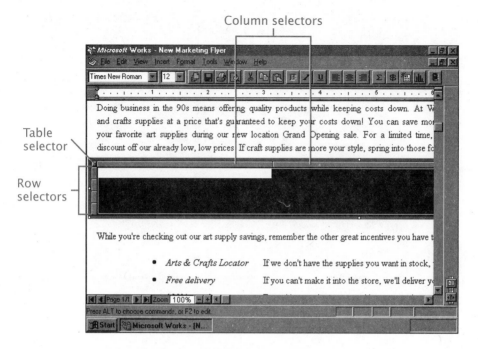

2   On the Format menu, click Column Width.

The Column Width dialog box appears.

3   Type **25**, and then press ENTER.

Each column in the table is resized to 25 characters. This means you can type 25 characters in a column before the text wraps to a new line. Your screen should look like the next illustration.

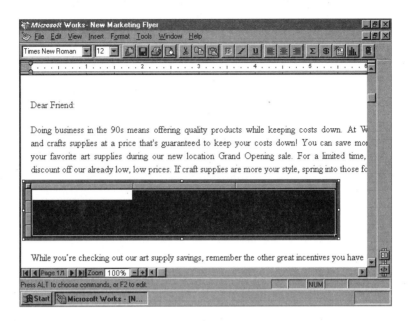

Add text to the table

1   Click in the upper left cell of the table to highlight the cell.

2   Type **Check out the savings on these great items:**

The text you type is entered in the highlighted cell. Notice that the row automatically expands to accommodate the text you type in the cell.

3   Press the DOWN ARROW key.

The highlight moves to the next row of cells.

4   Type the text in the table, as shown in the following illustration, pressing TAB to move between the cells.

Format the table

You can format text in a table the same as you would any other text in a document. You can also format the table cells with shading and lines. You can use *AutoFormats*, which are predefined table styles, to format your tables.

1   Click any cell in the table.

2 On the Format menu, click AutoFormat.

The AutoFormat dialog box appears.

3 In the Select A Format list box, click Art Deco Title.

A sample table format appears in the dialog box, as shown in the next illustration.

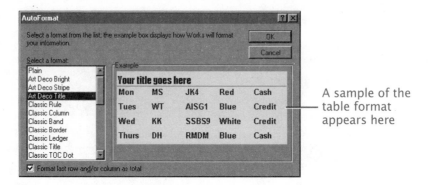

A sample of the table format appears here

4 Click the OK button.

The AutoFormat is applied to the table.

Center Align

5 Click to the right of the table, and then click the Center Align button on the toolbar.

The table is now centered in the document.

6 Scroll to the left to see the entire table. Your screen should match the following illustration.

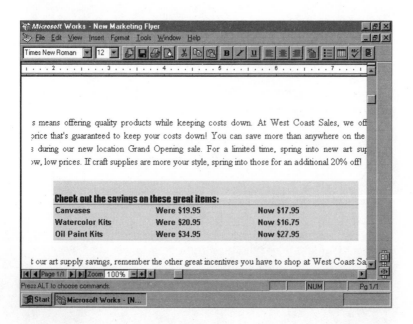

Using Fonts for Emphasis

A *font* is a set of characters with a specific design and a similar appearance. Each font has its own name, such as Arial or Times New Roman, which you use to identify and select the font. The size of a font is measured in *points*, with one point equal to approximately 1/72 inch. You generally use a 10-point or 12-point font for the main text in a document, and larger fonts for headlines and titles. You can change the style of a font by applying bold, italic, or underline styles. The following illustration shows examples of different fonts, point sizes, and styles.

Arial 10-point italic

Times New Roman 12-point Normal

<u>Roman 12-point underline</u>

Modern 14-point Normal

Arial 18-point Bold

You can improve the appearance and readability of text, emphasize key words and ideas, or fit more text on a printed page by using different fonts, sizes, and styles in a document. In the next exercises, you'll change the font, size, and style of text. You'll also use Easy Formats to apply formatting to text.

Change the font

1   Hold down CTRL and click the left margin.

    Works highlights all the text in the document.

Font Name

2   Click the arrow to the right of the Font Name list box on the toolbar.

    The Font Name list displays the names of the available fonts.

3   Click Arial to change the font of the highlighted text.

Change the font size

1   Starting with the paragraph near the top of the document that begins *Dear Friend:*, highlight all paragraphs down to the end of the document.

Font Size

2   Click the arrow to the right of the Font Size list box on the toolbar.

3   Click 10 to change the point size of the highlighted text.

NOTE The font size in your table isn't affected by font size changes you apply to the rest of the document.

4 Highlight the paragraph that begins *Arts & Crafts* in the letterhead at the top of the document.

5 Change the font size to 8.

Add bold, italic, and underline styles

1 Highlight the text *See you soon!* at the end of the document.

2 Click the Bold button on the toolbar to bold the highlighted text.

Bold

3 In the first paragraph, highlight the text *at a price that's guaranteed to keep your costs down!*

4 Click the Italic button on the toolbar to italicize the highlighted text.

Italic

5 At the end of the third bulleted paragraph, highlight the text *Everything. Guaranteed.*

6 Click the Underline button on the toolbar to underline the highlighted text.

Underline

7 Save your work.

Use Easy Formats

Easy Formats can simplify formatting the documents you create. If you want to apply existing formatting to other text in your document or text in any other document, you can assign that formatting to an Easy Format entry, and automatically apply it to new text.

1 In the letterhead at the top of the document, highlight the text *West Coast Sales*.

2 On the Format menu, click Easy Formats.

The Easy Formats dialog box appears.

You can also use the Easy Formats dialog box to define new formats.

Existing Easy Formats

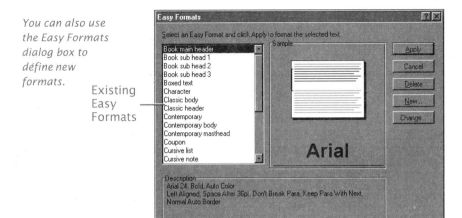

The Easy Formats dialog box displays a list of predefined Easy Formats.

3 Click the New button.

The New Easy Format dialog box appears.

Type the Easy Format name here

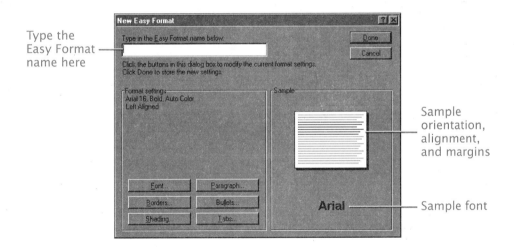

Sample orientation, alignment, and margins

Sample font

The New Easy Format dialog box displays the attributes of the highlighted text.

TIP Text does not have to be highlighted in order for Easy Formats to pick up the format. Easy Formats will display the attributes of any text where the insertion point is located.

You can accept the attributes of the selected text or add or remove attributes when naming the Easy Format.

4 Type **Large Bold**

5 Click the Paragraph button, click Center in the Alignment section, and then click the OK button.

The center-aligned attribute is added to the new Easy Format.

6 Click the Done button.

Large Bold is added to the list of existing Easy Formats.

7 Click the Close button to close the Easy Formats dialog box.

8 Position the insertion point anywhere in the text *See you soon!* at the end of the document.

Easy Formats

9 Click the Easy Formats button on the toolbar.

A list of Easy Formats appears.

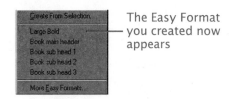

The Easy Format you created now appears

10 Click Large Bold.

The Large Bold Easy Format is applied to the text.

Your document should now match the following illustration.

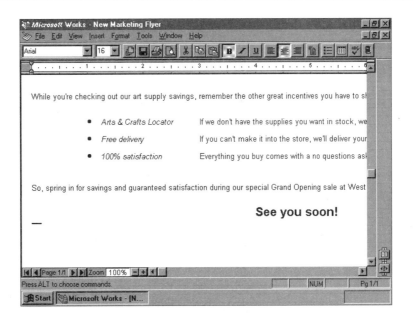

Adding Graphics to a Document

You decide that the picture above the company name could be changed. Adding pictures to your flyer can enhance the message to potential customers. *Clip art* is a collection of ready-made drawings and pictures. Works includes the ClipArt Gallery, which is a collection of clip art pictures organized by category that you can insert into your documents. In the next exercises, you'll insert and resize a clip art picture in your flyer.

Open the ClipArt Gallery

1 Press CTRL+HOME to position the insertion point at the top of the document.

2 Click the picture above the text *West Coast Sales* to select the graphic.

3 Press DELETE to delete the graphic.

4 On the Insert menu, click ClipArt.

The Microsoft ClipArt Gallery 2.0 dialog box appears.

If this is the first time you have used clip art, the Add New Pictures dialog box will appear in front of the Microsoft ClipArt Gallery 2.0 dialog box.

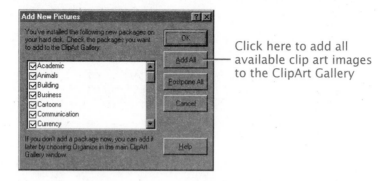

Click here to add all available clip art images to the ClipArt Gallery

5 Click the Add All button.

Works adds all available clip art images to the ClipArt Gallery, and then closes the Add New Pictures dialog box. The Microsoft ClipArt Gallery 2.0 dialog box is now available.

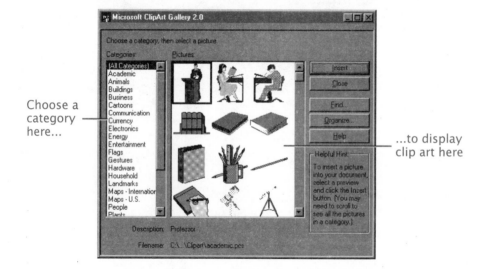

Choose a category here...

...to display clip art here

 NOTE If you have used clip art prior to this exercise, the Microsoft ClipArt Gallery 2.0 dialog box will appear when you click ClipArt on the Insert menu. You will not see the Add New Pictures dialog box.

Insert and resize a clip art picture

1 In the Categories list box, click Plants.

2   Double-click the single Palm Tree picture.

The clip art is inserted into the document, as shown in the next illustration.

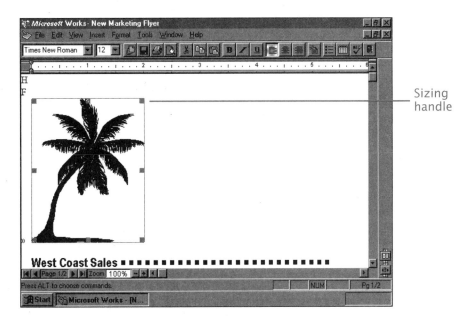

Sizing
handle

If the picture is too big or too small, you can resize it. Notice the small gray squares, called *sizing handles*, that appear on the picture borders.

3   Position the pointer on the lower right corner handle.

The pointer changes to the Resize pointer.

RESIZE

4   Drag the handle diagonally toward the top left corner until the right side of the picture border is at the .75-inch mark on the ruler.

5   Click outside the clip art picture.

Your document with the clip art picture should now match the following illustration.

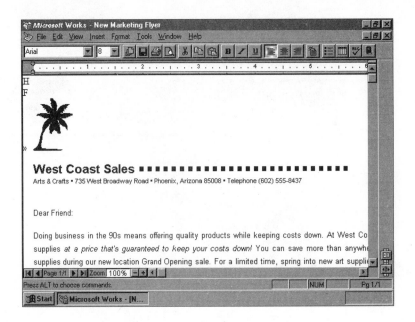

Printing Your Document

When you are satisfied with the content and appearance of a document, you can print it. In the next exercise, you'll print your flyer.

Print the document

1   On the File menu, click Print.

If this is the first time you have printed a document, the First-Time Help dialog box appears. Click Don't Display This Message In The Future, and then click the OK button.

The Print dialog box appears.

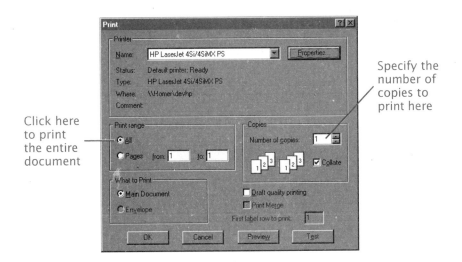

Specify the
number of
copies to
print here

Click here
to print
the entire
document

You can set the print options described in the following table.

To	Do this
Print multiple copies	Type the number of copies you want in the Number Of Copies text box.
Print the entire document	Click All in the Print Range section.
Print specific pages	Click Pages in the Print Range section and type the numbers of the first and last pages you want to print in the From and To text boxes.
Print a quick copy of the document with minimal formatting	Click the Draft Quality Printing check box.

Depending on the printer you are using and its resolution setting, your document may print on two pages instead of one.

2 Type **2** in the Number Of Copies text box, and then click the OK button.

Works prints two copies of the document, and the Printing dialog box appears.

The Printing dialog box shows the status of your print job and lists the printer that it is printing on. You can cancel the print job by clicking the Cancel button in the dialog box.

Print

TIP As a shortcut, you can click the Print button on the toolbar to print a document using the current Print dialog box settings.

One Step Further: Using WordArt

So far, you've learned to use a number of features to make your documents more attractive. Why not try one more feature, called *WordArt*, to create text objects with special effects. Some of the effects available in WordArt include flipping and rotating text, printing text in a circle or half-circle, changing the spacing between characters, and adding shadows and borders to text.

You have chosen "Grand Opening" as the catch phrase for your sale promotion. In the following exercises, you'll use WordArt to apply a special text effect to the phrase and insert it into your document.

Start WordArt

1 Position the insertion point two lines above the text *Dear Friend:*

2 Press ENTER to add a blank line between the business letterhead and the beginning of the letter.

Center Align

3 Click the Center Align button on the toolbar to center the insertion point in the blank line.

4 On the Insert menu, click WordArt.

The Enter Your Text Here dialog box appears.

In the Enter Your Text Here dialog box, you type the text to which you want to apply special effects.

Type the text

1 Type **Grand Opening**

Close

2 In the Enter Your Text Here dialog box title bar, click the Close button.

The dialog box closes, and the text appears in your document as an object with a shaded border. Notice that the toolbar now contains buttons you can use to apply special effects.

Special effects buttons

Apply special effects

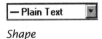

Shape

1 Click the arrow to the right of the Shape list box on the toolbar.

The Shape list appears.

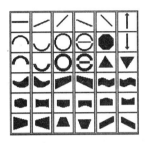

From the Shape list, you can select the angle or curve in which you want the text to appear.

2 Click the Wave 1 shape (the fourth shape down in the fifth column).

The wave effect is applied to the text. This effect will be more noticeable if you make the text larger.

Font Size

3 Click the arrow to the right of the Font Size list box on the toolbar.

The Font Size list appears.

4 Select 30.

The Size Change dialog box appears, asking you to confirm that you want to resize the WordArt object.

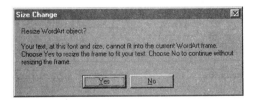

5 Click the Yes button to resize the WordArt object.

6 Click the Shadow button on the toolbar.

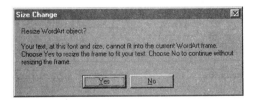

Shadow

The Shadow dialog box appears.

7   Click the second option from the left, and then click the OK button.

The Size Change dialog box appears again because adding a shadow to the text makes it larger.

8   Click the Yes button to resize the WordArt object.

9   Click twice outside the WordArt object.

Your screen should now match the following illustration.

10   Save New Marketing Flyer.

If you want to continue to the next lesson

Close

▶   Click the Close button in the New Marketing Flyer menu bar.

If you want to quit Works for now

Close

1   Click the Close button in the New Marketing Flyer menu bar.

2   In the Works Task Launcher dialog box, click the Exit Works button.

Lesson Summary

To	Do this	Button
Change margins	On the File menu, click Page Setup, click the Margins tab, type new margin settings, and then press ENTER.	
Change page orientation	On the File menu, click Page Setup, click the Source, Size & Orientation tab, click an Orientation option, and then click the OK button.	
Change alignment	Highlight the paragraphs you want to format, and then click an alignment button on the toolbar. For justified alignment, click Paragraph on the Format menu, click the Indents And Alignment tab, click Justified in the Alignment section, and then click the OK button.	
Indent paragraphs	Highlight the paragraphs you want to indent, and then drag the indent markers on the ruler.	
Insert tabs	Highlight the paragraphs you want to format, and then click where you want the tabs to be on the ruler.	
Change font	Highlight the text you want to format, click the arrow to the right of the Font Name list box on the toolbar, and then click a font.	
Change font size	Highlight the text you want to format, click the arrow to the right of the Font Size list box on the toolbar, and then click a font size.	
Change font style	Highlight the text you want to format, and then click the Bold, Italic, or Underline button on the toolbar.	
Create Easy Formats	Highlight the text from which you want to copy formatting, click Easy Formats on the Format menu, click the New button, type an Easy Format name, click the Done button, and then click the Close button.	

To	Do this	Button
Apply Easy Formats	Position the insertion point anywhere in the text you want to format, click the Easy Formats button on the toolbar, and then click the Easy Format to apply to the text.	
Insert a clip art picture	On the Insert menu, click ClipArt, and then double-click a picture in the ClipArt Gallery.	
Resize an object	Click the object, and then drag a sizing handle.	
Preview a document	Click the Print Preview button on the toolbar.	
Print a document	On the File menu, click Print, change print options, and then click the OK button. *or* Click the Print button on the toolbar.	
Insert WordArt text	On the Insert menu, click WordArt, type the text, close the Enter Your Text Here dialog box, and then use the toolbar to apply special effects.	

For online information about	Display the Help window, and then
Changing page margins	Click "Change margins and page orientation," and then click "To change margin settings"
Changing page orientation	Click "Change margins and page orientation," and then click "To change page orientation"
Changing spacing	Click "Indent, align, and space paragraphs," and then click "To add space before or after a paragraph"
Setting alignment	Click "Indent, align, and space paragraphs," and then click "To align or justify a paragraph"
Setting indents	Click "Indent, align, and space paragraphs," and then click "To set a custom indent"
Setting tabs	Click "Indent, align, and space paragraphs," and then click "To set a tab stop"

For online information about	Display the Help window, and then
Working with fonts	Click "Change how text looks (bold, italic, size, fonts,...), and then click the appropriate topic
Adding graphics	Click "Add pictures, charts, tables, and special text effects," and then click "To add a picture"
Using WordArt	Click "Add pictures, charts, tables, and special text effects," and then click "To add WordArt to a document"
Previewing documents	Click "Preview and print your document," and then click "To preview your document before printing"
Printing documents	Click "Preview and print your document," and then click "To print your document"

Preview of the Next Lesson

Congratulations! You are now able to create, edit, and format accurate and attractive documents that inform and capture the attention of the reader. If you want to learn how to add a personal touch to your documents and automate some of the tasks you have learned, move on to the next lesson, in which you'll learn how to create form letters, mailing labels, and envelopes; find and replace text; and use the spelling checker and thesaurus.

Creating Form Letters, Labels, and Envelopes

Estimated time
35 min.

In this lesson you will learn how to:

- Create form letters.
- Find and replace text.
- Check spelling and use the thesaurus.
- Create mailing labels.
- Create envelopes.

You are satisfied with the promotional flyer you created, but you would like to personalize it for your regular customers. You can increase the effectiveness of your documents even more by personalizing letters and flyers.

The information you have learned about the Works Word Processor so far is probably sufficient for simple letters, memos, or flyers. However, if you want to create more complex documents—such as form letters with personalized information and matching labels or envelopes—you'll need to learn more about the Word Processor. Creating form letters, mailing labels, and envelopes is more elaborate than creating promotional flyers. But don't worry! Works provides features that let you create complex documents quickly and easily.

TaskWizards are automated processes that you can use to create professional-looking documents and forms. Using a TaskWizard is easy. A series of screens appear with questions about the task you want to perform. All you need to do is answer the questions, and the TaskWizard will complete the task according to your specifications.

In this lesson, you'll create form letters to personalize your promotional flyers with each customer's name and address, find and replace text, check the spelling, use the thesaurus, and then use TaskWizards to print mailing labels and envelopes.

Creating Form Letters

Form letters are multiple copies of the same document with personalized information, such as names and addresses, inserted into each copy of the document. You create form letters by inserting information from a Works database file into a Word Processor document. The following steps outline the basic process of producing form letters.

- Create or open the document containing the general information you want to include in the form letters.

- Select the database file containing the personalized information you want to include in the form letters.

- Insert database fields in the document at locations where you want to merge personalized information from the database file.

- Preview and print the form letters.

In the next exercises, you'll personalize and print your flyers with each customer's name and address.

Start the form letter

1   Open Customer Marketing Flyer from the Works SBS Practice folder.

The file opens.

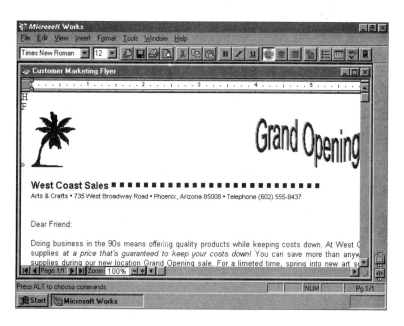

2   Maximize the document.

3   Position the insertion point on the blank line above the text *Dear Friend:*.

4   On the Tools menu, click Form Letters.

The Form Letters dialog box appears.

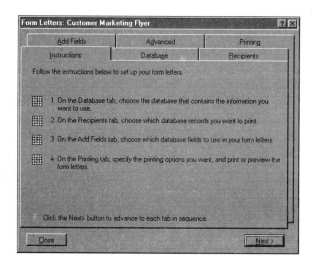

The Form Letters dialog box steps you through the process of creating a form letter by presenting you with a series of questions. You click the Next button to step through the process. The first tab in the dialog box, the Instructions tab, outlines the steps required to create a form letter. As you create the form letter, each step on the tab will be checked off as you complete it.

Choose the database and records

1 Click the Next button.

The Database tab appears, displaying database options.

Click here if you don't see the database you want
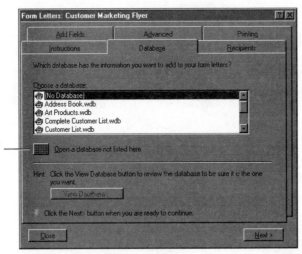

In the Database tab, you will specify the name of the database that contains the personalized information you want to put into the letters.

The Choose A Database list box lists the names of previously opened databases. If the database you want to use does not appear in the list box, you can click Open A Database Not Listed Here to find the database.

2 Click Open A Database Not Listed Here.

The Use Another File dialog box appears, displaying a list of available databases.

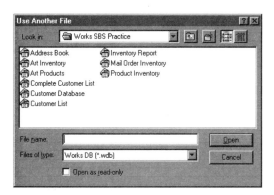

3 Click Customer Database, and then click the Open button.

Customer Database.wdb now appears in the Choose A Database list box.

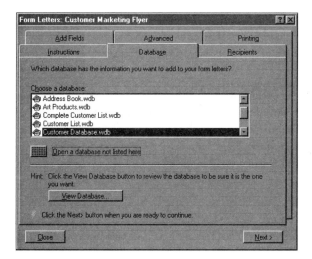

4 Click the Next button.

The Instructions tab reappears. Notice that the first step in the form letter procedure is checked off, indicating that you have selected a database.

5 Click the Next button.

The Recipients tab appears, showing a list of database record options.

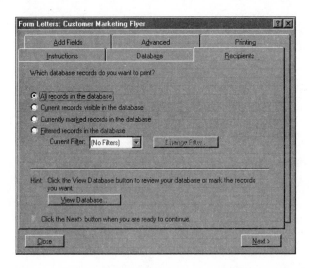

Since you want to include all your existing customers, you'll accept the default selection, All Records In The Database.

6 Click the Next button.

The Instructions tab reappears. Notice that the second step in the form letter procedure is checked off, indicating that you have selected which database records to include. If you don't want to return to the Instructions tab after completing each task, you can click the tab that corresponds to the next task.

Insert the database fields

1 Click the Add Fields tab.

The Add Fields tab appears, displaying a list of fields in the database.

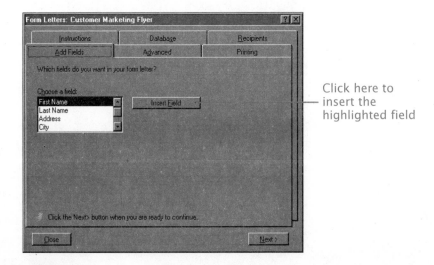

Click here to insert the highlighted field

2   Click the Insert Field button.

The First Name field is added to the document at the location of the insertion point.

3   Click the Insert Field button five more times.

The Last Name, Address, City, State, and Zip fields are added to the document.

Edit the letter

When you inserted the fields at the insertion point location, they were added as one paragraph. You can use the options on the Advanced tab to edit your letter.

1   Click the Advanced tab.

2   Click the Edit button.

The insertion point is positioned in the document and a secondary Form Letters dialog box appears.

NOTE   If the secondary Form Letters dialog box is covering the fields in the document, you can move the dialog box by clicking and dragging the title bar.

3   Position the insertion point to the left of the <<Address>> field, and then press ENTER to move the field to the next line.

4   Position the insertion point to the left of the <<City>> field, and then press ENTER.

5   Position the insertion point to the right of the <<Zip>> field, and then press ENTER.

6   Position the insertion point to the right of the <<City>> field and then type , (comma).

7   Double-click the word *Friend* directly below the database field placeholders, and then press DELETE.

8   Double-click the <<First Name>> field, and then click the Copy button on the toolbar.

Copy

Paste

9   Position the insertion point to the left of the colon (:) next to the word *Dear*, click the Paste button on the toolbar to paste the <<First Name>> field, and then press BACKSPACE to remove the extra space.

Your screen should now match the following illustration.

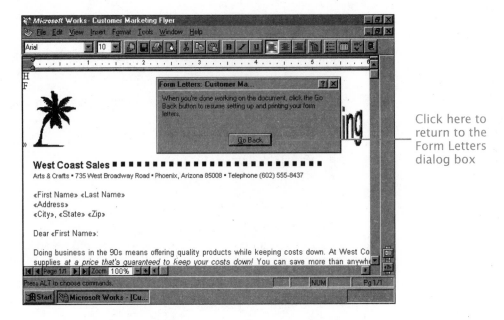

Click here to
return to the
Form Letters
dialog box

10 In the Form Letters dialog box, click the Go Back button.

The Advanced tab of the Form Letters dialog box appears.

Preview the form letters

Before printing, you can preview the form letters to make sure the personalized
information appears where it should.

1 Click the Printing tab.

The Printing tab appears, displaying a list of preview and printing options.

Click here to preview the form letters

Click here to print the form letters

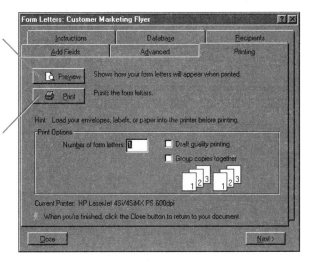

2 Click the Preview button.

A dialog box appears in which you confirm whether you want to preview all the records.

3 Click the OK button to preview all the records.

The first form letter appears in the Print Preview window.

4 Click the Zoom In button, and then click the Next button five times to preview all the form letters.

All the form letters contain personalized information at the location of each database field, as shown in the next illustration.

103

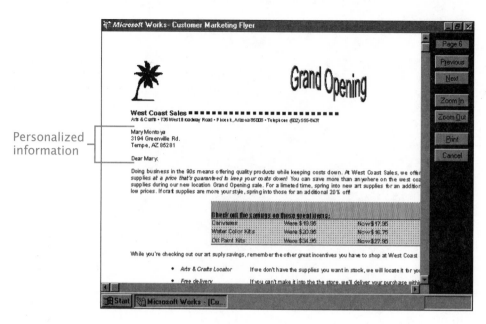

Personalized information

5 Click the Cancel button to close the Print Preview window.

Print the form letters

1 Click the Print button.

A dialog box appears in which you confirm whether you want to print all the records.

2 Click the OK button to print all the records.

The Printing dialog box appears, as shown in the next illustration.

Close

3 When your form letters have finished printing, click the Close button in the Form Letters dialog box.

4 Click the Save button on the toolbar to save your work.

Save

Finding and Replacing Text

Instead of scrolling through a document, you can use the find and replace features to quickly search for and replace a word or phrase. You can replace text throughout an entire document or in a highlighted block of text. In the next exercise, you'll replace the words *Grand Opening* with the word *Moving*.

Replace text

To position the cursor at the end of a document, press CTRL+END.

1 Press CTRL+HOME to position the insertion point at the top of the document.

2 On the Edit menu, click Replace.

The Replace dialog box appears.

 NOTE You can click Find on the Edit menu to search for words or phrases without replacing them.

3 Type **Grand Opening** in the Find What text box.

This is the text you want to find.

4 Press TAB to move to the Replace With text box, and then type **Moving**

This is the replacement text. The Replace dialog box should now appear as shown in the following illustration.

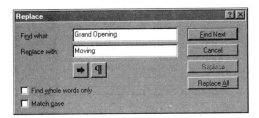

5 Click the Find Next button.

Works highlights the first instance of the words *Grand Opening*.

You can click the Replace All button to replace all instances of a word or phrase at the same time.

6 Click the Replace button.

Works replaces the first instance of *Grand Opening* with *Moving* and highlights the next instance.

7 Click the Replace button.

The next instance is replaced and a dialog box appears asking whether to continue searching from the beginning of the document.

8   Click the No button.

The search ends.

9   Click the Close button.

Checking the Spelling and Using the Thesaurus

Works has two accessories you can use to improve the quality of your documents. You can check the spelling in a document to find and correct misspelled words. If you find yourself using the same word repeatedly, you can use the thesaurus to look up a *synonym*, which is a different word with the same or similar meaning. In the next exercises, you'll check your flyer for misspelled words and look up a synonym.

Correct misspelled words

1   If the insertion point is not at the top of the document, press CTRL+HOME.

2   Click the Spelling Checker button on the toolbar.

Spelling Checker

You can check the spelling in only a portion of your document by highlighting that portion before you start the spelling check.

Works highlights the first misspelled word, *limeted*, and opens the Spelling dialog box.

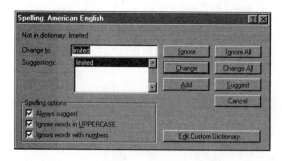

Notice that the Always Suggest check box is turned on, which indicates that Works will display a list of alternative words for every misspelled word it encounters.

3   Click the Change button.

Works changes *limeted* to *limited,* and highlights the next misspelled word, *suply.*

4   Click the Change button.

Works changes *suply* to *supply.* The next highlighted word, *the,* is a repeated word.

5   Click the Change button.

Works deletes the duplicate word and displays the Spelling Check Finished information box.

6 Click the OK button.

Find a synonym

1 In the paragraph that begins *While you're checking out...*, click anywhere in the word *supply*.

2 On the Tools menu, click Thesaurus.

The Thesaurus dialog box appears displaying a list of synonyms, as shown in the following illustration.

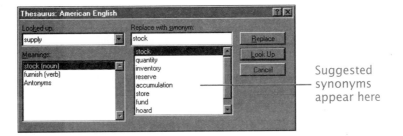

Suggested synonyms appear here

3 In the Replace With Synonym list box, click inventory, and then click the Replace button.

Works changes *supply* to *inventory* in the document.

4 Save Customer Marketing Flyer.

5 In the Customer Marketing Flyer menu bar, click the Close button.

The document closes and the Works Task Launcher dialog box appears.

Close

Creating Mailing Labels

After you print your form letters, you can use a TaskWizard to create mailing labels with matching names and addresses. In the next exercises, you'll use the Labels TaskWizard to create mailing labels for your flyers.

Start the TaskWizard

1   In the Works Task Launcher dialog box, click the TaskWizards tab if it isn't the displayed tab.

The TaskWizards tab contains the TaskWizards list, organized by category.

2   In the TaskWizards list, click Envelopes and Labels.

The Envelopes and Labels category expands to display a list of related TaskWizards.

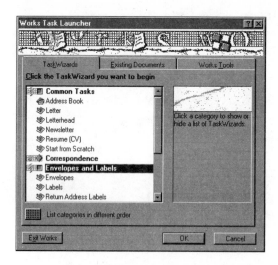

You can also click Labels on the Tools menu to create mailing labels.

3   Double-click Labels.

A secondary Works Task Launcher dialog box appears.

4   Click Yes, Run The TaskWizard.

If this is the first time you have used the Label TaskWizard, the First-Time Help dialog box appears. Click Don't Display This Message In The Future, and then click the OK button.

The Instructions tab in the Labels dialog box appears.

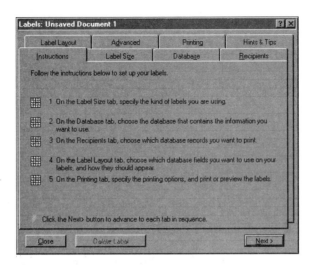

Notice that the Labels TaskWizard appears similar to the Form Letters dialog box. The Instructions tab lists the steps you follow to create labels. Like the Form Letters dialog box, you can click the Next button to step through the process, or click the tab of a specific task. As you create labels, each step in the Instructions tab will be checked off as you complete it.

Select a label size

1 Click the Label Size tab.

The Label Size tab contains a list of label sizes.

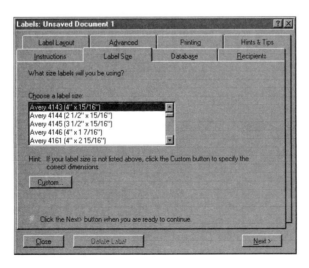

2   In the Choose A Label Size list box, scroll down and click Avery 5162 (4" x 1 1/3").

 NOTE   You can click the Custom button to specify label dimensions that are not in the Choose A Label Size list box.

Select a database and records

1   Click the Database tab.

The Database tab appears, displaying a list of available database files.

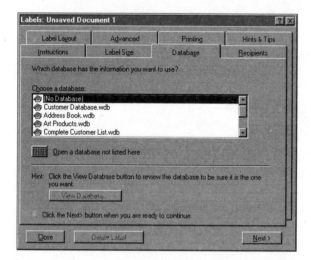

2   In the Choose A Database list box, click Customer Database.wdb.

3   Click the Recipients tab.

The Recipients tab appears, displaying a list of record options.

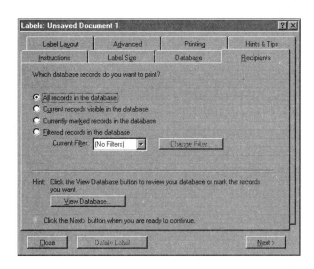

Since you want to include all the customers in the database, you'll accept the default selection, All Records In The Database.

Insert database fields

1 Click the Label Layout tab.

The Label Layout tab contains a list of database fields and a Label Layout box.

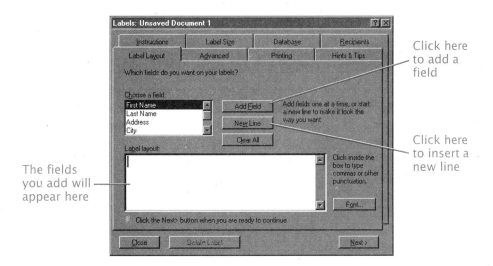

Click here to add a field

Click here to insert a new line

The fields you add will appear here

2 Click the Add Field button.

The First Name field is added to the Label Layout box.

3 Click the Add Field button again.

The Last Name field is added to the Label Layout box.

You can also press ENTER to begin a new line in the Label Layout box.

4 Click the New Line button.

A new line is added to the Label Layout box.

5 Add the Address field to the Label Layout box.

6 Press ENTER to begin a new line.

7 Add the City field to the Label Layout box, and then type , (comma).

8 Press SPACEBAR, and then add the State and Zip fields to the Label Layout box.

The Labels dialog box should now appear as follows.

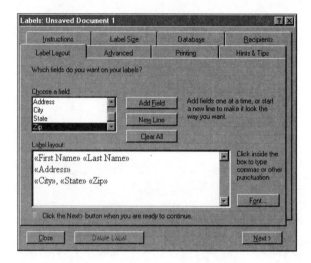

 NOTE If you want to create multiple copies of one label, such as a return address label, click Labels on the Tools menu, click Multiple Copies Of One Label, and then follow the steps on the Instructions tab of the Labels dialog box.

Preview the mailing labels

1 Click the Printing tab.

The Printing tab appears, displaying label printing options.

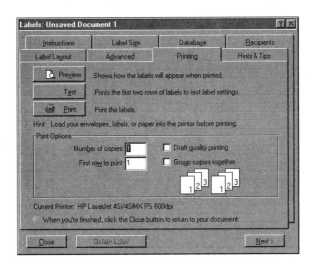

2 Click the Preview button.

An information box appears asking you to confirm that you want to preview all the database records.

3 Click the OK button to preview all the database records.

4 Click the Zoom In button to magnify the text.

Your Print Preview window should look like the following illustration.

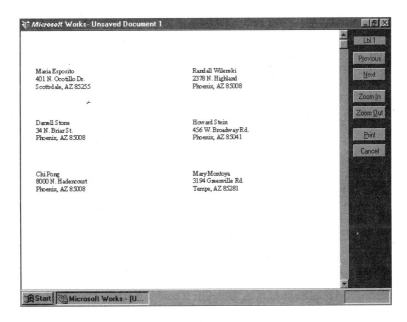

5 Click the Cancel button to close the Print Preview window.

Print the mailing labels

You can print your labels on a regular sheet of paper or on label stock. To make sure labels align properly, you can print a test row of labels.

1 Click the Test button.

A test row of labels prints and the Test Printing dialog box appears so you can print another test row, adjust the label settings, or print the remaining labels.

2 Click the Print button.

All the labels print.

3 Click the Close button.

The Labels dialog box closes and the label document appears.

4 Save the document as Customer Labels.

Close

5 In the Customer Labels document title bar, click the Close button.

The Works Task Launcher dialog box appears.

Creating Envelopes

If your printer can print directly on envelopes, you can avoid the extra time needed to attach mailing labels to the envelopes. You create personalized envelopes in much the same way you create mailing labels. In the next exercises, you'll create envelopes that match the personalized information in your form letters using the Envelopes TaskWizard.

Start the TaskWizard

1 Display the TaskWizards tab if it is not already displayed.

2 If the Envelope and Labels TaskWizards are not displayed, click Envelopes and Labels.

3 Double-click Envelopes.

A secondary Works Task Launcher dialog box appears.

4 Click Yes, Run The TaskWizard.

If this is the first time you have used the Envelopes TaskWizard, the First-Time Help dialog box appears. Click Don't Display This Message In The Future, and then click the OK button.

The Envelopes dialog box appears.

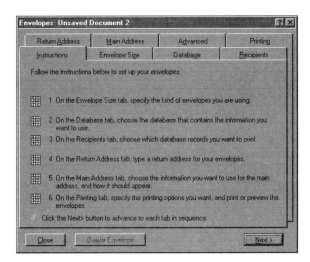

The Instructions tab in the Envelopes dialog box lists the steps you follow to create envelopes. You can click the Next button to step through the process, or click the tab of a specific task. As you create envelopes, each step in the Instructions tab will be checked off as you complete it.

Select an envelope size

1   Click the Envelope Size tab.

The Envelope Size tab contains a list of envelope sizes.

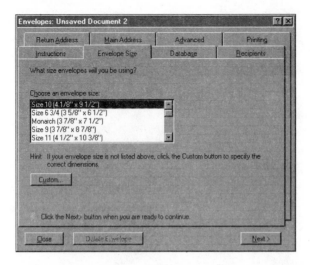

2   Click Size 10 (4 1/8" x 9 1/2"), if it is not already selected.

 NOTE   You can click the Custom button to specify dimensions for envelopes that are not listed in the Choose An Envelope Size list box.

Select a database and records

1   Click the Database tab.

The Database tab contains a list of existing database files.

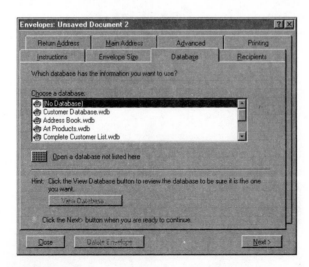

2 In the Choose A Database list box, click Customer Database.wdb.

3 Click the Recipients tab.

The Recipients tab contains a list of record options.

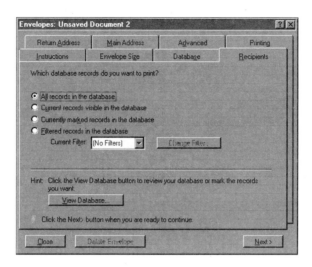

Since you want to include all the customers in the database, you'll accept the default selection, All Records In The Database.

Enter a return address

1 Click the Return Address tab.

The Return Address tab contains a text box in which you type the return address.

2 Type the return address shown in the following illustration, pressing ENTER to begin each new line.

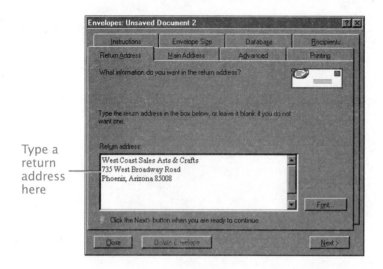

Type a
return
address
here

Insert database fields

1   Click the Main Address tab.

    The Main Address tab contains a list of database fields and a Main Address box.

2   Click the Add Field button.

    The First Name field is added to the Main Address box.

3   Add the Last Name field to the Main Address box.

4   Press ENTER to add a new line.

5   Add the Address field to the Main Address box.

6   Add a new line.

7   Click the Add Field button to insert the City field, and then type , (comma).

8   Press SPACEBAR, and then click the Add Field button twice.

    The State and Zip fields are added to the Main Address box.

    The Envelopes dialog box should now appear as follows.

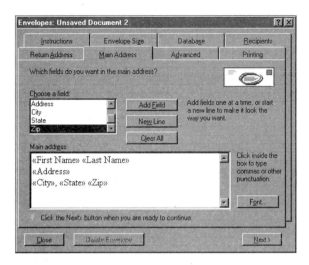

Preview the envelopes

1   Click the Printing tab.

The Printing tab contains envelope printing options.

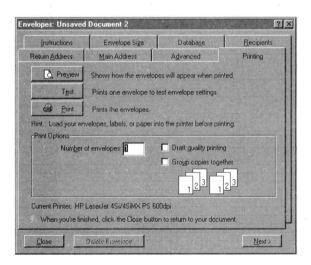

2   Click the Preview button.

An information box appears asking you to confirm that you want to preview all the database records.

3   Click the OK button to preview the database records.

Your Print Preview window should look like the following illustration.

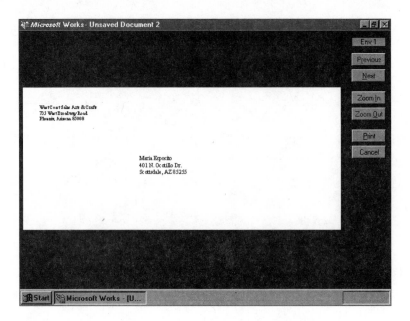

4   Click the Cancel button to close the Print Preview window.

Print the envelopes

1   Click the Print button.

An information box appears asking you to confirm that you want to print all of the database records.

2   Click the OK button to print all the envelopes.

3   Click the Close button.

The Envelopes dialog box closes, and the envelope document appears.

4   Save the document as Customer Envelopes.

Close

5   In the Customer Envelopes document title bar, click the Close button.

The Works Task Launcher dialog box appears.

One Step Further: Printing a Single Envelope

You can also print a single envelope without using your customer database or a TaskWizard.

Address and print a single envelope

Word Processor

1   In the Works Task Launcher dialog box, click the Works Tools tab.

2   Click the Word Processor button.

3   On the Tools menu, click Envelopes.

4   Click the Database tab.

Notice that *(No Database)* is selected. You choose this option to enter envelope addresses manually.

5   Click the Return Address tab.

Notice that the previously entered return address appears in the text box.

6   Click the Main Address tab.

7   In the Main Address box, type the following name and address:

**Laura Thomson
432 E. Aspen Rd.
Tempe, AZ 85281**

8   Click the Printing tab, and then click the Print button.

9   In the Envelope dialog box, click the Close button.

10   Close the envelope document without saving it.

If you want to continue to the next lesson

▶   Be sure the Works Task Launcher dialog box is open.

If you want to quit Works for now

▶   In the Works Task Launcher dialog box, click the Exit Works button.

Lesson Summary

To	Do this	Button
Create form letters	Click Form Letters on the Tools menu. Follow the directions and answer the questions that appear on the screen, clicking the Next button after you complete each step. When you have printed the letters, click the Close button.	
Find and replace text	On the Edit menu, click Replace, and then type the search and replacement text. To replace single instances, click the Find Next button, and then click the Replace button. To replace all instances, click the Replace All button.	
Correct misspelled words	Move the insertion point to the beginning of the document, and then click the Spelling Checker button on the toolbar.	ABC ✓
Find synonyms	Click on a word, and then click Thesaurus on the Tools menu.	
Create mailing labels	Double-click Labels under the Envelopes and Labels category in the TaskWizards tab of the Works Task Launcher dialog box. Follow the directions and enter the required data that appear on the screen, clicking the Next button after you complete each step. When you have printed the labels, click the Close button.	
Create envelopes	Double-click Envelopes under the Envelopes and Labels category in the TaskWizards tab of the Works Task Launcher dialog box. Follow the directions and enter the required data that appear on the screen, clicking the Next button after you complete each step. When you have printed the envelopes, click the Close button.	

For online information about	Display the Help window, and then
Creating form letters	Click the Index button at the bottom of the Help window, double-click in the Type A Word text box, type **form**, click "form letters: creating," and then click "To write a form letter WP"
Replacing text	Click "Correct mistakes," and then click "To find and replace text"
Using the Spelling Checker	Click "Correct mistakes," and then click "To check spelling"
Using the Thesaurus	Click the Index button at the bottom of the Help window, highlight the text in the Type A Word text box, type **th**, and then click "thesaurus"
Creating mailing labels	Click "Create envelopes or mailing labels," and then click "To create mailing labels"
Creating envelopes	Click "Create envelopes or mailing labels," and then click "To create envelopes"

Preview of the Next Lesson

In this lesson, you created form letters, labels, and envelopes. You also used the spell check and thesaurus utilities. In the next lesson, you'll learn how to link a spreadsheet to a document and use the TaskWizards to create your own template.

Using Links and Templates

Estimated time
20 min.

In this lesson you will learn how to:

- Copy and link data.
- Create your own templates.
- Use your own templates.

Each business quarter you create income statements to submit to your accountant. Although the spreadsheet data provides all the figures the accountant needs, a document describing and explaining the data would be helpful.

You can create a document that shows the data in spreadsheet form and contains explanatory text by pasting spreadsheet data into a Word Processor document. You paste the data using a link. A *link* is an electronic connection between a *source file* (the file from which you copy information) and a *destination file* (the file in which you paste the copied information). Any changes you make in the source file will be reflected in the destination file. In this case, the spreadsheet with the quarterly income figures will be the source file, and the Word Processor document will be the destination file.

You have also decided to start taking mail, phone, and fax orders from customers who are too far away to visit your store; however, you need customized order forms to send to these customers. You can use TaskWizards to create a price list order form, customize the information on the form, and then save it as a template. In this lesson, you'll copy and link spreadsheet data into a Word Processor document, create an order form template, and then use the template to enter an order.

Linking Spreadsheet Data to a Another File

Linking two documents created with different Works tools is as easy as copying and pasting. In the next exercises, you'll paste spreadsheet data into a Word Processor document with a link.

Open the Word Processor document

1   Open Income Document in the Works SBS Practice folder.

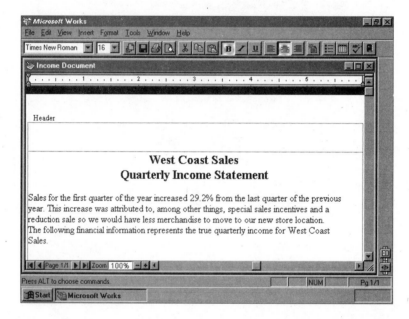

2   Maximize the document.

3   Position the insertion point on the second blank line under the first paragraph.

This is where you will paste the spreadsheet cells.

Open the spreadsheet

1   On the File menu, click Open.

The Open dialog box appears. Notice that even though you are in the Word Processor, all Works documents are displayed.

2   Double-click Quarterly Income.

The file opens in front of Income Document.

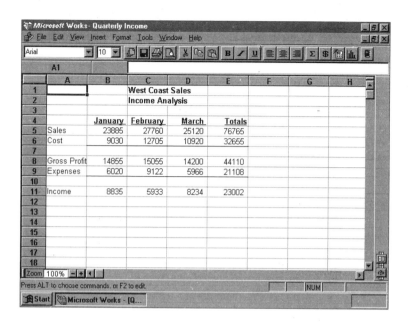

Copy the data with a link

1 Highlight cells A4 through E11, as shown in the following illustration.

Copy

2 Click the Copy button on the toolbar.

The data is copied.

3 On the Window menu, click 1 Income Document.

The Word Processor document appears.

> **TIP** You can also use the Cascade command on the Window menu so both application windows are visible on your desktop. Simply click a window title bar to make the window active.

4 Make sure the pointer is still positioned on the second blank line beneath the first paragraph, and then click Paste Special on the Edit menu.

The Paste Special dialog box appears.

You can paste the data in a number of formats; however, when you paste and link, you are restricted to using Microsoft Works 4.0 Sheet or Chart Object.

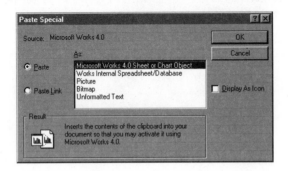

5 Click Paste Link.

Notice that the As options change to reflect your choice to paste and link.

6 Click the OK button.

If the First-Time Help dialog box appears, click Don't Display This Message In The Future, and then click the OK button.

The spreadsheet cells are pasted as an object in the Word Processor document, as shown in the following illustration.

You can paste data from one source document into many destination documents. When the data changes in the source document, it changes in all the destination documents as well.

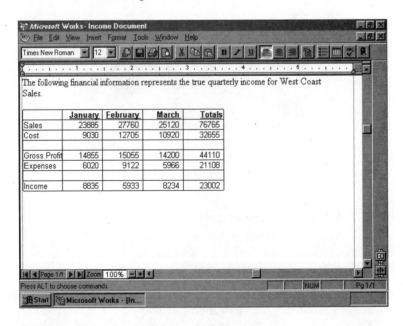

Notice that the information copied from the spreadsheet retains the original format.

Center Align

7 Click the Center Align button on the toolbar.

The spreadsheet object is centered on the page.

Update the data

You discover an error in the sales figure for March. Since the spreadsheet figures were pasted into the Word Processor document with a link, you can edit data in the spreadsheet and the changes will be reflected automatically in the Word Processor document.

1 On the Window menu, click 2 Quarterly Income.

The spreadsheet becomes the active window.

TIP   You can also double-click the spreadsheet object to make the spreadsheet the active window.

2 Move the highlight to cell D5.

3 Type **32887**, and then press ENTER.

4 On the Window menu, click 1 Income Document.

The change is reflected in the spreadsheet object, as shown in the next illustration.

	January	February	March	Totals
Sales	23885	27760	32887	84532
Cost	9030	12705	10920	32655
Gross Profit	14855	15055	21967	51877
Expenses	6020	9122	5966	21108
Income	8835	5933	16001	30769

NOTE   The destination file can be closed when a source file is updated. The data will be updated automatically the next time you open the destination file.

5 Save and then close Income Document.

6 Save and then close Quarterly Income.

Customizing a Template

You can create many standard business documents by using templates. *Templates* are predesigned documents with the basic layout, formatting, and sample text already in place. Templates save you time by eliminating the need to create and format documents—you just "fill in the blanks" and print. Works templates are accessed through the TaskWizards. You use the TaskWizard templates to quickly create sales invoices, income statements, newsletters, and so forth. You can also customize TaskWizard templates and save them as your own custom templates. In the next exercises, you'll use a TaskWizard to create a price list order form, enter information, and save the document as a custom template.

Open and complete the TaskWizard

You can start with a TaskWizard template, customize it, and save it as a user-defined, or custom template.

1 In the Works Task Launcher dialog box, click the TaskWizards tab if it isn't the displayed tab.

2 In the list of TaskWizards, click Business Management.

A list of business management TaskWizards appears.

3 Double-click Price List.

A secondary Works Task Launcher dialog box appears.

4 Click Yes, Run The TaskWizard.

The Price List TaskWizard appears.

To display more information about TaskWizards, click the Instructions button in the lower left section of the TaskWizard dialog box.

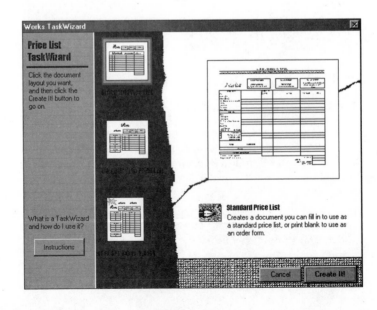

You will use the Standard Price List template, which is the default selection, for your order form.

5 Click the Create It! button.

The Standard Price List template opens.

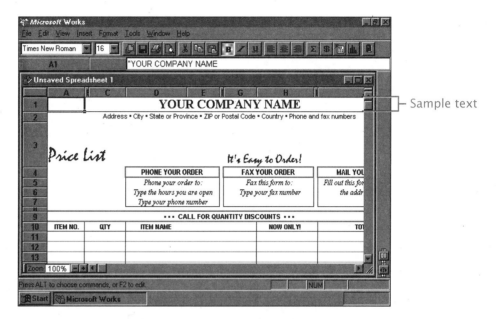

Sample text

The template is a spreadsheet that contains sample text, which you will replace with text of your own. You will also enter additional text, using the spreadsheet skills you have already learned.

6 Maximize the template window.

Enter constant information

Now that you have opened the template, you can enter the information necessary to create your custom price list template.

1 Type **West Coast Sales**, and then press ENTER.

The first line of sample text is replaced.

2 Click cell A2.

The cell contents display in the entry bar.

3 In the entry bar, double-click the word *Address*.

4 Type **735 West Broadway Road**, and then press SPACEBAR.

The word *Address* is replaced with *735 West Broadway Road*.

131

5   In the entry bar, double-click the word *City*.

6   Type **Phoenix**, and then press SPACEBAR.

    The sample text is replaced with *Phoenix*.

7   Replace the text *State or Province* with the text *Arizona*.

8   Replace the text *ZIP or Postal Code* with the text *85008*.

9   Highlight all the text to the right of the zip code, and then press DELETE.

    The remaining sample text is deleted from the header.

10 Press ENTER.

11 Double-click cell D6, highlight the text *"Type the hours you are open*, and then press DELETE to delete the sample text.

12 Type **(602) 555-8437**, and then press ENTER.

13 Double-click cell D7, highlight the text *"Type your phone number*, and then press DELETE to delete the sample text.

14 Double-click cell G6, highlight the text *"Type your fax number*, type **(602) 555-8787**, and then press ENTER.

    The sample text is replaced with your fax number. The spreadsheet should now match the following illustration.

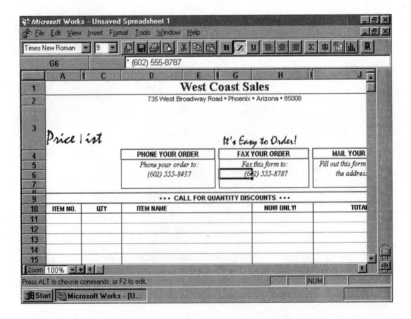

Save the document as a template

Now that you have customized the Standard Price List TaskWizard template, you can save it as a custom template and use it to create additional price lists.

Save

1   Click the Save button on the toolbar.

The Save As dialog box appears.

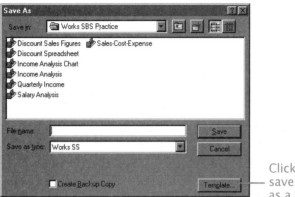

Click here to save a document as a template

2   Click the Template button.

The Save As Template dialog box appears.

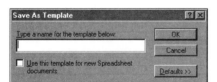

3   Type **Price List Order Form**, and then press ENTER.

The document is saved as a template. The spreadsheet remains unnamed.

Whenever you open a template, a new document is opened automatically. By default, the information you enter is saved to the document and not the template. When you save a document as a template, the document that was opened with the template still exists.

4   Close the spreadsheet document without saving it.

TIP   You can save a Works document as a template and as a document. Simply save the template and then resave it as a document.

Using the Price List Template

Now that you have created a custom template, you can use it to create new price list order forms for individual customers. All the custom information, such as the company name, address, and telephone and fax numbers, will appear automatically on each price list order form. All you need to do is enter information about the products each customer orders. In the next exercises, you'll enter product information, and then save the template as a document.

Open the template

1   In the Works Task Launcher dialog box, scroll down the list and click User Defined Templates.

The template you created in the previous exercises is listed.

2   Double-click Price List Order Form.

The template opens as a new spreadsheet document, as shown in the next illustration.

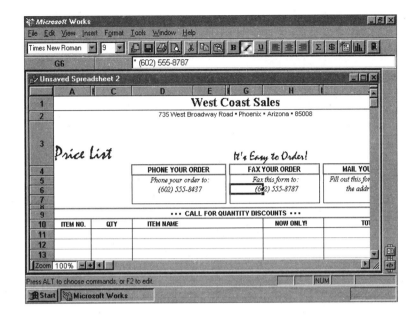

If you want to use the template more efficiently, you can enter the item number, name, and cost of each item in your inventory, and then save that information as part of your custom template.

Enter variable information

1 Maximize the spreadsheet.

2 Move the highlight to cell A11, type **131**, and then press TAB.

3 Type **24**, and then press TAB.

4 Type **Skein Worsted Weight Wool Yarn**, and then press TAB.

5 Type **4.35**, and then press ENTER.

The subtotal, *104.40*, is calculated automatically in cell J11. Scroll to the right to see the total. The spreadsheet should now match the following illustration.

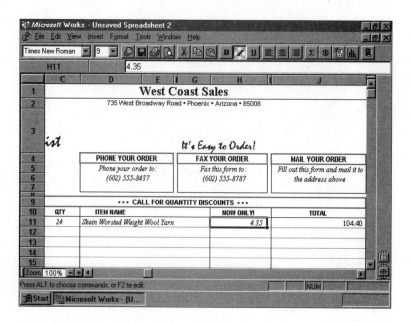

6 Scroll down and move the highlight to cell H49.

You need to enter the sales tax and shipping and handling amounts in order for the template to calculate the total cost.

7 Type **6.5**, and then press ENTER.

The sales tax, $6.79, is calculated automatically in cell J49.

8 Move the highlight to cell J50, type **5**, and then press ENTER.

The shipping and handling is added and the total cost is updated in cell J51. Scroll down to see the total. The spreadsheet should now match the following illustration.

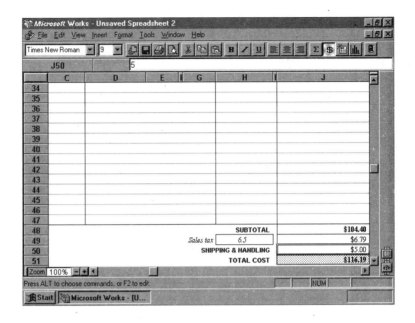

Save the template as a document

After you add the variable information to the template, you can save it as a document that you can open and edit the same as any other spreadsheet.

Save

1 Click the Save button on the toolbar.

The Save As dialog box appears.

2 Type **Johnson Order**, and then press ENTER.

The document is saved.

☒

Close

3 In the Johnson Order menu bar, click the Close button.

The Works Task Launcher dialog box appears.

One Step Further: Saving a Document as a Template

If the Works TaskWizard templates don't quite suit your needs, you can save an existing document as a custom template. You decide to use a spreadsheet document to create a template for updating income statements to send to your accountant.

Save an existing document as a template

You will use the Quarterly Income document as a template because you submit it to your accountant regularly. The existing document will be ideal once you change some basic information.

1 Open Quarterly Income.

2 Move the highlight to cell B4, type **Month1**, and then press the RIGHT ARROW key.

3 Type **Month2**, press the RIGHT ARROW key, type **Month3**, and then press ENTER.

4 Move the highlight to cell A1.

5 On the File menu, click Save As.

The Save As dialog box appears.

6 Click the Template button.

The Save As Template dialog box appears.

7 In the Type A Name For The Template Below text box, type **Monthly Income**

8 Press ENTER.

The file is now saved as a template you can use to create updated income statements.

Templates you create from documents are saved to the same template directory that you access from User Defined Templates in the Works Task Launcher dialog box.

9 Close Quarterly Income without saving.

If you want to continue to the next lesson

▶ Be sure the Works Task Launcher dialog box is open.

If you want to quit Works for now

▶ Click the Exit Works button in the Works Task Launcher dialog box.

Lesson Summary

To	Do this	Button
Link spreadsheet data to a Word Processor document	Open a Word Processor document, open a spreadsheet, and then highlight the spreadsheet cells to copy. Click the Copy button on the toolbar, display the Word Processor document, click Paste Special on the Edit menu, click Paste Link, and then click the OK button.	
Open a TaskWizard template	Click the TaskWizards tab in the Works Task Launcher dialog box, select a category, and then double-click a TaskWizard name.	
Save a TaskWizard template as a custom template	On the File menu, click Save As, click the Template button, type a template name, and then click the OK button.	
Open a custom template	Click the TaskWizards tab in the Works Task Launcher dialog box, click User Defined Templates, and then double-click the custom template you want to open.	
Save an existing document as a template	On the File menu, click Save As, click the Template button, type a template name, and then click the OK button.	

For online information about	Display the Help window, and then
Linking data between two documents	Click the Index button, type **link** in the Type A Word text box, and then click "linked objects: copying"
Using TaskWizard templates	Click the Index button, type **template** in the Type A Word text box, and then click "templates: Works 3.0 templates"
Using custom templates	Click the Index button, type **template** in the Type A Word text box, click "templates: creating," and then click "To create your own template"

Preview of the Next Lessons

In Part 3 of this book, you'll learn about formatting features that will make your spreadsheets attractive and easy to read; how to create, modify, and print charts of spreadsheet data; and how to use Works to communicate with other people through your modem.

Review & Practice

In the lessons in Part 2, "Creating Business Documents," you learned to work with complex documents by creating form letters, mailing labels, and envelopes. You learned how to add clip art and special text effects to your documents. You also learned how to link spreadsheet data to a Word Processor document and use TaskWizards and custom templates. If you want to practice these skills before you proceed with the lessons in Part 3, you can work through the Review & Practice section following this lesson.

Review & Practice

You will review and practice how to:

**Estimated time
45 min.**

- Format a document.
- Insert and format a table.
- Add clip art to a document.
- Create form letters and envelopes.
- Link spreadsheet data to a document.
- Use templates.

In this Review & Practice, you have an opportunity to fine-tune the skills you learned in the lessons in Part 2 of this book. You'll use what you learned about formatting a document, using tables, adding clip art, creating form letters and envelopes, linking spreadsheet data, and using templates to create personalized letters for your customers and a financial report to apply for a loan.

Scenario

During the past year, you have received several customer requests to hold arts and crafts classes at your store. You've decided to give the idea a try and are currently preparing to offer two classes. These preparations include advertising the classes, applying for a small loan to build a classroom workshop area, and creating gift certificates as an incentive for class enrollment. You'll create form letters to let customers know about the classes, prepare a preliminary loan application to your banker that includes spreadsheet data, and use a TaskWizard to create your gift certificates.

Step 1: Format a Document

1 Open Customer Classes Letter from the Works SBS Practice folder.

2 Maximize the document.

3 Open the Page Setup dialog box, and then click the Margins tab if it is not the displayed tab.

4 Set 1.5-inch left and right margins.

5 Highlight all the text from the date under the letterhead to the end of the document.

6 Change the font to Arial and the font size to 10 points.

7 Replace the text *Your name goes here* at the end of the document with your name.

8 Highlight the paragraph that begins *I am looking forward....*

9 Italicize the highlighted text.

10 Center align the highlighted text.

Your screen should now match the following illustration.

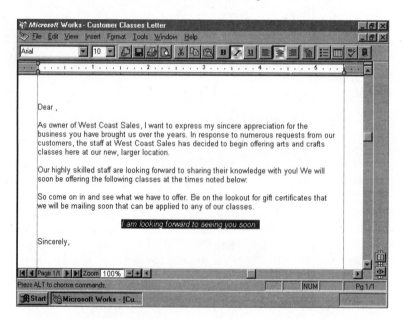

For more information on	See
Changing margins	Lesson 4
Changing the font, size, and style of text	Lesson 4
Changing the alignment of text	Lesson 4

Step 2: *Insert and Format a Table*

1   Insert a second blank line below the paragraph that begins *Our highly skilled staff....*

2   Add a three-row, two-column table.

3   Type the following text in the table, pressing TAB to move between table cells.

Class Offered	Class Time
Custom Photo Albums	Mon & Wed 6:00 PM
Silk Floral Arrangements	Tue & Thu 6:30 PM

4   Assign the Traditional Green AutoFormat to the table.

5   Use the Column Width dialog box to assign a width of 25 characters to each column.

6   Click to the right of the table, center the table, and then add a blank line beneath the table.

Your screen should look like the following illustration.

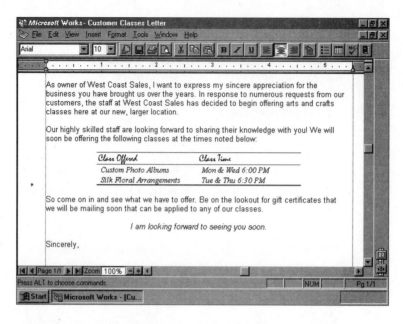

For more information on	See
Inserting a table	Lesson 4
Formatting a table	Lesson 4

Step 3: Add Clip Art and WordArt to a Document

1   Position the insertion point at the top of the document.

2   From the Insert menu, display the ClipArt Gallery.

3   From the Buildings category, insert the Store Front clip art picture.

4   Drag the lower right sizing handle until the picture is about 1 inch square.

5   Position the insertion point on the second blank line above the current date.

6   On the Insert menu, click WordArt.

7   Type **We're Listening!**, and then click the Close button in the Enter Your Text Here dialog box title bar.

8   Change the shape to the Wave 2 (the last shape in the fourth row of the Shapes drop-down list).

9   Change the font size to 12 points.

10   Click outside the WordArt object.

11   Center the WordArt object, and then click outside the object.

Your screen should match the following illustration.

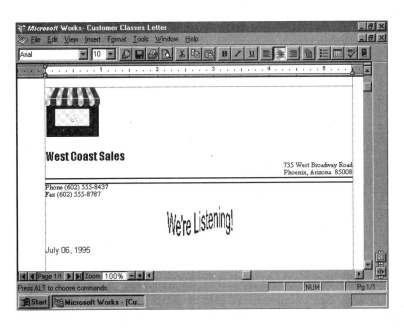

For more information on	See
Adding graphics	Lesson 4
Using WordArt	Lesson 4

Step 4: *Create Form Letters and Envelopes*

1   Position the insertion point on the blank line above the paragraph that begins *Dear....*

2   Open the Form Letters dialog box, select Customer Database.wdb, and specify to print all records in the database.

3   Insert the form letter field names below from Customer Database.wdb. Use the Advanced tab of the Form Letters dialog box to edit the field names as shown below:

<<First Name>> <<Last Name>>
<<Address>>
<<City>>, <<State>> <<Zip>>

Dear <<First Name>>,

4   Preview and print all the form letters, then close the Form Letters dialog box.

5   Save and close Customer Classes Letter.

6   Open the Envelopes TaskWizard.

7 Accept the default envelope size, select Customer Database.wdb, and specify to print all records in the database.

8 Type the following text for the return address:

West Coast Sales Arts & Crafts
735 West Broadway Road
Phoenix, AZ 85008

9 Add the fields shown below for the main address:

<<First Name>> <<Last Name>>
<<Address>>
<<City>>, <<State>> <<Zip>>

10 Preview and then print all the envelopes.

11 Close the TaskWizard, and then close the envelopes document without saving it.

For more information on	See
Creating form letters	Lesson 5
Previewing and printing form letters	Lesson 5
Creating envelopes	Lesson 5
Previewing and printing envelopes	Lesson 5

Step 5: Linking Spreadsheet Data

1 Open Loan Request from the Works SBS Practice folder.

2 Position the insertion point on the blank line following the paragraph that begins *I would like to request...*, and then press ENTER.

3 Open Quarterly Income.

4 Copy cells A4 through E11, and then paste them into the Loan Request document as a Works spreadsheet object with a link.

5 Center the spreadsheet object.

Your screen should now match the following illustration.

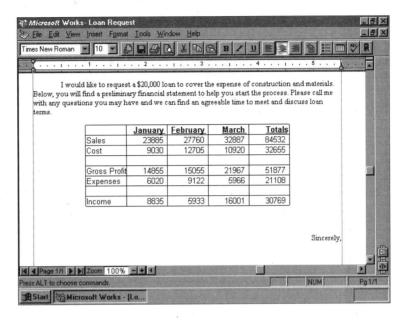

I would like to request a $20,000 loan to cover the expense of construction and materials. Below, you will find a preliminary financial statement to help you start the process. Please call me with any questions you may have and we can find an agreeable time to meet and discuss loan terms.

	January	February	March	Totals
Sales	23885	27760	32887	84532
Cost	9030	12705	10920	32655
Gross Profit	14855	15055	21967	51877
Expenses	6020	9122	5966	21108
Income	8835	5933	16001	30769

6 Save and then close Loan Request.

7 Close Quarterly Income.

For more information about	See
Linking spreadsheet data to another file	Lesson 6

Step 6: *Creating Custom Templates*

1 Run the Certificate TaskWizard from the Students and Teachers category.

2 Select the Gift Certificate layout, and then click the Create It button.

3 Highlight and then delete the $50 and $75 gift certificates.

4 In the $25 gift certificate, replace the text *the bearer* with the text *you.*

5 Replace the text *purchase* with the text *arts and crafts class.*

Your screen should now match the following illustration.

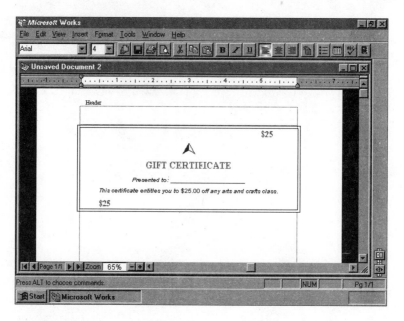

6 Save the document as a template using the name *Gift Certificate*.

7 Close the document without saving it.

For more information on	See
Customizing a template	Lesson 6

If you want to continue to the next lesson

▶ Be sure the Works Task Launcher dialog box is open.

If you want to quit Works for now

▶ Click the Exit Works button in the Works Task Launcher dialog box.

Illustrating and Communicating Information

Modifying Spreadsheets

In this lesson you will learn how to:

Estimated time
35 min.

- Perform calculations.
- Work with rows and columns.
- Change column widths.
- Change number formats.
- Change the alignment of cell entries.
- Change the font size and font style of cell entries.
- Add borders and shading to cells.
- Print spreadsheets.
- Protect cells from changes.

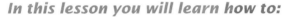

Now that West Coast Sales has relocated, you still see many areas for improvement. You decide to explore the possibilities for more growth by seeking investors. You have started a spreadsheet that analyzes your income to present to investors; however, you need to make the data easier to read. It could also use more visual appeal. In this lesson, you'll perform calculations and use the Spreadsheet formatting features to modify the appearance of your spreadsheet. You'll also use Spreadsheet features to protect your data from being altered.

Performing Calculations

You can use the Spreadsheet to make simple or complex calculations. In the next exercises, you'll work with formulas and functions, and use Easy Calc.

Enter formulas

Formulas must begin with an equal sign (=) and can contain numbers, cell references, other formulas, and mathematical operators (such as +, -, *, or /).

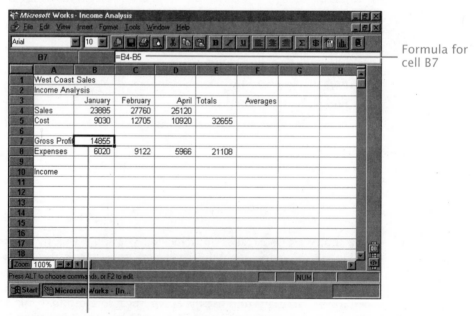

Maximize

1 In the Works SBS Practice folder, open Income Analysis, and then click the Maximize button in the Income Analysis title bar.

2 Move the highlight to cell B7.

You need to enter two formulas in your spreadsheet to calculate Gross Profit and Income. Gross Profit is Sales minus Cost. You can type an entire formula from the keyboard, or you can move the highlight to add cell references to a formula.

3 Type **=b4-b5**, and then press ENTER.

Works subtracts the number in cell B5 (Cost) from the number in cell B4 (Sales). The result of the formula (Gross Profit) appears in cell B7 and the formula appears in the entry bar, as shown in the following illustration.

Formula for cell B7

The result of the formula appears in the cell

You can copy a formula from one cell to other cells to perform the same calculation on other data in the spreadsheet.

4   Highlight cells B7 through D7, and then click Fill Right on the Edit menu.

The formula is copied from the first cell to the empty highlighted cells to calculate the gross profit for each month.

The cell references in the formula adjust after you copy them to the empty cells in the highlighted range. The formula in cell C7 adjusts to "=C4-C5," and the formula in cell D7 adjusts to "=D4-D5."

5   Move the highlight to cell B10.

Now you'll use the mouse to enter a formula to calculate Income. Income is Gross Profit minus Expenses.

6   Type = to begin the formula.

7   Click cell B7.

Works adds the cell reference to the formula.

8   Type -

The highlight moves back to the starting cell after you specify a mathematical operator.

9   Click cell B8 to add the cell reference to the formula.

10   Press ENTER to complete the Income formula.

Your spreadsheet should now look like the following illustration.

	A	B	C	D	E	F	G	H
1	West Coast Sales							
2	Income Analysis							
3		January	February	April	Totals		Averages	
4	Sales	23885	27760	25120				
5	Cost	9030	12705	10920	32655			
6								
7	Gross Profit	14855	15055	14200				
8	Expenses	6020	9122	5966	21108			
9								
10	Income	8835						
11								

11   Highlight cells B10 through D10, and then click Fill Right on the Edit menu.

The formula is copied from the first cell to the empty highlighted cells to calculate the income for each month.

Save

12   Click the Save button on the toolbar to save your work.

Enter functions

Functions are predefined formulas you can use to perform complex calculations in your spreadsheet. Using functions for calculations can save you time and help reduce errors in your spreadsheet.

153

Works functions and instructions for using them are listed by type in the online Help System.

Works contains 76 functions. You'll use the AVG and SUM functions to calculate a sales average and a sales total in your spreadsheet.

1 Move the highlight to cell F4.

Functions begin with an equal sign followed by a word or abbreviation that defines the action of the function.

2 Type **=avg(b4:d4)**

The range reference in parentheses is the *argument*, which specifies the range on which you want to perform the calculation. In this case, you will be averaging the numbers in cells B4 through D4. You must separate the cell references in the argument with a colon (:).

3 Press ENTER.

The AVG function averages the numbers in the specified range of cells and inserts the result, 25588.333, in cell F4.

4 Move the highlight to cell E4.

You will insert the total of the sales figures in columns B through D in cell E4 by using AutoSum, a Works feature that automatically highlights and totals a range of cells near the highlighted cell.

5 Click the AutoSum button on the toolbar.

AutoSum

Works inserts the SUM function in the entry bar and highlights an adjacent range of cells containing numbers. The SUM function will total the numbers in the highlighted range of cells. Your spreadsheet should match the following illustration.

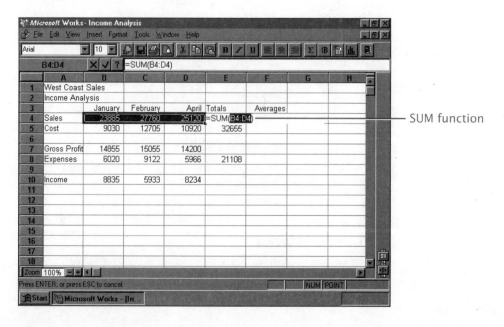

SUM function

Enter box

6 Click the Enter box on the entry bar.

Works inserts the SUM function in the cell and totals the highlighted numbers. Your spreadsheet should now match the following illustration.

	A	B	C	D	E	F	G	H
1	West Coast Sales							
2	Income Analysis							
3		January	February	April	Totals	Averages		
4	Sales	23885	27760	25120	76765	25588.333		
5	Cost	9030	12705	10920	32655			
6								
7	Gross Profit	14855	15055	14200				
8	Expenses	6020	9122	5966	21108			
9								
10	Income	8835	5933	8234				
11								

NOTE Clicking the Enter box is the same as pressing the ENTER key after completing a cell entry.

---

7 Total the gross profit in cell E7.

The result, 44110, appears in cell E7.

8 Total the income in cell E10.

The result, 23002, appears in cell E10.

9 Save your work.

Use Easy Calc

Easy Calc steps you through the process of creating a function to perform a calculation. You can use Easy Calc to step through any function available in the Spreadsheet. Easy Calc consists of a sequence of dialog boxes.

1 Move the highlight to cell F5.

2 Click the Easy Calc button on the toolbar.

Easy Calc

The first Easy Calc dialog box appears, displaying functions you can click to insert in your formula.

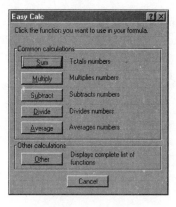

3 Click the Average button.

The second Easy Calc dialog box appears, displaying a text box in which you enter the range of cells that contain the numbers you want to calculate.

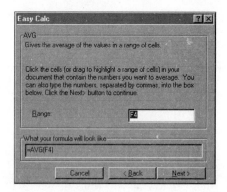

4 If necessary, move the dialog box so that row 5 is visible.

5 Highlight cells B5 through D5.

The highlighted range is entered into the Range text box.

The Easy Calc dialog box should appear as shown in the following illustration.

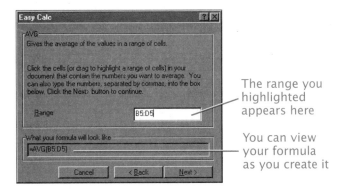

The range you
highlighted
appears here

You can view
your formula
as you create it

6 Click the Next button.

The third Easy Calc dialog box appears.

This is the cell
where the calculation
result will appear

The third Easy Calc dialog box shows you what the formula looks like before it is
inserted into the spreadsheet.

7 Click the Finish button.

The result of the formula is automatically inserted into the highlighted cell, as
shown in the next illustration.

	A	B	C	D	E	F	G	H
1	West Coast Sales							
2	Income Analysis							
3		January	February	April	Totals	Averages		
4	Sales	23885	27760	25120	76765	25588.333		
5	Cost	9030	12705	10920	32655	10885		
6								
7	Gross Profit	14855	15055	14200	44110			
8	Expenses	6020	9122	5966	21108			
9								
10	Income	8835	5933	8234	23002			
11								

Formula
result

157

You can copy a formula you create with Easy Calc to perform the same calculation on other data.

Copy

8 Click the Copy button on the toolbar.

The EasyCalc formula is copied.

9 Highlight cells F7 and F8, and then click the Paste button on the toolbar.

The result of the copied formula is inserted into the highlighted cells.

Paste

10 Move the highlight to cell F10, and then click the Paste button on the toolbar.

The result of the copied formula is inserted into cell F10.

The spreadsheet should now match the following illustration.

	A	B	C	D	E	F	G	H
1	West Coast Sales							
2	Income Analysis							
3		January	February	April	Totals	Averages		
4	Sales	23885	27760	25120	76765	25588.333		
5	Cost	9030	12705	10920	32655	10885		
6								
7	Gross Profit	14855	15055	14200	44110	14703.333		
8	Expenses	6020	9122	5966	21108	7036		
9								
10	Income	8835	5933	8234	23002	7667.3333		
11								

11 Save your work.

Making the Spreadsheet Easy to Read

The rows and columns of data in your spreadsheet are too close together, and the spreadsheet needs data for the month of March. You can insert blank rows and widen the columns to make your spreadsheet easier to read and add new data by inserting a column and entering the numbers. You can also change number formats, change cell alignment and fonts, and add borders and shading to enhance the appearance of your spreadsheet. In the next exercises, you'll insert rows and columns, change column widths, and add data. You'll also change number formats and enhance the appearance of your data.

Insert rows

You can insert blank rows to increase the amount of space between the spreadsheet title and the monthly entries, and between the monthly entries and the Sales data.

1 Click the row label for row number 4 to highlight the entire row, as shown in the next illustration.

Click the row
label to
highlight the
entire row

	A	B	C	D	E	F	G	H
1	West Coast Sales							
2	Income Analysis							
3		January	February	April	Totals	Averages		
4	Sales	23885	27760	25120	76765	25588.333		
5	Cost	9030	12705	10920	32655	10885		
6								
7	Gross Profit	14855	15055	14200	44110	14703.333		
8	Expenses	6020	9122	5966	21108	7036		
9								
10	Income	8835	5933	8234	23002	7667.3333		
11								

*You can
delete a row by
highlighting it,
and then clicking
Delete Row on
the Insert menu.*

2 On the Insert menu, click Insert Row.

Works inserts a new row above the highlighted row. The number of rows you highlight determines the number of rows that will be inserted into the spreadsheet.

3 Drag across row labels 3 and 4 to highlight the rows.

You can also click with the right mouse button to display *context-sensitive* menu commands, which are commands specific to your selection, instead of clicking commands on the menu bar.

4 Use the right mouse button to click the highlighted area, and then click Insert Row.

Works inserts two new rows into the spreadsheet, as shown in the following illustration.

	A	B	C	D	E	F	G	H
1	West Coast Sales							
2	Income Analysis							
3								
4								
5		January	February	April	Totals	Averages		
6								
7	Sales	23885	27760	25120	76765	25588.333		
8	Cost	9030	12705	10920	32655	10885		
9								
10	Gross Profit	14855	15055	14200	44110	14703.333		
11	Expenses	6020	9122	5966	21108	7036		
12								
13	Income	8835	5933	8234	23002	7667.3333		
14								

Insert a column

To enter the March data, you'll need to insert a column.

1   Click the column label D to highlight the entire column.

The number of columns you highlight determines the number of columns that will be inserted into the spreadsheet.

2   Use the right mouse button to click the highlighted area, and then click Insert Column.

Works inserts a new column to the left of the highlighted column. You can now enter the data for March in the new column.

3   Highlight cells E5 through E13, and then click the Copy button on the toolbar.

Copy

4   Move the highlight to cell D5, and then click the Paste button on the toolbar.

Paste

The data and formulas in cells E5 through E13 are copied to cells D5 through D13.

Although the data you copied to the new column is not the data for March, you also copied formulas, which adjusted when they were pasted to the new location. You will need to change the data entries, but you will not need to enter new formulas.

5   Change the entry in cell D5 to **March**

6   Change the entry in cell D7 to **31000**

As you change the entry for the March Sales figure, every existing formula that refers to cell D7 updates to reflect the new data. As you enter the rest of the data for March, other formulas will also update.

7   Change the entry in cell D8 to **12468**

8   Change the entry in cell D11 to **5820**

Your spreadsheet should now match the following illustration.

	A	B	C	D	E	F	G	H
1	West Coast Sales							
2	Income Analysis							
3								
4								
5		January	February	March	April	Totals	Averages	
6								
7	Sales	23885	27760	31000	25120	107765	26941.25	
8	Cost	9030	12705	12468	10920	45123	11280.75	
9								
10	Gross Profit	14855	15055	18532	14200	62642	15660.5	
11	Expenses	6020	9122	5820	5966	26928	6732	
12								
13	Income	8835	5933	12712	8234	35714	8928.5	
14								

Change column widths

If cell entries are too long for the width of a column, or if you want to add space between columns, you can change column widths.

1 Drag across column labels B through G to highlight the columns.

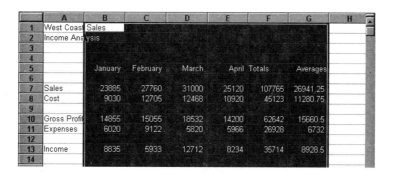

2 Use the right mouse button to click the highlighted area, and then click Column Width.

The Column Width dialog box appears. Initially, all columns are preset to a width of 10 characters.

3 Type **12**

The Column Width dialog box should now appear as shown in the following illustration.

4 Press ENTER.

Columns B through G are now each 12 characters wide.

Adjust pointer

TIP You can also drag the border next to a column label to change the width of a single column. When you place the pointer on the border, it changes to the Adjust pointer.

---

5 Double-click column label A.

Works automatically adjusts the column to accommodate the width of the longest entry. This feature is called the *best fit*.

TIP You can also click the Best Fit button in the Column Width dialog box to change a column width to the best fit.

Change number formats

You can format numbers in your spreadsheet to display as currency, dates, percentages, and so forth.

1   If necessary, click the right horizontal scroll arrow until columns B through G are visible.

2   Highlight cells B7 through G7.

3   On the Format menu, click Number.

   The Format Cells dialog box appears, displaying the Number tab.

4   In the Format section, click Currency.

   The Currency format displays numbers with a leading dollar sign, thousands separators, and a specified number of decimal places (numbers that appear to the right of the decimal point).

5   Type **0** to specify the number of decimal places.

   The Format Cells dialog box should now look like the following illustration.

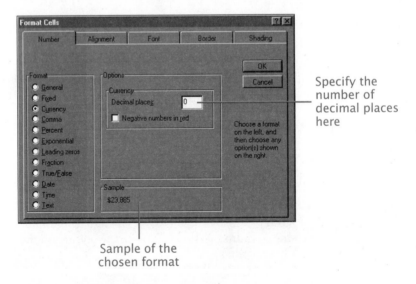

Specify the number of decimal places here

Sample of the chosen format

6   Press ENTER to apply the new number format.

   The numbers in the highlighted cells now appear in the Currency format with no decimal places.

7 Highlight cells B8 through G11.

8 On the Format menu, click Number.

9 In the Format section, click Comma.

The Comma format displays numbers with thousands separators and a specified number of decimal places.

10 Type **0** to specify the number of decimal places.

11 Press ENTER.

The numbers in the highlighted cells now appear in the Comma format with no decimal places.

12 Highlight cells B13 through G13.

Currency

13 Click the Currency button on the toolbar.

Clicking the Currency button applies the Currency format with two decimal places.

Your screen should now match the following illustration.

	B	C	D	E	F	G	H
1							
2							
3							
4							
5	January	February	March	April	Totals	Averages	
6							
7	$23,885	$27,760	$31,000	$25,120	$107,765	$26,941	
8	9,030	12,705	12,468	10,920	45,123	11,281	
9							
10	14,855	15,055	18,532	14,200	62,642	15,661	
11	6,020	9,122	5,820	5,966	26,928	6,732	
12							
13	$8,835.00	$5,933.00	$12,712.00	$8,234.00	$35,714.00	$8,928.50	
14							

TIP To avoid cluttering the spreadsheet with dollar signs, apply the Currency format to only the first and last rows of numbers in the spreadsheet.

14 Save your work.

Emphasizing Information

Your spreadsheet is looking better, but you can enhance its appearance even more by using the Spreadsheet formatting features. You can change alignment to emphasize certain cell entries, change the font size and style to accentuate text, use borders to differentiate sections of your spreadsheet, and use shading to emphasize column labels. In the following exercises, you'll change the alignment of cell entries, change the font size and font style of text entries, and add borders and shading.

Change the alignment of cell entries

Right Align

Center Align

1 Move the highlight to cell F5.

2 Click the Right Align button on the toolbar.

   The cell entry aligns with the right border of the cell, matching the rest of the cell entries in row 5.

3 Move the highlight to cell A10.

4 Click the Center Align button on the toolbar.

   The entry is now centered in the cell, distinguishing it from the other entries in column A.

5 Move the highlight to cell A13, and then click the Center Align button.

6 Highlight cells A1 through G2.

7 On the Format menu, click Alignment.

   The Format Cells dialog box appears, displaying the Alignment tab.

8 In the Horizontal section, click Center Across Selection.

   The Format Cells dialog box should now match the following illustration.

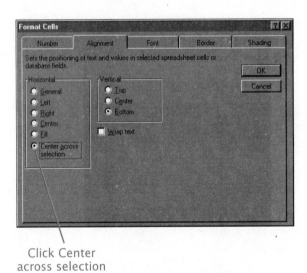

Click Center
across selection

9 Click the OK button.

   Your screen should now match the following illustration.

164

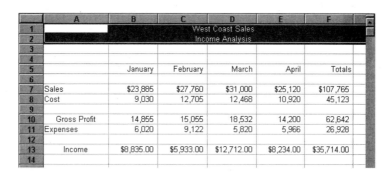

	A	B	C	D	E	F
1			West Coast Sales			
2			Income Analysis			
3						
4						
5		January	February	March	April	Totals
6						
7	Sales	$23,885	$27,760	$31,000	$25,120	$107,765
8	Cost	9,030	12,705	12,468	10,920	45,123
9						
10	Gross Profit	14,855	15,055	18,532	14,200	62,642
11	Expenses	6,020	9,122	5,820	5,966	26,928
12						
13	Income	$8,835.00	$5,933.00	$12,712.00	$8,234.00	$35,714.00
14						

Notice that the cell entries are now centered within the highlighted block. Although the text appears to be in cells C1 through D2, it is actually the contents of cell A1.

Change the font size and font style of text entries

Font Size

Bold

Italic

1 Move the highlight to cell A1.

Notice that the text *West Coast Sales* appears in the entry bar even though it is not highlighted on your screen.

2 Click the arrow to the right of the Font Size list box on the toolbar, and then select 16.

The font size increases, making the text larger.

3 Click the Bold button on the toolbar.

Now the spreadsheet title is bold.

4 Move the highlight to cell A2.

5 Click the Italic button on the toolbar.

The spreadsheet subtitle is now italicized, as shown in the following illustration.

Title is large and bold

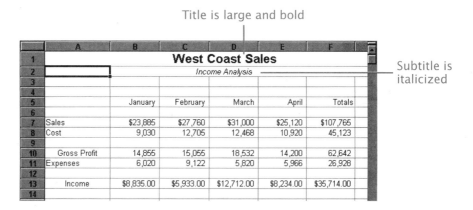

Subtitle is italicized

Bold

6 Highlight cells B5 through G5.

7 Click the Bold button on the toolbar to apply the bold style to the column headings.

8 Click cell H5.

Your spreadsheet should now match the next illustration.

	B	C	D	E	F	G	H
1			**West Coast Sales**				
2			*Income Analysis*				
3							
4							
5	**January**	**February**	**March**	**April**	**Totals**	**Averages**	
6							
7	$23,885	$27,760	$31,000	$25,120	$107,765	$26,941	
8	9,030	12,705	12,468	10,920	45,123	11,281	
9							
10	14,855	15,055	18,532	14,200	62,642	15,661	
11	6,020	9,122	5,820	5,966	26,928	6,732	
12							
13	$8,835.00	$5,933.00	$12,712.00	$8,234.00	$35,714.00	$8,928.50	
14							

Add borders

To undo an existing border and line style, select the existing border in the Format Cells dialog box, and then select the blank line style.

Adding borders can help differentiate the Cost, Expenses, and Income sections of your spreadsheet.

1 Highlight cells B8 through G8.

2 On the Format menu, click Border.

The Format Cells dialog box appears, displaying the Border tab.

3 In the Border section, click Bottom.

NOTE If you apply the wrong border or line style to a cell, immediately click Undo Format on the Edit menu to remove the border or line style.

4 In the Line Style section, click the third line style from the top.

The Format Cells dialog box should now match the following illustration.

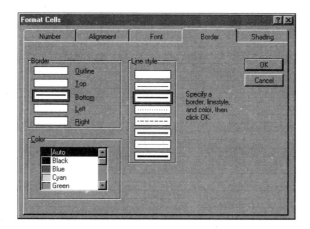

5 Click the OK button, and then click outside the highlighted area to view the border that now appears along the bottom of cells B8 through G8.

6 Highlight cells B11 through G11.

7 On the Format menu, click Border.

8 In the Border section, click Bottom.

9 In the Line Style section, click the third line style from the top, and then click the OK button.

10 Add a double-line border to the bottom of cells B13 through G13.

Now it's easier to differentiate the sections of the spreadsheet.

You may find it easier to see your formatting changes if you hide the horizontal and vertical gridlines that separate the rows and columns of the spreadsheet. To hide the gridlines, click Gridlines on the View menu. Click Gridlines on the View menu again if you want to redisplay the gridlines.

11 Press CTRL+HOME to move the pointer to cell A1.

Your spreadsheet should match the following illustration.

	A	B	C	D	E	F
1			**West Coast Sales**			
2			*Income Analysis*			
3						
4						
5		January	February	March	April	Totals
6						
7	Sales	$23,885	$27,760	$31,000	$25,120	$107,765
8	Cost	9,030	12,705	12,468	10,920	45,123
9						
10	Gross Profit	14,855	15,055	18,532	14,200	62,642
11	Expenses	6,020	9,122	5,820	5,966	26,928
12						
13	Income	$8,835.00	$5,933.00	$12,712.00	$8,234.00	$35,714.00
14						

Add shading

1 Highlight cells A5 through G5.

2 On the Format menu, click Shading.

The Format Cells dialog box appears, displaying the Shading tab.

3 In the Shading section, click the fourth shading pattern from the top.

The Format Cells dialog box should now look like the following illustration.

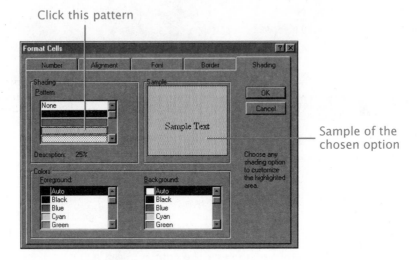

Click this pattern

Sample of the chosen option

4 Click the OK button.

The highlighted cells are now shaded.

5 Save your work.

Printing Your Spreadsheet

When you are satisfied with the accuracy and appearance of your spreadsheet, you can print it. Before you print, you can preview the spreadsheet to review the layout and spot any areas that require changes. In the next exercises, you'll preview the spreadsheet, change the margins and page orientation, and print the spreadsheet.

Preview the spreadsheet before printing

Print Preview

1 Click the Print Preview button on the toolbar.

Your spreadsheet appears in the Print Preview window.

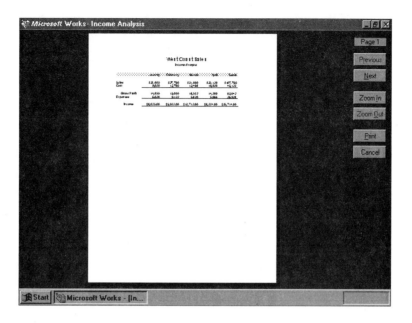

If the data in the Print Preview window is too small for you to read, you can click the spreadsheet with the Zoom pointer to magnify the view.

2 Magnify the view to preview your spreadsheet.

 TIP You can also click the Zoom In and Zoom Out buttons to change the magnification of the view.

---

3 Click the Cancel button to close the Print Preview window.

Change margins

You can change the left and right margins to center the spreadsheet horizontally on the page.

1 On the File menu, click Page Setup.

The Page Setup dialog box appears, displaying the Margins tab.

2 Double-click the Left Margin text box, and then type **1.75**

3 Press TAB to move to the Right Margin text box, type **1.75**, and then press TAB.

The Sample section of the dialog box illustrates the new left and right margin settings.

169

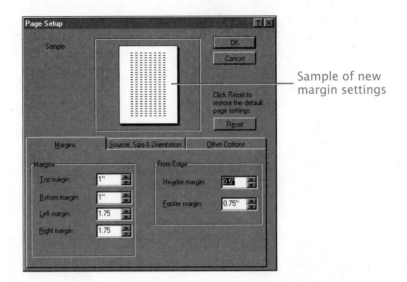

Sample of new
margin settings

NOTE   You can click the Reset button in the Page Setup dialog box to change the margins back to their original settings.

The new margin settings will not be applied to your spreadsheet until you click the OK button. Before you do that, however, you can specify more settings in other sections of the Page Setup dialog box, and then apply all the changes simultaneously.

Change the page orientation

Your spreadsheet is now seven columns wide and you've increased the width of the left and right margins. The data would fit better if the page was turned horizontally. Horizontal page orientation would also provide extra space that you can use if you need to increase the width of columns.

1   Click the Source, Size & Orientation tab.

The current page orientation is portrait (vertical), as shown in the Sample section of the dialog box.

2   In the Orientation section, click Landscape.

The Sample section of the dialog box now illustrates the new landscape (horizontal) orientation.

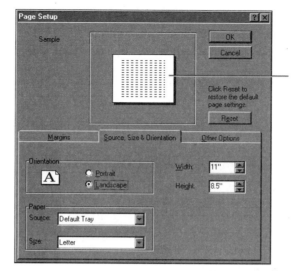

Sample of landscape
orientation

3   Click the OK button to apply the new margin and orientation settings.

Print Preview

4   Click the Print Preview button on the toolbar to view the new margins and the
page orientation.

Your spreadsheet in the Print Preview window should now look like the following
illustration.

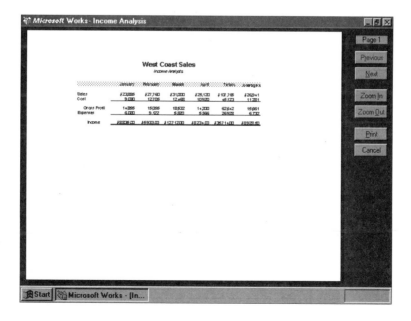

5 Click the Cancel button to close the Print Preview window.

6 Save your work.

Print the spreadsheet

1 On the File menu, click Print.

The Print dialog box appears.

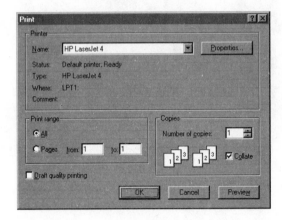

2 Type **2** in the Number of Copies text box.

3 Click the OK button to print two copies of the spreadsheet.

Print

 TIP You can click the Print button on the toolbar to print a spreadsheet using the current Print dialog box settings.

Protecting Your Data

You can use *locked cells* and *cell protection* to safeguard cell entries from changes or deletions.

Cells are protected from changes when they are locked and cell protection is turned on. Initially, all cells in a spreadsheet are locked and cell protection is turned off. Since cell protection isn't on, you can change or delete any cell entry. You can unlock cells in which you will allow changes, and then turn on cell protection to protect the other cells in the spreadsheet. In the next exercises, you'll unlock cells and use cell protection.

Unlock cells

Because the Sales, Cost, and Expenses data may change, you can unlock the cells containing that data. Because the data in the Gross Profit, Income, Totals, and Averages cells contains formulas that will not change, you can keep those cells locked.

1 Highlight cells B7 through E8.

2 On the Format menu, click Protection.

The Format Protection dialog box appears.

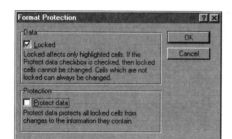

The highlighted cells are locked but not protected. Notice that the Locked check box is shaded. You must click once to turn the check box on; you click again to turn it off.

3 In the Data section, click the Locked check box twice to turn it off, and then click the OK button.

The highlighted cells are now unlocked.

4 Highlight cells B11 through E11.

5 On the Format menu, click Protection.

6 Turn off the Locked check box, and then click the OK button.

Turn on cell protection

Now that you have unlocked the cells in which you will allow changes, you must turn on cell protection to protect the rest of the spreadsheet.

1 On the Format menu, click Protection.

2 In the Protection section, turn on the Protect Data check box, and then click the OK button.

The locked cells are now protected from changes or deletions. However, you can still change or delete the entries in the unlocked cells.

3 Move the highlight to cell A8.

4 Type **Cost of Goods**, and then press ENTER.

Because cell A8 is locked, the following message box appears.

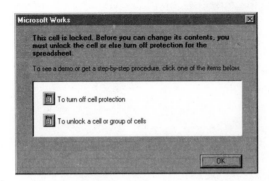

5 Click the OK button to close the message box.

6 Move the highlight to cell E7.

7 Type **30923**, and then press ENTER.

Since the cell is unlocked, you can change the entry.

8 Save your work.

One Step Further: Creating a Header

Your spreadsheet looks great, but it doesn't identify the data as specifically for investors. You can create a *header*, which is a line of information that prints at the top of every page, to identify your spreadsheet.

Create a header

You must turn off cell protection before you can create the header.

1 On the Format menu, click Protection.

2 Turn off the Protect Data check box, and then click the OK button.

3 On the View menu, click Headers And Footers.

For more information about footer and header codes, see "How to use footer and header codes" in the online Help index.

The View Headers And Footers dialog box appears.

You can use *footer and header codes*, which are the characters that you enter before the footer and header text, as a shortcut for specifying text, dates, and alignment.

4 Type **&lInvestor Relations&r&d**

This header will print the text "Investor Relations," left-aligned and the current date, right-aligned. The View Headers And Footers dialog box should now look like the following.

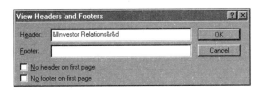

 NOTE The character you type after the first ampersand (&) is a lowercase "L," not the number 1.

5 Press ENTER.

6 Preview the spreadsheet to view the header.

Your spreadsheet should now look like the following illustration.

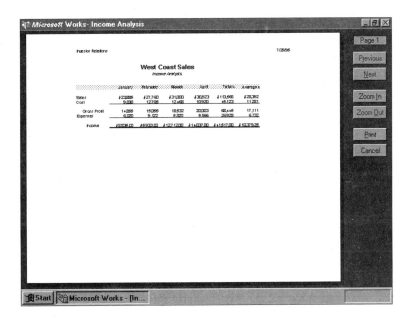

7 Click the Print button in the Print Preview window to print the spreadsheet.

8 Save your work.

If you want to continue to the next lesson

▶ Click the close button in the Income Analysis menu bar.

If you want to quit Works for now

➤ Click the Exit Works button in the Works Task Launcher dialog box.

Lesson Summary

To	Do this	Button
Insert rows or columns	Highlight as many rows or columns as you want to insert. Use the right mouse button to click the highlighted area, and then click Insert Row or Insert Column.	
Change column widths	Highlight the columns you want to change. Use the right mouse button to click the highlighted area, click Column Width, type the new column width, and then press ENTER.	
Change the number format	Highlight the cells you want to change, and then click Number on the Format menu. Select a format, type the number of decimal places, and then press ENTER.	
Change the alignment of cell entries	Highlight the cells you want to change, and then click the Left Align, Center Align, or Right Align button on the toolbar.	
Change the font size of text entries	Highlight the cells you want to change, click the arrow to the right of the Font Size list box on the toolbar, and then select a font size.	12
Change the font style of text entries	Highlight the cells you want to change, and then click the Bold, Italic, or Underline button on the toolbar.	B I U
Add borders	Highlight the cells to which you want to add borders, and then click Border on the Format menu. Select a border, select a line style, and then click the OK button.	

To	Do this	Button
Add shading	Highlight the cells to which you want to add shading, and then click Shading on the Format menu. Select a shading pattern, and then click the OK button.	
Hide or display gridlines	On the View menu, click Gridlines.	
Preview a spreadsheet	Click the Print Preview button on the toolbar.	
Change margins	On the File menu, click Page Setup. Click the Margins tab, type new margin settings, and then press ENTER.	
Change the page orientation	On the File menu, click Page Setup. Click the Source, Size & Orientation tab, select the desired orientation, and then click the OK button.	
Print a spreadsheet	Click the Print button on the toolbar.	
Unlock cells	Highlight the cells you want to unlock, click Protection on the Format menu, turn off the Locked check box, and then click the OK button.	
Turn on cell protection	Click Protection on the Format menu, turn on the Protect Data check box, and then click the OK button.	
Turn off cell protection	Click Protection on the Format menu, turn off the Protect Data check box, and then click the OK button.	
Create a header	On the View menu, click Headers And Footers, type the header codes and text, and then press ENTER.	

For online information about	Display the Help window, and then
Entering calculations	Click "Calculate (add, subtract, formulas, functions...)," and then click the appropriate topic for the type of calculation you want to do
Changing the page setup	Click "Change how things look on the page," and then click "To change margin settings" or "To change page orientation"
Formatting rows and columns	Click "Change how text, numbers, and dates look," and then click the appropriate topic
Previewing and printing spreadsheets	Click "Preview and print your spreadsheet or chart," and then click the appropriate topic

Preview of the Next Lesson

In this lesson, you learned to perform calculations and enhance the appearance of your spreadsheet. In the next lesson, you'll work with spreadsheet charts, which are visual representations of spreadsheet data. You'll learn the basics of creating and enhancing spreadsheet charts.

Creating Charts

In this lesson you will learn how to:

Estimated time
25 min.

■ Create bar, line, and pie charts.

■ Add titles and labels to charts.

■ Name and save charts.

■ Insert charts into other documents.

■ Change from one chart type to another.

■ Preview and print charts.

Charts are visual representations of numerical data in a spreadsheet. You use charts to illustrate, analyze, and interpret information represented by your spreadsheet. Because charts are visual, they can often communicate information more effectively than the text and numbers in the spreadsheet.

You decide to create charts with the income analysis spreadsheet to send to potential investors. In this lesson, you'll use the chart feature of the spreadsheet to create, enhance, and print charts.

Creating a Chart

After you finish a spreadsheet, you can use charts to display your information visually. To create a chart, highlight spreadsheet data, specify a chart type, and then let Works create the chart for you automatically. You can choose one of 12 basic types of charts in Works.

In the next exercises, you'll create a bar chart to illustrate the relationship between the Sales and Income data.

Create a bar chart

You use *bar charts* to compare data illustrated with side-by-side or stacked bars.

1   Open Income Analysis Chart in the Works SBS Practice folder.

Maximize

2   In the Income Analysis Chart title bar, click the Maximize button.

3   Highlight cells A7 through E7.

The sales data you want to chart is highlighted.

New Chart

4   Click the New Chart button on the toolbar.

The New Chart dialog box appears. The bar chart type is currently selected.

Available chart types   Sample of current chart type

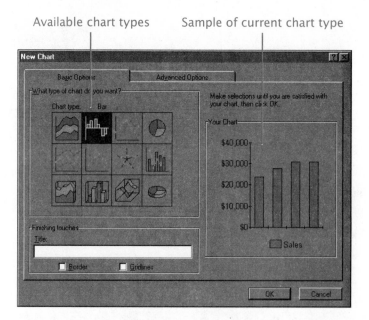

Notice that a sample of the chart type appears in the right side of the dialog box.

> **NOTE**   If this is the first time you have created a chart, the First-Time Help dialog box appears. Click Don't Display This Message In The Future, and then click the OK button.

5   Click the OK button.

Works creates a bar chart based on the highlighted Sales data in the spreadsheet.

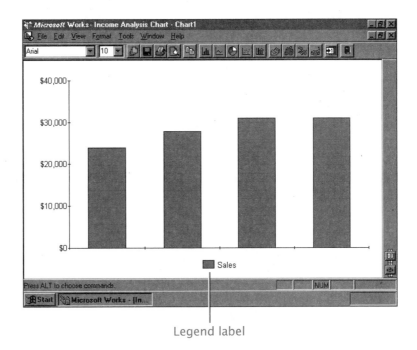

Legend label

Each bar in the chart represents the sales data in one column of the highlighted cells of your spreadsheet. The set of bars is a Y-series. A *Y-series* is a group of related data plotted along the vertical edge of the chart, in this case, Sales. The data plotted along the horizontal line at the bottom of the chart is an *X-series*. In this instance, the categories represented by the X-series will be months. You will add the information for this data later in the lesson. The text and box that appear below the chart is a legend label. *Legend labels* are text or symbols that identify the Y-series data in a chart, which in this case is Sales.

Add another series

The purpose of this bar chart is to show the relationship between two Y-series values: Sales and Income. Since these values are not adjacent in the spreadsheet, you cannot add them to the chart at the same time. You must add the second series after Works draws the initial chart.

1 On the View menu, click Spreadsheet to switch to the spreadsheet window.

2 Highlight cells B13 through E13.

The income data you want to chart is highlighted.

Copy

3 Click the Copy button on the toolbar.

Works copies the Income values.

4 On the Window menu, click 2 Income Analysis Chart - Chart1 to switch to the chart window.

181

5   On the Edit menu, click Series.

The Edit Series dialog box appears.

Notice that the data from the first Y-series appears in the 1st text box.

6   Click in the 2nd text box.

7   Click the Paste button in the Edit Series dialog box.

Works pastes the range reference of the highlighted cells into the 2nd text box, as shown in the following illustration.

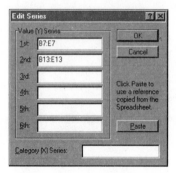

8   Click the OK button.

Works adds the second Y-series to the chart.

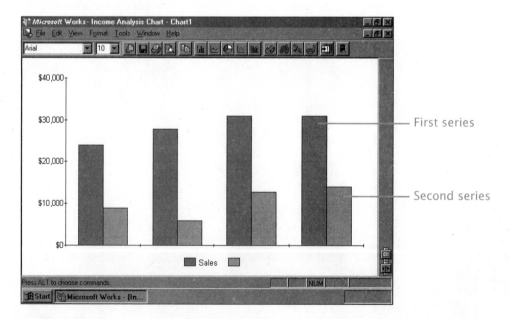

9   Save your work.

Making the Chart More Informative

You can enhance your bar chart by adding identifying titles and labels. In the next exercises, you'll add titles and labels and change the font of the chart text.

Add chart titles and subtitles

1   On the Edit menu, click Titles.

The Edit Titles dialog box appears. You can specify a title by entering text or by typing a cell reference in the Chart Title text box. If you type a cell reference, any text contained in the reference cell will appear as the chart title.

2   In the Chart Title text box, type **a1**

The text in cell A1, *West Coast Sales*, will appear as the chart title.

3   Press TAB to move to the Subtitle text box, and then type **Sales to Income Analysis**

This text will appear in the chart as a subtitle. The Edit Titles dialog box should match the next illustration.

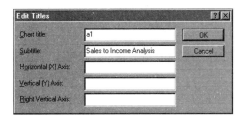

4   Press ENTER.

Your bar chart should now look like the following illustration.

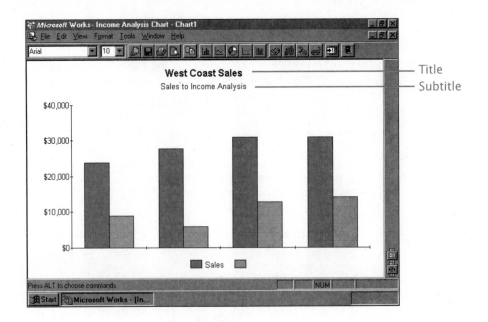

Title
Subtitle

Add category labels

Since your bar chart represents data for the months of January through April, you'll add labels to identify the month that corresponds to each set of bars. These labels, called *category labels*, are the X-series for the chart.

Copy

1   On the View menu, click Spreadsheet.

2   Highlight cells B5 through E5, and then click the Copy button on the toolbar.

The text contained in the highlighted cell range is copied.

3   On the Window menu, click 2 Income Analysis Chart - Chart1.

4   On the Edit menu, click Paste Series.

The Paste Series dialog box appears.

5   In the Use Selection For Series section, click Category.

The Paste Series dialog box should now appear as shown in the next illustration.

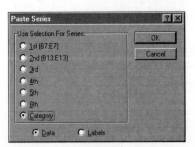

6 Click the OK button.

The category labels appear beneath each set of bars, as shown in the following illustration.

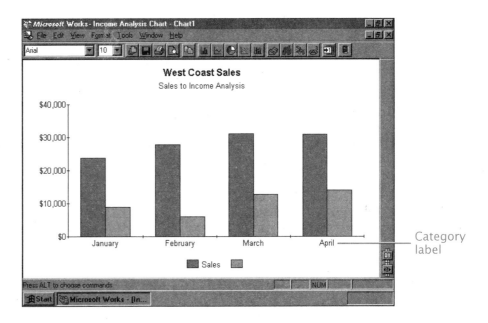

Add a legend label

Your chart currently has a legend label that identifies the Sales series. You can add another legend label to identify the Income series.

1 On the Edit menu, click Legend/Series Labels.

The Edit Legend/Series Labels dialog box appears.

Notice that the cell reference for the 1st Value Series appears in the dialog box.

2 Click in the 2nd Value Series text box, and then type **a13**

The text in cell A13, *Income*, will appear as the legend label. The Edit Legend/Series Labels dialog box should now look like the following illustration.

185

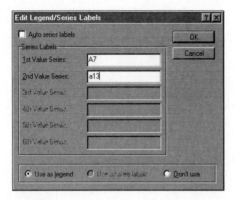

3 Press ENTER to add the legend label to the chart.

Add data labels

Data labels display the spreadsheet values that a series represents in a chart. You can add data labels so you can identify data without referring back to the spreadsheet.

1 On the Edit menu, choose Data Labels.

The Edit Data Labels dialog box appears.

2 Turn on the Use Series Data check box, and then click the OK button.

By turning on this check box, you specify to use the spreadsheet values, represented by the series in the chart, as the data labels. These values are the same values contained in cells B7:E7 and B13:E13 in your spreadsheet. The data labels appear above each bar, as shown in the following illustration.

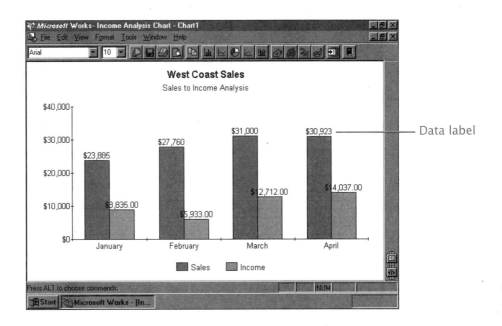

Data label

Change the font of chart text

You can further enhance the information in your chart by changing the font and size of the chart text. You can use two fonts in each chart; one for the chart title and another for the other text.

1 Click *West Coast Sales* to select the chart title.

A selection box appears around the title.

Font Size

2 Click the arrow to the right of the Font Size list box on the toolbar, and then click 14.

The font size for the title is increased.

3 Click a blank area of the chart to remove the selection box from the chart title.

4 On the Format menu, click Font And Style.

The Format Font And Style - Tick Labels, Data Labels, Etc. dialog box appears.

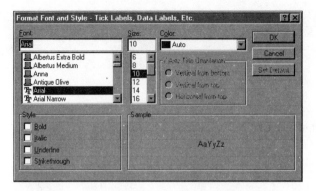

5 In the Size list box, click 8 to specify 8-point type. Points are a unit of measurement used with fonts.

6 In the Style section, click the Italic check box, and then click the OK button.

The chart labels are now smaller and italicized, as shown in the following illustration.

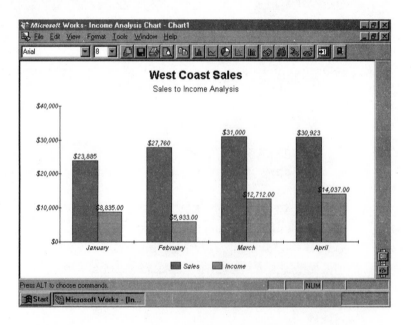

Name the chart

Works automatically names each chart you create *Chart1*, *Chart2*, and so on. If you create multiple charts in a spreadsheet, you can assign more descriptive names to help you find and switch to a specific chart quickly.

1　On the Tools menu, click Rename Chart.

The Rename Chart dialog box appears.

2　Type **Sales/Inc Bar**

The Rename Chart dialog box should now match the following illustration.

If you change information in a spreadsheet upon which a chart is based, Works automatically updates the chart to match the new data.

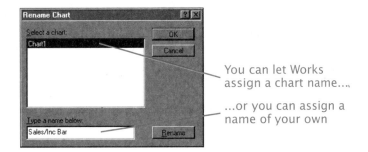

You can let Works assign a chart name...

...or you can assign a name of your own

3　Click the Rename button.

The new chart name appears in the Select A Chart list box and the application title bar.

4　Click the OK button.

5　Save your work.

The spreadsheet and the chart are saved together.

Printing Your Chart

Your chart is now ready to print. Before you print the chart, you can preview it to see if you need to make any last minute changes. In the next exercises, you'll preview your chart, change the page orientation, and then print the chart.

Preview a chart

Print Preview

1　Click the Print Preview button on the toolbar.

Notice that your chart appears in black and white in the preview window.

The bar chart would look better with a horizontal (landscape) page orientation.

2　Click the Cancel button.

Change the page orientation

The page orientation of a chart is not affected by the orientation of the associated spreadsheet. You can set different page orientations for a spreadsheet and its charts.

1　On the File menu, click Page Setup.

2 Click the Source, Size & Orientation tab if it isn't the displayed tab.

3 In the Orientation section, click Landscape, and then click the OK button.

4 Preview the chart to view the new page orientation.

5 Click the Cancel button to close the print preview window.

Print a chart

Print

1 Click the Print button on the toolbar.

Works prints the chart.

 TIP If you want to print multiple copies of a chart, click Print on the File menu and specify the number of copies.

---

2 When the chart has finished printing, save your work.

Working with Line Charts

You can create as many as eight charts for a single spreadsheet. They can all be the same type of chart or a combination of different chart types. In the next exercises, you'll create a line chart, and then change the chart type.

Create a line chart

A *line chart* shows changes in numerical data over a period of time. Data is illustrated with one or more lines. You will create a line chart to show fluctuations in Sales and Cost values in your first quarter.

1 Display the spreadsheet window.

2 Highlight cells A7 through E8.

Since the Sales and Cost values are adjacent in the spreadsheet, you can highlight them together and Works will chart the values simultaneously.

New Chart

3 Click the New Chart button on the toolbar.

4 In the What Type Of Chart Do You Want section, click the third chart in the first row (line chart).

5 In the Finishing Touches section, click the Title text box.

The text you type in this text box will appear as a title at the top of the chart.

6 Type **First Quarter: Sales vs Cost**

The New Chart dialog box should now look like the following illustration.

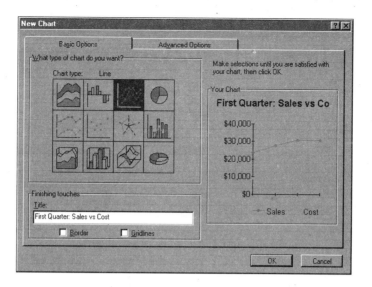

7 Press ENTER.

Works creates a line chart based on the highlighted sales and cost data in the spreadsheet.

Your screen should now look like the following.

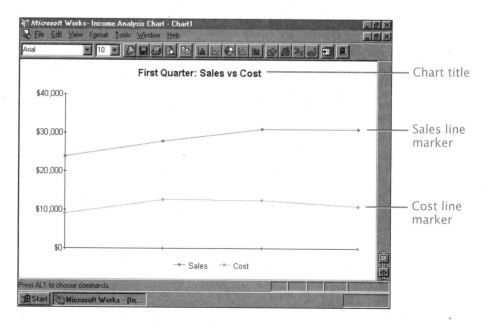

The top line in the chart represents the Sales data contained in the highlighted cells. The bottom line represents the Cost data. Each line is a Y-series.

191

8 On the Tools menu, click Rename Chart.

9 Type **Sales/Cost Line**

The chart name is now more descriptive.

10 Click the Rename button, and then click the OK button.

Change the chart type

If you want to view your data in a different way, you don't have to create additional charts; you can simply change the chart type of an existing chart.

3-D Line Chart

1 Click the 3-D Line Chart button on the toolbar.

The Chart Type dialog box appears.

2 Click the Variations tab.

The Variations tab appears, displaying 3-D line chart options and information.

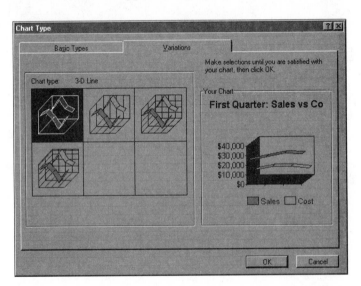

3 Click the last option in the first row, and then click the OK button.

The chart type changes to a 3-D line chart with gridlines.

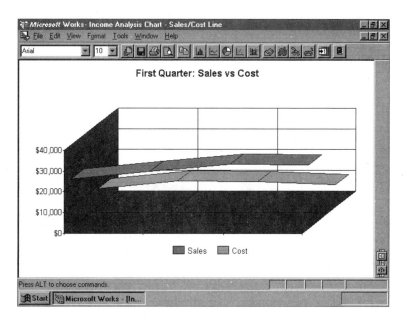

4   Save your work.

Working with Pie Charts

In addition to the charts you have already created, you can create another type of chart, to show the relationship between monthly income and total income in your spreadsheet. A pie chart is ideal for this purpose. A *pie chart* is a circle divided into slices. Each slice in a pie chart represents a single value in a Y-series. The entire pie chart illustrates the relationship of each value to all values in the Y-series. In the next exercises, you'll create a pie chart and add data labels that show the income value of each month in the first quarter.

Create a pie chart

New Chart

1   Display the spreadsheet.
2   Highlight cells B13 through E13.
3   Click the New Chart button on the toolbar.
4   Click the fourth chart type in the first row (pie chart).
5   Click the Title text box, and then type **West Coast Sales Income**
6   Press ENTER to create the pie chart shown in the following illustration.

193

A pie chart can represent only one series.

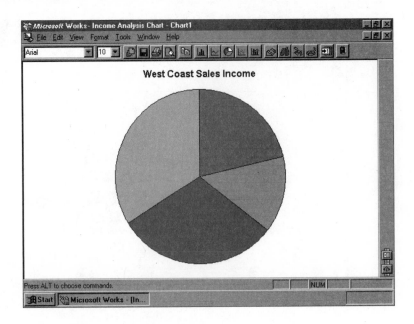

Add data labels

1 On the Edit menu, click Data Labels.

The Format Data Labels dialog box appears.

2 In the 1st Label section, click Cell Contents.

3 Click the Cell Range text box, and then type **b5:e5**

The entries in cells B5 through E5 (the month labels January through April) will appear as data labels.

4 In the (2nd Label) section, click Values.

The Format Data Labels dialog box should now appear as follows.

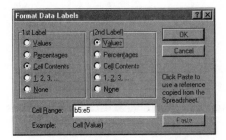

5   Click the OK button.

The data labels appear next to each pie slice, as shown in the following illustration.

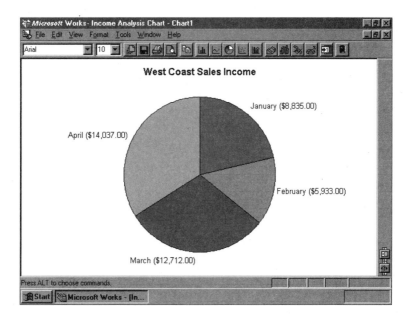

6   On the Tools menu, click Rename Chart.

7   Type **Income Pie**

8   Click the Rename button, and then click the OK button.

9   Save your work.

Inserting a Chart into Another Document

A chart is an object, which you can paste from one application in Works to another application.

Open the document

You will insert the bar chart into a cover letter you have prepared for investors.

1   Open Investor Letter in the Works SBS Practice folder.

The document opens in the Word Processor.

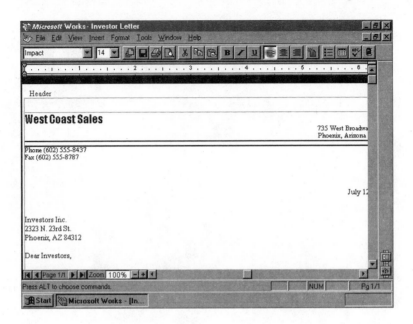

2 Maximize the Investor Letter window if it isn't already maximized.

Insert the chart

1 Scroll down and position the insertion point on the blank line above the paragraph that begins *Please contact us....*

2 On the Window menu, click 2 Income Analysis Chart - Sales/Inc Bar.

3 Click the Copy button on the toolbar.

4 On the Window menu, click 5 Investor Letter.

5 Click the Paste button on the toolbar.

Works pastes the chart into the document. Notice that the chart proportionally decreases in size within the document margins.

6 Preview the Investor Letter document to see how the chart looks in the document.

Your screen should match the following illustration.

Copy

Paste

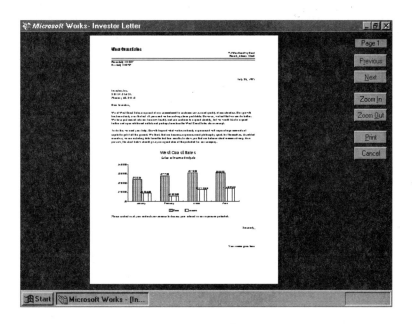

NOTE Since screen resolution varies from one computer to another, your screen may look different than the illustration shown above. In particular, the size of your chart may appear to be different. If the chart is larger, your letter may scroll to two pages. You can change the size of the chart by completing the following steps.

7 Click the Cancel button in the Print Preview window.

8 Click the chart to select it.

9 Position the pointer on the lower right sizing handle. *Sizing handles* are small squares that appear on the border of a selected object.

The pointer now appears as the Resize pointer.

RESIZE

10 Drag the sizing handle up and to the left to make the chart smaller, or down and to the right to make the chart larger.

Center Align

11 Click the Center Align button in the toolbar to center the chart between the left and right document margins.

12 Print the Investor Letter document.

13 Save and then close Investor Letter.

197

One Step Further: Changing Colors and Fill Patterns

You can change colors and fill patterns to help your chart look better when printed or to improve its appearance onscreen.

Change colors and fill patterns

1   On the Format menu, click Shading And Color.

The Format Shading And Color dialog box appears.

If you print your chart in black and white, you may want to choose contrasting colors and patterns for better distinction.

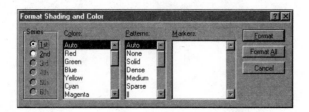

2   In the Colors list box, click Dark Magenta.

3   Scroll down in the Patterns list box, click Dark //, and then click the Format button.

The color and fill pattern of the first series changes to thick, diagonal, dark magenta stripes.

4   In the Series section, click 2nd.

5   In the Colors list box, click Dark Cyan.

6   Scroll down in the Patterns list box, click Light \\, and then click the Format button.

Now the color and fill pattern of the second series changes to thin, diagonal, dark cyan stripes.

7   Click the Close button to close the Format Shading And Color dialog box.

Your screen should now match the following illustration.

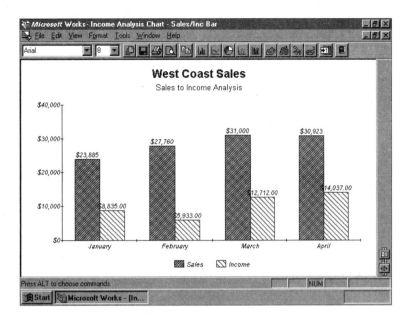

Print

8   Click the Print button on the toolbar to print the chart.

9   Save the spreadsheet and chart.

If you want to continue to the next lesson

➤   Close the spreadsheet and charts.

If you want to quit Works for now

1   Close the spreadsheet and charts.

2   Click the Exit Works button in the Works Task Launcher dialog box.

Lesson Summary

To	Do this	Button
Create a new chart	In the spreadsheet, highlight the values that you want to plot. Click the New Chart button on the toolbar, click a chart type, and then click the OK button.	

To	Do this	Button
Add a series	Highlight the cells containing the series values in the spreadsheet. Click the Copy button on the toolbar, switch to the chart window, and then click Series on the Edit menu. Click in a series text box, click the Paste button, and then click the OK button.	
Add chart titles	On the Edit menu, click Titles, type cell references or text in the text boxes, and then press ENTER.	
Add category labels	Highlight the cells containing the category labels in the spreadsheet, and then click the Copy button on the toolbar. Switch to the chart window, click Paste Series on the Edit menu, click Category, and then click the OK button.	
Add data labels	On the Edit menu, click Data Labels, click the Use Series Data check box, and then click the OK button.	
Change the font or font size of the chart title	Click the chart title to select it, and then click a new font or font size on the toolbar.	
Change the font or font size of other chart text	Be sure the chart title is not selected. Click Font And Style on the Format menu. Then select a font, font size, and style, and click the OK button.	
Name a chart	On the Tools menu, click Rename Chart, and then click the chart you want to rename. Type the new chart name, click the Rename button, and then click the OK button.	

To	Do this	Button
Change the chart type	Click a chart type button on the toolbar, and then double-click a chart option in the dialog box that appears.	
Insert charts into other documents	Click the Copy button on the toolbar, and open the document to which you want to copy the chart. Position the insertion point where you want to paste the chart, click Paste on the Edit menu, and then click the OK button.	
Preview a chart	Click the Print Preview button on the toolbar.	
Change the page orientation	On the File menu, click Page Setup, click the Source, Size & Orientation tab, click an Orientation option, and then click the OK button.	
Print a chart	Click the Print button on the toolbar.	
Save a chart	Click the Save button on the toolbar.	
Change colors and fill patterns	On the Format menu, click Shading And Color. Click a Series option, click a new color and pattern, click the Format button, and then click the Close button.	

For online information about	Display the Help window, and then
Creating new charts	Click "Create a chart," and then click "To create a chart"
Enhancing charts	Click "Change a chart," and then click the appropriate topic
Printing charts	Click "Preview and print your spreadsheet or chart," and then click "To print a chart"

Preview of the Next Lesson

In this lesson, you learned to use the chart feature of the Spreadsheet to create, enhance, and print charts. In the next lesson, you'll learn how to use the Communications tool. You'll start a Communications session, connect and reconnect to another computer, and quit a Communications session. You'll also transfer files from one computer to another and automate connections between computers.

Communicating Information to Another Computer

Estimated time
20 min.

In this lesson you will learn how to:

- Start and quit a Communications session.
- Connect and reconnect to another computer.
- Send and receive files.
- Record and play back scripts.

IMPORTANT In order to complete the exercises in this lesson, you'll need a modem and access to an information service, a bulletin board, or a friend's computer that has communication capabilities.

With the Works communication tool and a modem, you can send and receive information to and from another computer and connect to online services and bulletin boards.

A *modem* is a device that a computer uses to send or receive information over telephone lines. Modems can be internal, inside your computer, or external, in a separate box connected to your computer by a cable.

You can connect to *online information services* for the latest news, sports, medical, legal, and other information. Some services have sites that allow you to interact with that information so you can buy and sell stock, make travel reservations, or purchase products. Some popular information services include CompuServe, Prodigy, GEnie, and America Online. Before you can connect or "sign on" to an information service, you need to obtain an account or subscription. The service will then provide you with a phone number, communications settings, and sign-on/sign-off procedures. You can find starter kits for many services at your local computer software store.

Bulletin boards are usually smaller local services that you can use to exchange information about a specific subject. Many bulletin boards are affiliated with computer magazines and newspapers or local computer clubs. Before you can connect to a bulletin board, you need to contact the organization that operates the bulletin board and obtain such information as the telephone number, communications settings, a password, and sign-on/sign-off procedures.

Instead of mailing information about West Coast Sales to potential investors, you can use the Communications tool and your modem to send the data electronically. In this lesson, you'll learn the basics of using the Communications tool, including how to connect to another computer and how to send and receive information.

Getting in Touch

 IMPORTANT The following exercises are written for users who are both using Works. If a participant is using a different communications package, some steps and results could vary. Regardless of which packages you use, your computer's modem settings must be compatible with the settings of the other computer's modem. Users should refer to the documentation of the package they are using for the appropriate modem settings. Works users can refer to online Help.

Using your computer to communicate with another computer is similar to talking on the telephone—you dial a number, make a connection, and have a conversation. However, instead of using your voice, you communicate by typing and reading text on the screen, exchanging documents, or selecting menu options to view information. You can use the Communications tool to make computer-to-computer connections to online information services, bulletin boards, or a friend's or business associate's computer.

Before you can connect to the computer of a friend or business associate, you must make sure that both computers have compatible communications applications.

In the following exercises, you'll connect to another computer for the first time, quit a communications session, and reconnect to the other computer.

> **NOTE** Before you start the next exercises, be sure you have the phone number of an online service, a bulletin board, or a friend's computer and that the other computer is ready to answer your call.

Connect to another computer for the first time

Communications

1 In the Works Task Launcher dialog box, click the Works Tools tab.

2 Click the Communications button.

Works opens a new Communications document and the Easy Connect dialog box appears.

You can also use an online service or bulletin board to complete the exercise; however, some of the steps and results may vary.

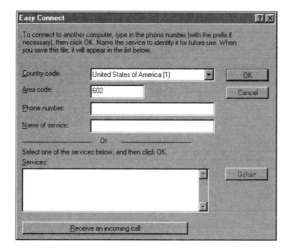

> **TROUBLESHOOTING** If your modem is not yet set up in Windows 95, a message box displays informing you that there are no configured communications devices. Click the Yes button to have Windows 95 configure your modem, and then click the Communications button again to start a communications session.

3 In the Phone Number text box, type the number of the computer to which you want to connect.

You can include a prefix or area code in the number, for example 1-500-555-4567. Hyphens are optional.

TIP   Insert commas in a phone number when you need a pause during dialing. For example, to dial 9 for an outside line and pause before dialing a number, type 9,555-4567. If you need a longer pause, use two or more commas.

4   In the Name Of Service text box, type **SBS Connection**

The name you enter in the Name Of Service text box will appear on the Phone menu and in the Easy Connect dialog box so you can reconnect to the other computer without retyping the information.

5   Click the OK button.

The Dial dialog box appears.

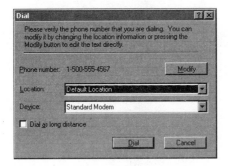

You use the Dial dialog box to confirm the telephone number and the modem configuration.

6   Click the Dial button.

Works dials the number and displays the Dial Status dialog box, which tracks the progress of the connection operation.

Notice that *DIAL* appears in the status bar.

When the connection is made, the SBS Connection window appears, as shown in the following illustration.

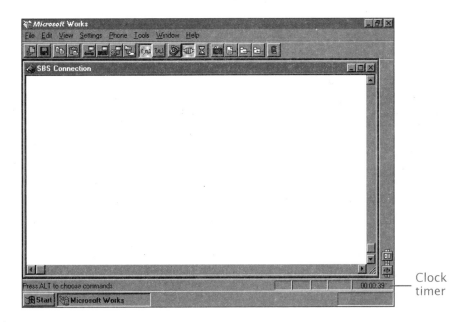

Clock
timer

This is the window in which you will type and receive your messages. Notice the clock timer that appears in the status bar, which indicates the connection was successful.

 IMPORTANT If Works cannot make a connection, it displays a message box indicating the nature of the problem. For example, the communications settings might be incorrect or your modem might not be connected properly. You'll need to resolve the problem before you can make a connection.

If you connected to an online service or bulletin board, you might see a menu or other instructions on your screen and be requested to type a password, identification number, or other sign-on information.

7 Type a short greeting informing the other person that you are in the process of learning how to use the Works Communications tool.

 NOTE If your text does not appear on the screen as you type, click Terminal on the Settings menu and then turn on the Local Echo check box.

8 Have the other person type a response.

Comments should be visible on your screen.

207

TIP   You can press ENTER twice to prompt the other person that you have finished typing and are waiting for a response.

If you are connected to an information service or bulletin board, perform the required steps to properly sign off from the other computer.

Quit a communications session

When you are finished with your communication session, you need to sign off and disconnect from the other computer.

IMPORTANT   Always sign off from an information service or bulletin board before you disconnect or you might receive unnecessary phone charges for the time it takes the service to recognize that you have disconnected.

Dial/Hangup

1   Click the Dial/Hangup button on the toolbar.

A message box appears asking you if it's OK to disconnect.

2   Click the OK button to disconnect.

When you start and quit a communications session, Works saves the communications document with the name of the service you typed in the Easy Connect dialog box. If you didn't specify a service name, Works uses the prefix "PH" and the number you dialed as the document name; for example, PH9,555-4567.wcm.

3   In the SBS Connection title bar, click the Close button. Do not save changes if you are prompted to do so.

Close

The Communications document closes.

Reconnect to another computer

The receiver must be ready to reconnect before you can begin this exercise.

Communications

1   Click the Communications button.

The Easy Connect dialog box appears, listing the names of the last eight services to which you connected.

2   In the Services list box, double-click SBS Connection.

The Dial dialog box appears.

3   Click the Dial button.

Works dials the number and displays the Dial Status dialog box to inform you of the progress of the connection operation.

Dial/Hangup

TIP You can click the Dial/Hangup button on the toolbar to quickly dial the phone number of the last service to which you were connected.

If you reconnected to an online service or bulletin board, follow the required sign-on and sign-off procedures.

4   When the other computer responds, type a short greeting informing the other person that the reconnection is successful.

TIP   If you get a busy signal or if the other computer doesn't respond, you can click Dial Again on the Phone menu to quickly redial the last number.

5   When you are finished communicating with the other computer, perform the required sign-off procedures.

6   Click the Dial/Hangup button, and then click the OK button.

Dial/Hangup

Exchanging Information

When you transfer a file from your computer to another computer, the other computer saves the file on its disk. When you receive a file from another computer (sometimes called *downloading*), the file is saved on your disk.

In the next exercises, you'll transfer files.

NOTE   Before you start the next exercises, be sure you have the phone number of an online service, a bulletin board, or a friend's computer and that the other computer is prepared to send and receive files.

Send a file

You can send ASCII or binary files to another computer. An *ASCII* file contains text, punctuation, and spaces without formatting so the file can be read between different applications. A *binary* file is a formatted file. Save your file as a text file if you want to send it as an ASCII file.

1   Connect to the computer to which you will send the file.

2   Ask the other computer user what transfer protocol they are using.

3   Click the Transfer Settings button on the toolbar.

Transfer Settings

The Settings dialog box appears showing the Transfer settings.

Select the same
transfer protocol the
other computer is using

4   Select the same transfer protocol the other computer is using, and then click the OK button.

5   On the Tools menu, click Send File.

The Send File dialog box appears.

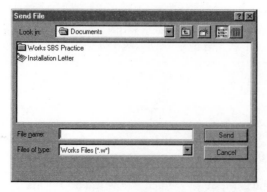

6   Change to the Works SBS Practice folder.

7   Click Investor Letter, and then click the Send button.

NOTE To send a file successfully, the receiver must click Receive File on the Tools menu as you send the file. Inform the receiver of the time frame in which you will send the file (such as 30 seconds).

Works begins sending the file to the other computer and displays a message box that indicates the progress of the transfer. You can press ESC if you want to cancel a file transfer before it is completed.

8 After the file transfer is completed, click the Dial/Hangup button on the toolbar to disconnect from the other computer.

Dial/Hangup

Receive a file

If you connected to an online service or bulletin board, perform the required sign-off procedures after the file transfer is complete.

1 Connect to the computer from which you will receive the file.

2 Be sure the other computer is using the same transfer protocol you are using.

3 Ask the other computer user to send the file to your computer.

4 On the Tools menu, click Receive File.

The Receive File dialog box appears.

5 Change to the Works SBS Practice folder.

6 If you are using the Xmodem protocol, type **Received File** in the File Name text box.

NOTE If you are using the Ymodem, Zmodem, or Kermit protocol, the file will be received with its original name. Works will begin the file transfer without displaying the Receive File dialog box.

7 Click the Save button.

Works begins transferring the file to your computer and displays a message box that indicates the progress of the transfer.

8 Click Open on the File menu, and then open the Works SBS Practice folder, if it isn't already open.

9 In the Files Of Type list box, click All Files (*.*).

10 Verify that the file you received is in the directory, and then close the Open dialog box.

11 Click the Dial/Hangup button on the toolbar to disconnect from the other computer.

Dial/Hangup

Close

12   In the Communications document window, click the Close button.

The document closes and the Works Task Launcher dialog box appears.

Automating Your Connections

You can use *scripts*, which are recorded sequences of keystrokes and commands, to automate repetitive or lengthy communication tasks. After you record a script, you can play it back and Works will automatically perform the series of tasks you recorded.

You can record *sign-on scripts*, which automate the steps you take to sign on to a service, or *other scripts*, which automate tasks you perform after you sign on to a service, such as navigating through a series of menus to access a particular section of an online service.

In the next exercises, you'll record a sign-on script and play back a script.

Record a sign-on script

1   Connect to the other computer.

2   After you are connected to the other computer, click Record Script on the Tools menu.

The Record Script dialog box appears.

3   In the Type Of Script section, click Sign-on, and then click the OK button.

The text "Recording a script" appears in the status bar.

4   Perform the procedures required to sign on to the computer or service.

Works records your entries and the other computer's responses.

5   On the Tools menu, click End Recording.

6   Click the Save button on the toolbar.

Save

The sign-on script is saved with the document. The next time you open SBS Connection, Works will automatically connect and sign on to the other computer or service.

7   Perform the required sign off proceducres.

8   Disconnect from the other computer.

Play back a script

1   Connect to the other computer.

    Works automatically plays back the sign-on script and signs on to the computer or service.

2   Perform the required sign-off procedures.

3   Click the Dial/Hangup button on the toolbar to disconnect from the other computer.

Dial/Hangup

4   Close the Communications document window.

One Step Further: Recording Scripts for Other Tasks

Record a script for other tasks

After you connect and sign on to a computer service, you can record scripts to automate other tasks.

1   Connect to the other computer.

2   On the Tools menu, click Record Script.

3   In the Type Of Script section, click Other.

4   In the Type A Name For The Script Below text box, type **Test Script**

    A script name can contain as many as 15 characters, including spaces.

5   Click the OK button.

    The text "Recording a script" appears in the status bar.

6   Perform any sequence of steps, such as choosing a series of menu items.

    Works records your actions and the other computer's responses.

7   On the Tools menu, click End Recording.

8   Click the Save button on the toolbar.

    The script is saved with the Communications document.

Save

9   Perform the required sign-off procedures.

10 Click the Dial/Hangup button on the toolbar to disconnect from the other computer or service.

Dial/Hangup

11 Close the Communications document window.

213

Play Back the Script

1   Connect to the other computer.

2   On the Menu bar, click Tools.

    A list of available scripts appears on the Tools menu.

Click here to play back your script

3   Click 2 Test Script.

    Works plays back the sequence of keystrokes and commands recorded in the script.

4   Perform the required sign-off procedure.

5   Disconnect from the other computer, and then close the communications document window.

If you want to continue to the next lesson

➤   Be sure the Works Task Launcher dialog box is open.

If you want to quit Works for now

➤   Click the Exit Works button in the Works Task Launcher dialog box.

Lesson Summary

To	Do this	Button
Connect to another computer for the first time	Click the Communications button in the Works Task Launcher dialog box, type a phone number and service name in the Easy Connect dialog box, click the OK button, and then click the Dial button. When the other computer responds, type a greeting or the required sign-on information.	
Quit a Communications session	Perform the steps required to sign off from the other computer, click the Dial/Hangup button on the toolbar, and then click the OK button.	
Reconnect to another computer	Click the Communications button in the Works Task Launcher dialog box. In the Easy Connect dialog box, double-click the name of the service in the Services list box, and then click the OK button. When the other computer responds, type a greeting or the required sign-on information.	
Send a file to another computer	Connect to the other computer and be sure both computers are using the same transfer protocol and settings. On the Tools menu, click Send File, click a folder and filename, and then click the OK button.	

To	Do this	Button
Receive a file from another computer	Connect to the other computer and be sure both computers are using the same transfer protocol and settings. On the Tools menu, click Receive File. If you are using the Xmodem protocol, click a folder and type a filename, and then click the OK button.	
Record a sign-on script	Connect to another computer, click Record Script on the Tools menu, click Sign-on in the Type Of Script section, and then click the OK button. Perform the procedure required to sign on to the other computer or service, click End Recording on the Tools menu, and then click the Save button on the toolbar.	
Record a script for other tasks	Connect and sign on to another computer, click Record Script on the Tools menu, click Other in the Type Of Script section, type a name in the Script text box, and then click the OK button. Perform the steps you want to record, click End Recording on the Tools menu, and then click the Save button on the toolbar.	
Play back a sign-on script	Open the Communications document that contains the script, and then click the OK button.	
Play back a named script	Click the name of the script on the Tools menu.	

For online information about	Display the Help window, and then
Connecting to another computer	Click "Connect to another computer or service," and then click "To connect to another computer" or "To connect to an information service or bulletin board"
Sending files	Click "Send text or files," and then click "To send a file"
Receiving files	Click "Receive text or files," and then click "To receive a file"
Recording and playing back scripts	Click "Record the sign-on procedure or other repetitive tasks," and then click "To record a sign-on sequence (script)" or "To record repetitive tasks"

Preview of the Next Lessons

In this lesson, you learned the basics of using the Communications tool. In Part 4 of this book, you'll learn how to use the Database tool by sorting, finding, replacing, and filtering database information. You'll learn how to add pictures and calculations to a database, and create, modify, and print database reports.

Review & Practice

In the lessons in Part 3, "Illustrating and Communicating Information," you learned how to enter formulas and functions; edit, format, and print spreadsheets; as well as how to use a number of advanced features to create and work efficiently with complex spreadsheets. You also learned how to create, modify, and print spreadsheet charts and how to communicate through your modem. If you want to practice these skills and test your understanding before you proceed with the lessons in Part 4, you can work through the Review & Practice section following this lesson.

Review & Practice

Estimated time
20 min.

You will review and practice how to:

- Use formulas and functions.
- Format a spreadsheet.
- Protect cells.
- Create a spreadsheet chart.
- Connect and communicate with another computer.
- Quit a Communications session.
- Reconnect and send a file to another computer.

In this Review & Practice, you'll have an opportunity to fine-tune the skills you learned in the lessons in Part 3 of this book. You'll use what you have learned about formatting spreadsheets, protecting cells, creating charts, and using the Communications tool to create and send a salary analysis to investors by modem.

Scenario

One of the investors has requested additional information from you. The investor wants to review your employee salary data. You decide to modify an existing spreadsheet and add a chart, and then send the information to the investor by modem.

Step 1: Use Formulas and Functions

1   Open Salary Analysis in the Works SBS Practice folder, and then maximize the document window.

2   In cell F19, enter a formula that calculates a 4% raise from the 1994 Salary figure.

 NOTE   A 4% raise is the previous year's salary (E19) multiplied by 4% (.04), and then added to the previous year's salary.

3   In cell B20, use the SUM function to calculate the total salaries for all employees for 1991.

4   Copy the function in cell B20 to cells C20 through G20.

5   In cell H20, use Easy Calc to calculate the average of the raises shown in column H.

Your spreadsheet should now match the following illustration.

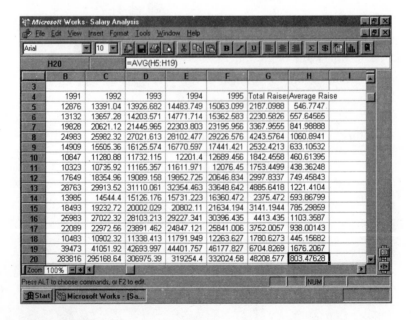

For more information on	See
Entering formulas	Lesson 7
Entering functions	Lesson 7

Step 2: *Format a Spreadsheet*

1 Change the width of columns A through G to 12, and change the width of column H to the best fit.

2 Highlight row 4, and then insert one row.

3 Highlight row 6, and then insert one row.

4 Highlight row 22, and then insert one row.

5 Change the number format of cells B7 through H7 and B23 through H23 to Currency with no decimal places.

6 Change the number format of cells B8 through H21 to Comma with no decimal places.

7 Center align the entries in row 5.

8 Highlight cells A1 through H3.

9 Display the Alignment tab of the Format Cells dialog box, and then center the entries across the current selection.

10 Bold the entries in cells A5 through H5.

11 Change the font size and style of the entry in cell A1 to 16-point bold.

12 Bold the entries in cells A23 thorugh H23.

13 Highlight cells A5 through H5.

14 Display the Shading tab of the Format Cells dialog box, and then apply the fourth shade style from the top.

15 Highlight cells A21 through H21.

16 Display the Border tab of the Format Cells dialog box, and then apply the second line style as a bottom border.

17 Press CTRL+HOME to move the highlight to cell A1.

Your spreadsheet should now match the following illustration.

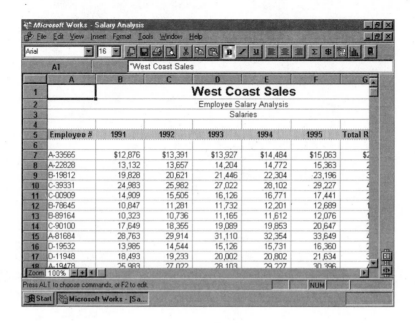

For more information on	See
Changing column widths	Lesson 7
Inserting rows	Lesson 7
Changing number formats	Lesson 7
Changing the alignment of cell entries	Lesson 7
Changing the font size and font style of text entries	Lesson 7
Adding borders and shading to cells	Lesson 7

Step 3: Protect Cells

1 Highlight cells B7 through F21.

2 Open the Format Protection dialog box, and then unlock the highlighted cells.

3 Turn on cell protection.

4 Save Salary Analysis.

For more information on	See
Unlocking cells	Lesson 7
Using cell protection	Lesson 7

Step 4: Create a Spreadsheet Chart

1 Highlight cells B23 through F23, and then open the New Chart dialog box.

2 Specify the Bar chart type and the chart title "Salary Analysis."

3 Create the chart.

4 Open the Edit Titles dialog box and add the subtitle "Total Salaries by Year."

5 Select the chart title and change its font size to 14.

6 Remove the selection box from the chart title.

7 Italicize the other chart text.

8 Display the spreadsheet, and then copy cells B5 through F5.

9 Display the chart, display the Edit Data Labels dialog box, and then paste the data in the 1st text box.

10 Click the OK button.

11 Open the Rename Chart dialog box, name the chart "Salaries," and then save Salary Analysis.

Your completed chart should look like the following illustration.

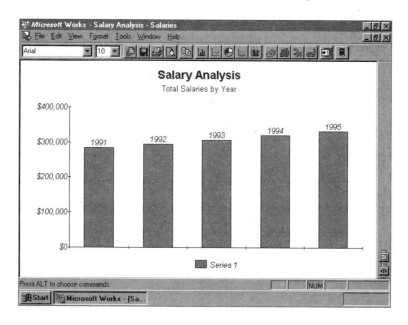

For more information on	See
Creating and modifying charts	Lesson 8

Step 5: Print a Spreadsheet and a Chart

1   Display the Source, Size & Orientation tab of the Page Setup dialog box.

2   Change the Orientation setting to Landscape.

3   Switch to the spreadsheet and then change the page orientation of the spreadsheet to Landscape.

4   Change the top margin of the spreadsheet to 2.5 inches and the left margin to 2 inches.

5   Preview the spreadsheet.

6   Print the spreadsheet.

7   Switch to the Salaries chart, and then preview and print the chart.

8   Save your work.

9   Close the Salary Analysis spreadsheet and the Salaries chart.

For more information on	See
Changing the page orientation	Lesson 7
Changing margins	Lesson 7
Previewing and printing a spreadsheet	Lesson 7
Previewing and printing a chart	Lesson 8

 NOTE   Before you start the following exercise, be sure you have the phone number of another user whose computer has communications capabilities and that the other computer is ready to answer your call.

Step 6: Communicate with Another Computer

1   Open a new Communications document.

2   In the Easy Connect dialog box, type the phone number and service name for the computer you are calling, and then connect to the other computer.

3   Type the following message to the other computer user.

   The meeting to review our finances with you is set for Tuesday of next week. I will send you our investor information file within the next hour. I am including the salary analysis as requested.

4   Have the other computer user type a confirmation message and reply.

5   Type a closing message to the other computer user; for example, **Goodbye**

6   Hang up and disconnect from the other computer.

For more information on	See
Connecting to another computer for the first time	Lesson 9
Quitting a Communications session	Lesson 9

Step 7: Reconnect and Send a File to Another Computer

1   Open the Easy Connect dialog box.

2   Reconnect to the same computer you connected to in Step 6.

3   Be sure you are using the same transfer protocol the other computer is using.

4   Send the file Salary Analysis to the other computer.

5   After the file transfer is completed, disconnect from the other computer.

For more information on	See
Sending a file	Lesson 9

If you want to continue to the next lesson

Close

1   Click the Close button in the Communications document title bar.

2   Be sure the Works Task Launcher dialog box is displayed.

If you want to quit Works for now

Close

1   Click the Close button in the Communications document title bar.

2   Click the Exit Works button in the Works Task Launcher dialog box.

Keeping Track of Information

Part 4

Customizing a Database

In this lesson you will learn how to:

- Update database information.
- Organize your database.
- Make your database easy to use.
- Add a drawing object to your database form.
- Use calculations.
- Print records.

Estimated time
50 min.

You can view database information in different ways. For example, you can look up specific information for a particular record or organize your data in groups or in alphabetical order. In this lesson, you'll learn different ways to update, organize, and enhance the information in a database. You'll also add a logo to a database form, calculate a value in a database, and print database records.

Updating Database Information

You use the find feature to locate specific records in a database. In Form view, you can search for a specific item in a record, and then edit that record. In List view, you can search for items in all the records, and then print the resulting list.

The replace feature enables you to make changes to multiple records using a single command. For example, you can reduce the price of all items priced at $34.99 to $30.89 or change the cost for a group of supplies by using a single command. In the next exercises, you'll use the find and replace features in Form and List view.

Find a record in Form view

You want to find the selling price of the Easel item. Since you are looking for only one record, you'll use Form view.

1 Open Art Inventory in the Works SBS Practice folder, and then maximize the form window.

2 On the Edit menu, click Find.

   The Find dialog box appears.

3 In the Find What text box, type **easel**

   The characters you type are *search characters*, which specify the text of the entry you want to locate.

   The Find dialog box should look like the following illustration.

Search characters

The Next Record option specifies to find only the next instance of the search characters; the All Records option specifies to find all instances of the search characters.

NOTE You don't need to match the capitalization of the text for which you're searching to find an entry. When you type *easel*, Works will find *easel*, *Easel*, and *EASEL*.

4 Press ENTER.

   Works finds and displays the next record that contains the search characters.

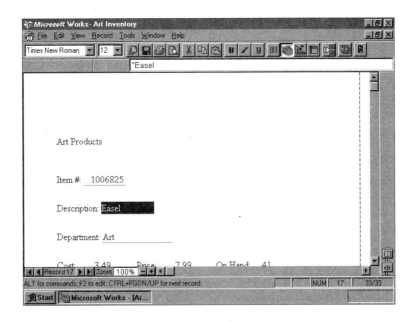

Find records in List view

If you want to find more than one record, you can use List view. You will use List view to create a list of all supplies in the Flowers department.

List View

1 Click the List View button on the toolbar to switch to List view.

2 Click the Department field name to highlight that field for every record.

When you highlight a field before beginning a search, Works searches only that field, rather than the entire database. Search characters that appear in fields other than the highlighted field will not be in the list.

3 On the Edit menu, click Find.

4 Type **flowers** in the Find What text box.

5 In the Match section, click All Records, and then click the OK button.

Works finds and displays all records with *Flowers* in the Department field.

✓		Item #	Description	Department	Cost	Price	On H
☐	2	1002248	Silk carnation individual count	Flowers	0.68	1.25	
☐	7	1003019	Silk leaves 5 count	Flowers	0.29	0.99	
☐	13	1004748	Ceramic bud vase unpainted	Flowers	1.25	3.55	
☐	23	1008727	Ceramic bud vase painted	Flowers	1.75	4.55	
☐	25	2001112	Styrofoam 5" cube green	Flowers	0.35	0.99	
☐	28	2001422	Styrofoam 10" cube white	Flowers	0.7	1.98	
☐	31	2001562	Styrofoam 5" cube white	Flowers	0.35	0.99	
☐	32	2001595	Silk rose individual count	Flowers	0.78	1.45	
☐	34						

231

Print

6 Click the Print button on the toolbar to print your list.

Before you can begin another search, you must display all the database records.

7 On the Record menu, point to Show, and then click 1 All Records.

All the records in the database are displayed so you can begin another search.

Use a wildcard in a search

You don't have to enter the exact search text to find entries in your database. You can type a *wildcard character* to take the place of one or more characters in your search. Wildcard characters include the question mark (?), which replaces a single character, and the asterisk (*), which replaces any number of characters. You will use a wildcard to create a list of products in your inventory with a price between $1.00 and $1.99.

1 Highlight the Price field for all the records.

2 On the Edit menu, click Find.

3 Type **1.*** in the Find What text box.

The search characters specify to list records that contain a 1, a period, and any number of characters after the period.

NOTE You can substitute the ? wildcard for a single character. For example, if you type 197?, the ? wildcard takes the place of a single character, and specifies that records containing four characters, with 197 as the first three characters, will appear in the list.

---

4 In the Match section, click All Records, and then click the OK button.

Works finds and displays all records for the products that are between $1.00 and $1.99.

☑	Item #	Description	Department	Cost	Price	On H
☐ 2	1002248	Silk carnation individual count	Flowers	0.68	1.25	
☐ 15	1005883	Ceramic paint 2 oz. individual cold	Art	0.79	1.25	
☐ 20	1007993	Paint thinner 2 oz.	Art	0.75	1.55	
☐ 28	2001422	Styrofoam 10" cube white	Flowers	0.7	1.98	
☐ 32	2001595	Silk rose individual count	Flowers	0.78	1.45	
☐ 34						

5 Print the list.

Replace information in List view

You decide to rename the Flowers department to the Floral department. As a result, you'll need to replace all occurrences of *Flowers* with *Floral* in the Department field.

1 On the Record menu, point to Show, and then click 1 All Records.

All records in the database appear.

2 Highlight the Department field for all records.

3 On the Edit menu, click Replace.

The Replace dialog box appears.

4 Type **flowers** in the Find What text box, press TAB to move to the Replace With text box, and then type **Floral**

The Replace dialog box should now match the following illustration.

Search characters
Replacement characters

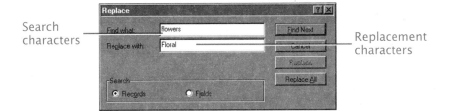

 IMPORTANT   You must type replacement text exactly the way you want the text to appear. Works inserts the replacement text into the records exactly as it appears in the Replace With text box.

---

5 Click the Replace All button.

Works replaces all instances of *Flowers* with *Floral* in the Department field.

		Item #	Description	Department	Cost	Price	On H
☐	1	1002247	Satin fabric solid colors 20 yard r	Fabric	26.87	59.99	
☐	2	1002248	Silk carnation individual count	Floral	0.68	1.25	
☐	3	1002302	Cotton fabric assorted prints 20 y	Fabric	18.65	34.99	
☐	4	1002517	Oil paint palette	Art	5.75	12.25	
☐	5	1002979	Cotton fabric solid colors 20 yard	Fabric	17.65	32.99	
☐	6	1002995	Scissors	Fabric	3.39	5.95	
☐	7	1003019	Silk leaves 5 count	Floral	0.29	0.99	
☐	8	1003023	Sketching pad 8" by 10" white	Art	1.29	4.35	
☐	9	1003031	Sketching pad 8" by 10" ivory	Art	1.29	4.35	
☐	10	1003037	Soft bristle brush 1"	Art	2.69	6.25	
☐	11	1003194	Canvas 8" by 10" white	Art	5.25	10.75	
☐	12	1003361	Clear plastic 30 yard roll	Fabric	21.67	44.99	
☐	13	1004748	Ceramic bud vase unpainted	Floral	1.25	3.55	
☐	14	1004749	Artist brush set	Art	4.95	10.5	

6 Save your work.

Organizing Your Data

Works can sort as many as three fields at a time.

It can be time consuming to find specific information in a large database. You can *sort*, or rearrange, your records to view them in a specified order. Sorting doesn't change the contents of your database; it lets you look at the information in a different way.

Works can sort more than one field at a time. For example, you can sort your art inventory database by specifying the department as the first sort field and the description as the second sort field. As a result, records in the same department will be grouped together and listed in alphabetical order by description within each group.

You can sort database records in Form view or in List view, although List view is usually more appropriate for viewing records after they are sorted. In the next exercise, you'll sort your art inventory database in List view by department and then by description.

Sort database records

1 On the Record menu, click Sort Records.

The Sort Records dialog box appears.

NOTE If this is the first time you have sorted records in the database, a First-Time Help dialog box appears. Click Don't Display This Message In The Future, and then click the OK button.

You can sort records in ascending or descending order within each field. Ascending order is A through Z or 0 through 9; descending order is Z through A or 9 through 0.

In the Sort Records dialog box, you specify the fields by which to sort the information and the order in which to display the fields.

2 In the Sort By section, click the arrow to the right of the list box, and then click Department.

Department will be the first sort field.

3 In the first Then By section, click the arrow to the right of the list box, and then click Description.

Description will be the second sort field.

The Sort Records dialog box should now look like the following illustration.

Primary sort field

Secondary sort field

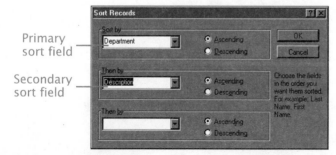

4 Click the OK button.

The records are now sorted alphabetically by department, and then by description, as shown in the next illustration.

	Item #	Description	Department	Cost	Price	On H...
1	1004749	Artist brush set	Art	4.95	10.5	
2	1008726	Canvas 12" by 14" white	Art	5.75	12.25	
3	1003194	Canvas 8" by 10" white	Art	5.25	10.75	
4	2001514	Ceramic paint 10 color assortmen	Art	3.99	7.55	
5	1005883	Ceramic paint 2 oz. individual colc	Art	0.79	1.25	
6	1008740	Charcoal pencils 5 pack	Art	1.35	2.99	
7	1007304	Colored pencils 10 pack	Art	1.24	2.76	
8	1006825	Easel	Art	3.49	7.99	
9	2005975	Enamel paint 10 color assortment	Art	2.99	6.55	
10	1002517	Oil paint palette	Art	5.75	12.25	
11	1007993	Paint thinner 2 oz.	Art	0.75	1.55	
12	2001454	Pastel crayon 20 pack assortmen	Art	4.69	9.95	
13	1006282	Pastel crayon 50 pack assortmen	Art	6.87	12.95	
14	1003031	Sketching pad 8" by 10" ivory	Art	1.29	4.35	
15	1003023	Sketching pad 8" by 10" white	Art	1.29	4.35	
16	1003037	Soft bristle brush 1"	Art	2.69	6.25	
17	2001420	Soft bristle brush 2"	Art	2.75	6.5	
18	1003361	Clear plastic 30 yard roll	Fabric	21.67	44.99	

Making Your Database Easy to Use

You can use the Database formatting features to improve the appearance of your database and make field entries easier to read and locate. In the next exercises, you'll change the size and number formats of fields. You'll also change the alignment of field entries, and work with fonts, borders, and shading to improve the appearance of your database form.

Change the size of fields

You change the size of a field to accommodate the size of information in the field. You can also change the amount of space between columns of data. The size of a field does not affect the amount of data you can store in the field, but only the amount of data that appears on the screen and on a printed sheet.

1 Click the Description field for record number 20.

Currently, you can't see the entire description because the field is too small. You can show the entire description by increasing the size of the field.

2 On the Format menu, click Field Width.

The Field Width dialog box appears.

You can also drag a field name border to change the width of a field.

3 Type **35** in the Column Width text box, and then press ENTER.

The field width changes from 28 to 35 characters, and you can now see the entire contents of the field.

4 Move the highlight to the Cost field name.

You decide to make the field smaller so that there is more room for the Description field.

5 Double-click the Cost field name.

Works automatically adjusts the field size to accommodate the width of the longest entry. This feature is called *best fit*. Your screen should now look like the following illustration.

Double-click here
to get the best fit

	Item #	Description	Department	Cost	Price
3	1003194	Canvas 8" by 10" white	Art	5.25	10.75
4	2001514	Ceramic paint 10 color assortment	Art	3.99	7.55
5	1005883	Ceramic paint 2 oz. individual colors	Art	0.79	1.25
6	1008740	Charcoal pencils 5 pack	Art	1.35	2.99
7	1007304	Colored pencils 10 pack	Art	1.24	2.76
8	1006825	Easel	Art	3.49	7.99
9	2005975	Enamel paint 10 color assortment	Art	2.99	6.55
10	1002517	Oil paint palette	Art	5.75	12.25
11	1007993	Paint thinner 2 oz.	Art	0.75	1.55
12	2001454	Pastel crayon 20 pack assortment	Art	4.69	9.95
13	1006282	Pastel crayon 50 pack assortment	Art	6.87	12.95
14	1003031	Sketching pad 8" by 10" ivory	Art	1.29	4.35
15	1003023	Sketching pad 8" by 10" white	Art	1.29	4.35
16	1003037	Soft bristle brush 1"	Art	2.69	6.25
17	2001420	Soft bristle brush 2"	Art	2.75	6.5
18	1003361	Clear plastic 30 yard roll	Fabric	21.67	44.99
19	1008041	Colored plastic 30 yard roll	Fabric	22.67	46.99
20	1002302	Cotton fabric assorted prints 20 yard roll	Fabric	18.65	34.99

6 Click the Description field for record number 1.

Form Design

You can also highlight a field and then drag a sizing handle, which is one of the small squares that appear on the bottom and right borders of a highlighted field, to change the size of a field in Form Design.

7 Click the Form Design button on the toolbar to switch to Form Design.

Although you changed the size of the Description field in List view, the field size did *not* change in Form Design. You will change the size of the Description field in Form Design so you can see the entire field contents on the database form.

8 On the Format menu, click Field Size.

The Format Field Size dialog box appears.

9 Type **35** in the Width text box, and then press ENTER.

The field width changes to 35 characters. The new field width affects all records you view in Form Design and in Form view.

Change number formats

1 Click the Cost field, hold down CTRL, and then click the Price field.

Both the Cost and Price fields should now be highlighted, as shown in the following illustration.

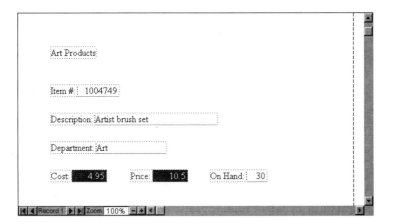

2 Use the right mouse button to click either of the highlighted fields, and then click Format Field.

The Field tab of the Format dialog box appears.

3   In the Format section, click Number.

A list of number formats appears in the Appearance list box.

4   In the Appearance list box, click the third option from the top of the list (currency).

The Field tab of the Format dialog box should now appear as follows.

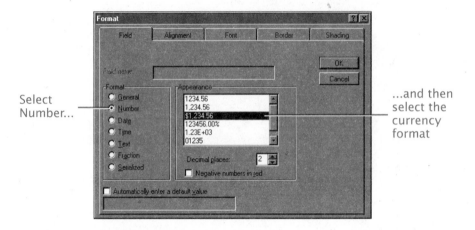

Select
Number...

...and then
select the
currency
format

The Currency format displays numbers with a leading dollar sign, thousands separators, and two decimal places.

5   Click the OK button to apply the new number format to the highlighted field entries.

The Cost and Price field entries now appear in the Currency format with two decimal places, as shown in the next illustration.

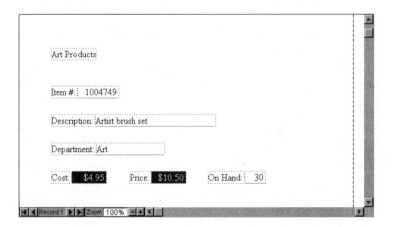

Change the alignment of field entries

So far, you've made your database easier to read by changing field sizes and number formats. You can emphasize the Cost and Price fields by changing the alignment of the data in these fields.

1 Make sure the Cost and Price fields are still highlighted. If they aren't, click the Cost field, hold down CTRL, and then click the Price field.

2 Use the right mouse button to click either of the highlighted fields, and then click Alignment.

   The Alignment tab of the Format dialog box appears.

3 In the Horizontal section, click Center.

4 Click the OK button.

   The entries are centered within the borders of each field. When you change the alignment of a field in Form Design or in List view, the alignment also changes in the other views.

Change the font, size, and style of text

Your database form currently contains all the information you need, but it's difficult to distinguish some of the fields from their field names because all of the text looks the same. You can add visual appeal to your form and make it easier to read by changing the font, size, and style of the text.

1 Position the pointer above and to the left of the label *Art Products*.

2 Drag the pointer diagonally to the bottom right corner of the database form.

   A dotted rectangle appears as you drag the pointer.

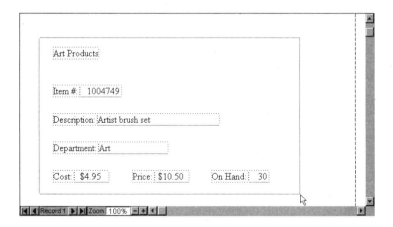

3 Release the mouse button.

All of the enclosed objects are now highlighted, including the field names and field entries.

Font Name

4 Click the arrow to the right of the Font Name list box on the toolbar, and then click Arial.

The font of the highlighted text changes from Times New Roman to Arial.

Bold

5 Click the Bold button on the toolbar.

The highlighted text is now bolded.

6 Click a blank area of the form to remove the highlighting.

7 Hold down CTRL, and then click each of the fields to highlight all of them.

Only the fields are highlighted. The field names and the *Art Products* label should not be highlighted. Your screen should match the following illustration.

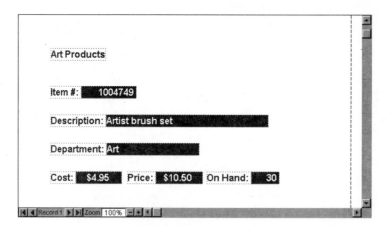

Font Size

8 Click the arrow to the right of the Font Size list box on the toolbar, and then click 10.

The font size of the field entries changes from 12 to 10.

Bold

9 Click the Bold button on the toolbar to turn off bold for the field entries.

10 Change the font size of the label *Art Products* to 24.

Italic

11 Click the Italic button on the toolbar to italicize the label.

The changes you made will affect every record in the database. Your form should now look like the following illustration.

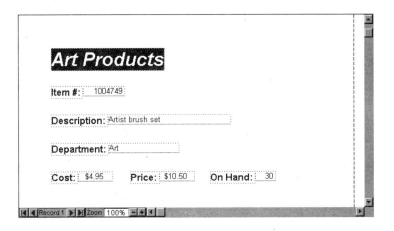

Add borders

You decide to draw attention to the Price field by adding a border.

1 Highlight the Price field.

2 Use the right mouse button to click the highlighted field, and then click Border.

   The Border tab of the Format dialog box appears.

3 In the Line Style section, click the third line style from the top to select it.

   The Border tab of the Format dialog box should match the next illustration.

Select this
line style

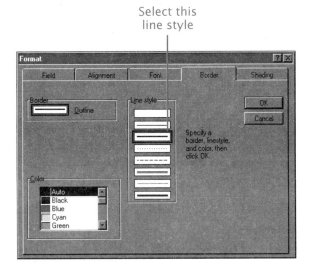

4 Click the OK button to add the border to the field.

241

5 Click a blank area of the form to see the border.

Add shading

1 Highlight the *Art Products* label.

2 Use the right mouse button to click the highlighted label, and then click Shading.

The Shading tab of the Format dialog box appears.

3 In the Shading section, click the seventh shading pattern from the top.

You have to scroll down in the Pattern list box to see the seventh pattern. The Shading tab of the Format dialog box should now look like the following.

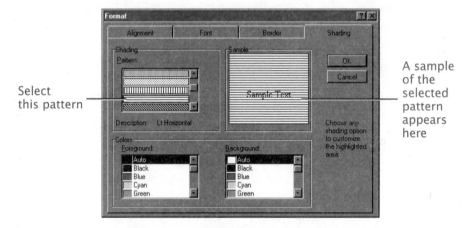

Select this pattern

A sample of the selected pattern appears here

4 Click the OK button to add the shading to the label.

5 Click a blank area on the form to see the shading.

Your database form should now match the following illustration.

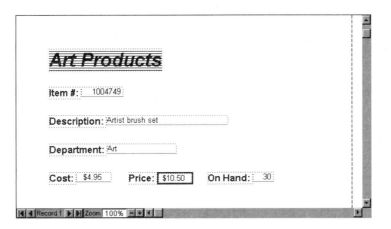

6 Save your work.

Adding a Drawing Object to Your Database Form

You decide to add a company logo to your form. Microsoft Draw is a drawing application in Works you can use to create drawings in your documents. You can use Microsoft Draw to design a company logo, create drawings to illustrate important points in a report, or draw lines that divide a form into sections. You can use the drawing tools to create objects such as rectangles, circles, lines, arcs, polygons, or blocks of text. To create a drawing, you position the insertion point at the location where you want the drawing, start Microsoft Draw, and use the drawing tools to draw objects. When your drawing is complete, you exit Microsoft Draw and insert the drawing into your document. In the next exercises, you'll use Microsoft Draw to create a logo.

Start Microsoft Draw

1 Position the insertion point at the coordinates X1.83" Y1.00".

2 On the Insert menu, click Drawing.

Microsoft Draw starts and opens the drawing window.

Maximize

3 In the drawing window, click the Maximize button to maximize the drawing window.

The components of the drawing window are shown in the following illustration.

243

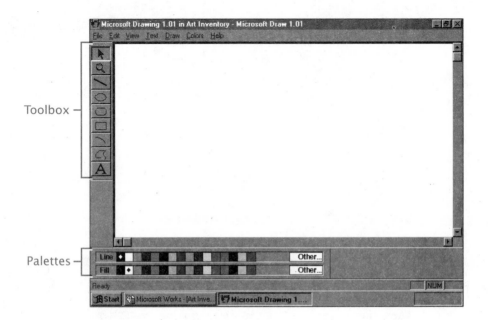

Draw objects

To draw an object, you click a drawing tool in the toolbox, move the pointer into the drawing area, and drag the pointer.

Oval

1   Click the Oval tool in the toolbox.

Notice that the name of the selected tool appears in the status bar when you click and hold down the mouse button.

2   Move the pointer into the center of the drawing area.

The pointer appears in the shape of cross hairs (+).

3   Drag the mouse down and to the right to draw an oval in the center of the drawing area, as shown in the following illustration. Release the mouse button when the oval is the size you want.

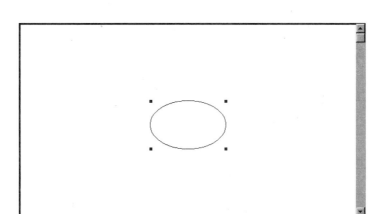

NOTE If your drawing does not resemble the illustration, you can press DELETE to delete the object, and then you can draw it again. You can also click Undo on the Edit menu to delete the last object drawn.

Rounded Rectangle

4 Click the Rounded Rectangle tool in the toolbox.

5 Draw a rectangle through the midsection of the oval, as shown in the following illustration.

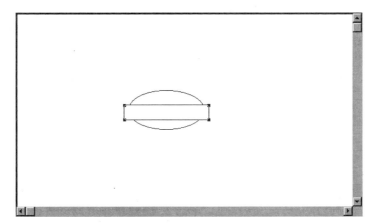

TIP You can draw a perfect square or circle with the Rectangle or Oval tool by holding down SHIFT while you drag the pointer.

Change the interior color

You can use the two *palettes* at the bottom of the drawing window to change the colors and patterns of objects. You use the Line palette to change the color or pattern of lines and the borders of objects. You use the Fill palette to change the interior color or pattern of objects.

Pointer

1   Click the Pointer tool in the toolbox.

2   In the drawing area, click the oval.

Sizing handles appear around the oval, indicating that it is selected. You must select an object before you can modify it.

3   Click the charcoal gray color box in the Fill palette.

The interior of the oval is now charcoal gray. The interior color of the rectangle remains white, providing a visible contrast between the objects.

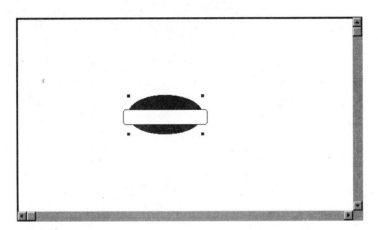

Add text

Text

1   Click the Text tool in the toolbox.

2   In the drawing area, click inside the rectangle near the left border.

The text insertion point appears in the rectangle.

3   Type **West Coast Sales**, and then press ENTER.

You'll format the text to enhance its appearance.

4   If handles don't appear around the text object, click the text to select it.

5   On the Text menu, click Font to display the Font dialog box.

6   In the Font list box, click Times New Roman.

246

7 In the Font Style text box, click Bold.

The Font dialog box should now match the following illustration.

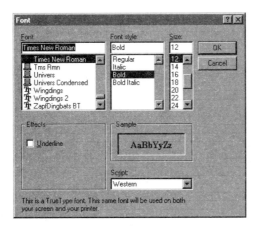

8 Click the OK button, and then click a blank section of the drawing area to see the text changes.

Your drawing should now look similar to the following illustration.

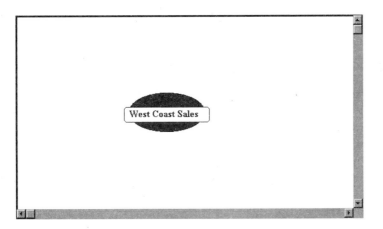

 TIP If your text object is not correctly positioned, you can move it by clicking the text object and then dragging it to a new position.

Insert the drawing

After your logo is complete, you can insert it into your document.

1 On the File menu, click Exit And Return.

The following message box appears.

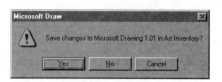

2 Click the Yes button to update the form.

The drawing is inserted into the form. Your form should now look like the following illustration.

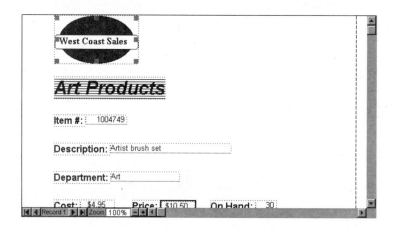

You can drag the bottom-right sizing handle diagonally to resize the logo.

Calculating Field Values

You can use a formula in your database to calculate the value of products in your inventory. In order to calculate the value, you need to add a field and then enter the formula. In the next exercises, you'll add a field and enter a formula.

Add a field

1 Position the insertion point at X1.83" Y4.75".

2 Type **Inventory Value:**

Your database form should now look like the following.

3   Press ENTER.

The Insert Field dialog box appears.

4   In the Format section, click Number, and then click the third option in the Appearance list box.

The Inventory Value field will display entries in the Currency format.

The Insert Field dialog box should match the following illustration.

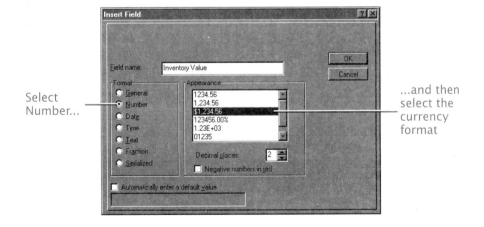

Select Number...

...and then select the currency format

5 Click the OK button to insert the new field into the form.

6 Change the font of the Inventory Value label to Arial and make it boldface.

Your form should now match the following illustration.

Enter a formula

The formula you will enter into the Inventory Value field will use the contents of other fields to make the calculation. So far, there are no entries for the Inventory Value field because you set up inventory value to be the result of a calculation. All formulas begin with an equal sign (=) and can contain field names, mathematical operators (+, -, *, and /), and numbers.

List View

1 Click the List View button on the toolbar, scroll to the right, and then double-click the Inventory Value heading to resize the column.

2 Highlight the Inventory Value field for record number 1.

3 Type **=price*on hand**

This formula calculates the inventory value by multiplying the values in the Price field by the values in the On Hand field.

Your screen should now match the following illustration.

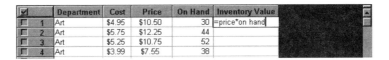

4 Press ENTER.

The formula calculates an inventory value for every record in the database, as shown in the next illustration.

You can also enter a formula in Form view.

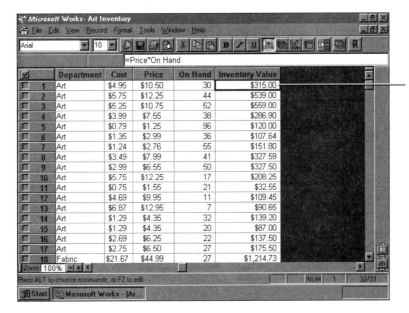

Entering a formula in one record creates the formula for all records

Notice that the entries in the Inventory Value column are displayed in the Currency format.

Printing Your Database Records

You can print your database records in Form view or in List view. In Form view, you usually print records one at a time. In List view, you print multiple records in a table format. You can selectively print records by hiding records and then printing either the hidden or the displayed records. You can also add headers and footers, change the page orientation and printing options, and preview the records before you print.

In the next exercises, you'll print a list of your best selling products, and add a header and a footer to the list.

Select records for printing

1 Drag across record numbers 1 through 4 to highlight the records, as shown in the following illustration.

Drag across
these record
numbers to
highlight the
rows

		Department	Cost	Price	On Hand	Inventory Value
	1	Art	$4.95	$10.50	30	$315.00
	2	Art	$5.75	$12.25	44	$539.00
	3	Art	$5.25	$10.75	52	$559.00
	4	Art	$3.99	$7.55	38	$286.90
	5	Art	$0.79	$1.25	96	$120.00
	6	Art	$1.35	$2.99	36	$107.64

2 On the Record menu, click Hide Record.

Records 1 through 4 are now hidden and are not available for printing.

3 Highlight records 30 through 33.

4 On the Record menu, click Hide Record.

Records 30 through 33 are now hidden and are not available for printing.

*There are other
ways to select
records for
printing. In
Lesson 11, you'll
learn how to use
filters to select
records that
match certain
conditions.*

5 On the Record menu, point to Show, and then click 4 Hidden Records.

Now the hidden records are the only records that appear and are available for printing. Your screen should look like the following illustration.

		Department	Cost	Price	On Hand	Inventory Value
	1	Art	$4.95	$10.50	30	$315.00
	2	Art	$5.75	$12.25	44	$539.00
	3	Art	$5.25	$10.75	52	$559.00
	4	Art	$3.99	$7.55	38	$286.90
	30	Floral	$0.78	$1.45	167	$242.15
	31	Floral	$0.70	$1.98	22	$43.56
	32	Floral	$0.35	$0.99	42	$41.58
	33	Floral	$0.35	$0.99	39	$38.61
	34					

Preview records before printing

1 Click the Print Preview button on the toolbar.

The selected records appear in the Print Preview window.

Print Preview

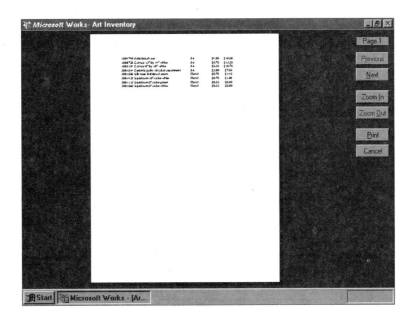

After viewing the records, you decide to add field names, change the page orientation, and use a header and a footer to add a title and the current date.

2 Click the Cancel button to close the Print Preview window.

Change the page setup

1 On the File menu, click Page Setup.

The Page Setup dialog box appears showing margin options.

2 Display the Source, Size & Orientation tab and change the page orientation to landscape.

The Sample section illustrates the new orientation.

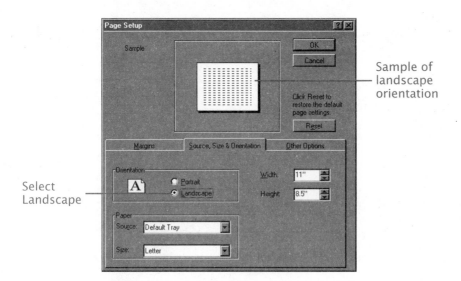

Sample of
landscape
orientation

Select
Landscape

3 Click the Other Options tab.

4 Click the Print Record And Field Labels check box.

This specifies to print the record and field labels. The Other Options tab of the Page Setup dialog box should now match the following illustration.

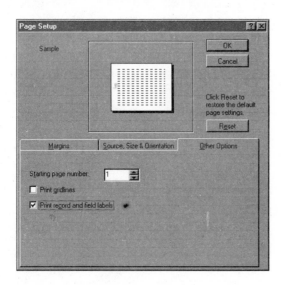

5 Click the OK button.

Add a header and a footer

For more information about header and footer codes, see "How to use footer and header codes" in the Works online Help index.

1 On the View menu, click Headers And Footers.

The View Headers And Footers dialog box appears.

2 In the Header text box, type **&cBest Selling Art Products**

The header will print *Best Selling Art Products* centered at the top of the page.

3 Press TAB to move to the Footer text box, and then type **&r&d**

This footer will print the current date, right-aligned, at the bottom of the page. The View Headers And Footers dialog box should now look like the following illustration.

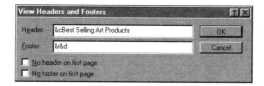

4 Press ENTER.

5 Preview the document.

Your screen should look like the following illustration.

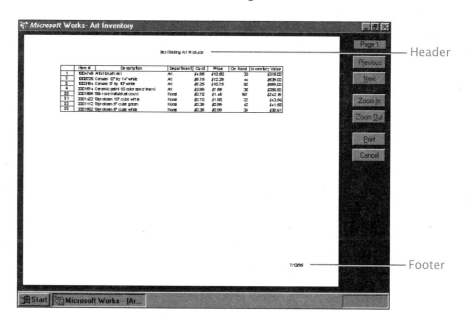

Magnify the view if you have difficulty seeing the text.

6 Click the Print button in the Print Preview window to print the list.

 TIP If you want to print multiple copies of the report, click Print on the File menu, and specify the number of copies.

After you print the list, you need to redisplay all of the database records so they are available for other operations.

7 On the Record menu, point to Show, and then click 1 All Records.

8 Save your work.

One Step Further: Creating a Blank Form

When you want to add new items to your database, you can prepare the information for data entry by writing it on blank database forms. You create the blank database forms by printing blank records in Form view.

Print a blank form

1 Switch to Form view.

2 On the File menu, click Page Setup.

3 Display the Source, Size & Orientation tab, and then change the orientation to portrait.

Portrait orientation is often more appropriate for printing in Form view.

4 On the View menu, click Headers And Footers.

The View Headers And Footers dialog box appears. You don't need the header and footer on a blank database form.

5 Press DELETE, press TAB, press DELETE, and then press ENTER to delete the header and footer text and close the dialog box.

Last Record

6 In the bottom left corner of the database window, click the Last Record button to display a blank record.

7 On the File menu, click Print.

The Print dialog box appears.

 NOTE If this is the first time you have printed using the File menu, a First-Time Help dialog box appears. Click Don't Display This Message In The Future, and then click the OK button.

8 In the What To Print section, click Current Record Only.

The Print dialog box should match the following illustration.

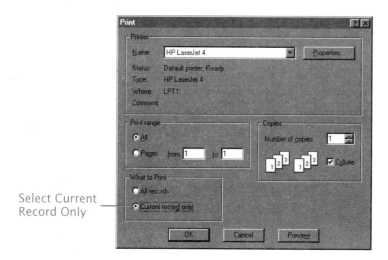

Select Current
Record Only

9 Click the OK button to print the blank form.

10 Save your work.

If you want to continue to the next lesson

⊠
Close

➤ Click the Close button in the Art Inventory menu bar.

If you want to quit Works for now

⊠
Close

1 Click the Close button in the Art Inventory menu bar.

2 Click the Exit Works button in the Works Task Launcher dialog box.

Lesson Summary

To	Do this	Button
Find a record	On the Edit menu, click Find, type the characters you want to find, and then press ENTER.	
Display all records after a search	On the Record menu, point to Show, and then click 1 All Records.	

To	Do this	Button
Replace information	On the Edit menu, click Replace, type the characters you want to find, press TAB, type the replacement characters, and then click the Replace All button.	
Sort database records	On the Record menu, click Sort Records, and select the fields by which you want to sort. Click Ascending or Descending for each field, and then click the OK button.	
Change the size of a field	In Form Design, highlight the field, click Field Size on the Format menu, type a new field width, and then press ENTER. In List view, move the highlight to the field you want to change, click Field Width on the Format menu, type a new field width, and then press ENTER.	
Change a number format	Highlight the field you want to change, and click Field on the Format menu. Click a format, click an appearance for the format, type the number of decimal places, and then press ENTER.	
Change the alignment of field entries	Highlight the fields you want to change, click Alignment on the Format menu, click an Alignment option, and then click the OK button.	

To	Do this	Button
Change the font of text	Highlight the labels and fields you want to change, click the arrow to the right of the Font Name list box on the toolbar, and then click a font.	Times New Roman ▾
Change the font size of text	Highlight the labels and fields you want to change, click the arrow to the right of the Font Size list box on the toolbar, and then click a font size.	12 ▾
Change the font style of text	Highlight the labels and fields you want to change, and then click the Bold, Italic, or Underline button on the toolbar.	**B** *I* U
Add a border	Highlight the field or label to which you want to add a border, click Border on the Format menu, select a line style, and then click the OK button.	
Add shading	Highlight the field or label to which you want to add shading, click Shading on the Format menu, click a shading pattern in the Pattern list box, and then click the OK button.	
Start Microsoft Draw	Place the insertion point in a document or form, and then click Drawing on the Insert menu.	
Change the interior color of an object	Click the object, and then click a color box in the Fill palette.	
Add text to a drawing	Click the Text tool in the toolbox, click in the drawing area, and then type the text.	A

To	Do this	Button
Change the font of a text object	Click the text object, click Font on the Text menu, and then click a font.	
Change the font size of a text object	Click the text object, click Font on the Text menu, and then click a size.	
Change the font style of a text object	Click the text object and then click Bold, Italic, or Underline on the Text menu.	
Enter a formula	Highlight the field in which you want to place the formula, type =, enter field names, operators, or numbers, and then press ENTER.	
Hide records	Highlight the records in List view, and then click Hide Record on the Record menu.	
Change the page orientation	On the File menu, click Page Setup, click the Source, Size & Orientation tab, click an Orientation option, and then click the OK button.	
Print records with field labels	On the File menu, click Page Setup, click the Other Options tab, click the Print Record And Field Labels check box, and then click the OK button.	
Add a header and a footer	On the View menu, click Headers And Footers, type the header and footer text and codes, and then press ENTER.	
Print records	Click the Print button on the toolbar.	
Print a blank form	Display a blank record in Form view, click Print on the File menu, click Current Record Only, and then click the OK button.	

For online information about	Display the Help window, and then
Finding and replacing database information	Click "Find, sort, or filter information," and then click "To replace specific text or numbers"
Sorting database records	Click "Find, sort, or filter information," and then click "To sort a database in alphabetic or numeric order"
Formatting text	Click "Change how text looks (bold, italic, size, fonts,...)" and then click the appropriate topic
Printing a database	Click the Index button, type **printing**, click "Printing database records," and then click the appropriate topic

Preview of the Next Lesson

In this lesson, you updated and sorted database information, formatted fields, added graphics and formulas, and printed database records. In the next lesson, you'll learn how to manipulate the information in your database. You'll use filters to select records that match certain conditions, add data to a document, and convert the data into a spreadsheet.

Locating and Copying Information

Estimated time
20 min.

In this lesson you will learn how to:

- Create and apply filters.
- Add database information to a Word Processor document.
- Convert database information into a spreadsheet.

In addition to updating and sorting information, you can use Database features to manipulate your data in other ways. You can use filters to display only the information you want to see. For example, in a large database, such as a product inventory, you can apply a filter to display items with less than 10 units in stock. When you use a filter, Works displays only the records that match the description defined by the filter and hides the rest.

You can also use the information in a database to create or enhance other documents. For example, you can use a filter to display certain records and then add that data to other documents for illustrative purposes or to share important information with others without having to show the entire database. You can also convert database records into a spreadsheet to perform more advanced calculations on your data.

In this lesson, you'll learn how to use filters to display records that contain specific information and use that information in a Word Processor memo. You'll also convert database data into a spreadsheet.

Displaying Specific Information in a Database

In order to display the information you want in a database, you can create a filter. *Filters* are conditional statements that specify the criteria a record must match in order to be displayed. For example, if a filter specifies to display records for items in the Art department that cost from $10.00 through $15.00, the record would have to meet the following criteria: 1) the item must be from the Art department, 2) the cost cannot be less than $10.00, 3) the cost cannot be more than $15.00.

When you apply a filter, Works searches the database and displays only the records that match the conditions specified by the filter.

In the following exercises, you'll use filters to display specific information.

Display records that match in a single field

The easiest type of filter you can create is one that displays records with matching values in a single field. For example, if you want to check your inventory for items only in the Art department, you can create a filter that displays only records with *Art* in the Department field.

1   Open Product Inventory in the Works SBS Practice folder, and then maximize the database window.

Works opens the database.

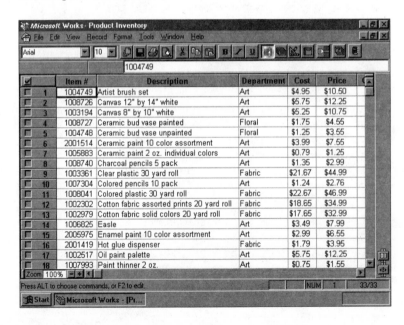

2   On the Tools menu, click Filters.

The Filter Name dialog box appears, and the Filter dialog box appears behind it.

You name the filter so that you can apply it again without having to re-enter the criteria.

 NOTE If this is the first time you have named a filter, a First-Time Help dialog box appears. Click Don't Display This Message In The Future, and then click the OK button.

3 Type **Art Department**, and then press ENTER.

The Filter dialog box appears.

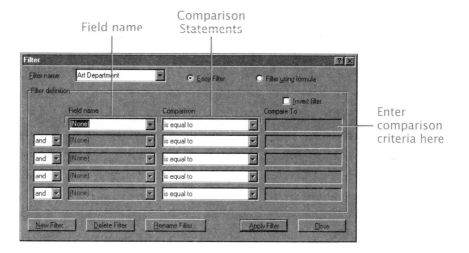

The Filter dialog box contains the Field Name, Comparison, and Compare To components that you use to create the conditional statements for a filter. The Field Name component lists the fields you can select from in the database. The Comparison component lists phrases you use to match the field name with the Compare To criteria. The Compare To component is where you enter the value or criteria, such as a number, formula, or item, that you want to compare to the field name.

4 Click the arrow next to the first Field Name list box, and then click Department.

Notice that the Comparison text box already contains a default comparison phrase.

5   Click the first Compare To text box, and then type **Art**

The Filter dialog box should now match the following illustration.

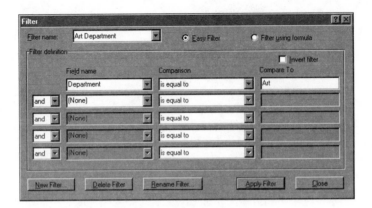

6   Click the Apply Filter button.

Works displays only the records with *Art* in the Department field, as shown in the following illustration.

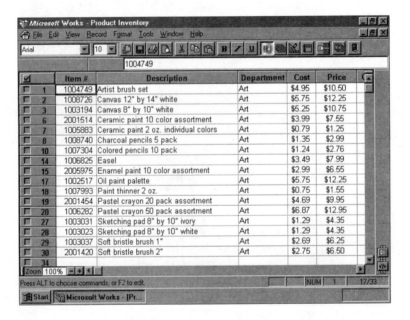

Display records that match in more than one field

You can also create filters that display records with matching values in more than one field. For example, you can display records for products in the Floral department in which the number of items in the On Hand field is less than 50.

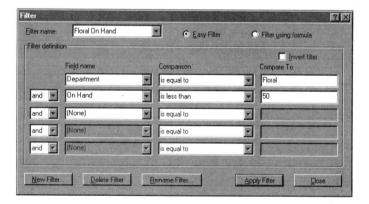

Filters

1 Click the Filters button on the toolbar.

The Filter dialog box appears. Notice that the current filter, *Art Department*, is displayed in Filter Name list box.

2 Click the New Filter button.

The Filter Name dialog box appears.

3 Type **Floral On Hand,** and then press ENTER.

The Filter dialog box appears.

4 Click the arrow to the right of the first Field Name list box, and then click Department.

5 Click the first Compare To text box, and then type **Floral**

6 Click the arrow to the right of the second Field Name list box, and then click On Hand.

7 Click the arrow to the right of the second Comparison list box, and then click Is Less Than.

8 Click the second Compare To text box, and then type **50**

The Filter dialog box should now match the following illustration.

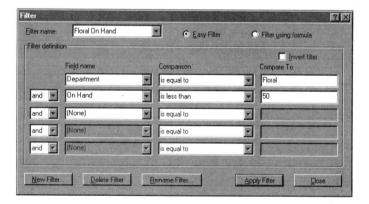

The *and* that appears between the first and second conditional statements specifies that Works will display only records that match both criteria.

9 Click the Apply Filter button, and then scroll right to see the On Hand field.

Works displays the records with *Floral* in the Department field and a value less than *50* in the On Hand field, as shown in the following illustration.

267

✓		Description	Department	Cost	Price	On Hand	I▲
□	5	Ceramic bud vase unpainted	Floral	$1.25	$3.55	1	
□	26	Silk rose individual count	Floral	$0.78	$1.45	9	
□	31	Styrofoam 10" cube white	Floral	$0.70	$1.98	22	
□	33	Styrofoam 5" cube white	Floral	$0.35	$0.99	39	
□	34						

Display records using wildcards

You can use wildcards in filters to represent text. For example, if you want to display records for fabrics in solid colors only, you can use a wildcard to specify that the records displayed for fabrics must contain the word *solid* somewhere in the Description field.

Filters

1 Click the Filters button on the toolbar.

  The Filter dialog box appears.

2 Click the New Filter button.

  The Filter Name dialog box appears.

3 Type **Solid Colors**, and then press ENTER.

  The Filter dialog box appears.

4 Click the arrow to the right of the first Field Name list box, and then click Description.

5 Click the first Compare To text box, and then type ***solid***

  The Filter dialog box should now appear as follows.

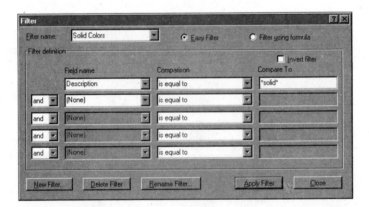

By typing *solid*, you specify that the word *solid* must appear in the Description field, but any text can appear before or after the word *solid*.

6 Click the Apply Filter button.

  Works displays the records for fabrics that contain the word *solid* anywhere in the description.

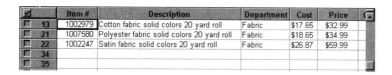

☑	Item #	Description	Department	Cost	Price	
☐ 13	1002979	Cotton fabric solid colors 20 yard roll	Fabric	$17.65	$32.99	
☐ 21	1007580	Polyester fabric solid colors 20 yard roll	Fabric	$18.65	$34.99	
☐ 22	1002247	Satin fabric solid colors 20 yard roll	Fabric	$26.87	$59.99	
☐ 34						
☐ 35						

Display records that match any of several conditions

So far, you've used filters to select records that match a single condition or multiple conditions. However, you don't have to limit a filter to finding records that match all the conditions specified. You can display records that match any of two or more conditions. For example, you can list records with a price greater than or equal to $10.00 in either the Art or Fabric department.

Filters

1 Click the Filters button on the toolbar, and then click the New Filter button.

2 Type **Low Stock** and then press ENTER to name the filter.

3 Click the arrow to the right of the first Field Name list box, and then click Department.

4 Click the first Compare To text box, and then type **Art**

5 Click the arrow to the right of the list box that appears between the first and second conditional statements, and then click Or.

   The Or option specifies that Works will display records that match one or both of the first two conditions.

6 Click the arrow to the right of the second Field Name list box, and then click Department.

7 Click the second Compare To text box, and then type **Fabric**

8 Click the arrow to the right of the third Field Name list box, and then click Price.

9 Click the arrow to the right of the third Comparison list box, and then click Is Greater Than Or Equal To.

   This option specifies that records must have a number greater than or equal to the value specified in the Compare To text box.

10 In the third Compare To text box, type **$10.00**

   The Filter dialog box should now match the following illustration.

Select or

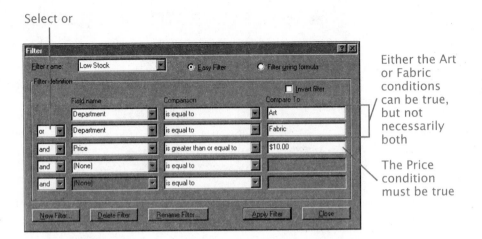

Either the Art
or Fabric
conditions
can be true,
but not
necessarily
both

The Price
condition
must be true

11 Click the Apply Filter button.

Works displays the records in the Art and Fabric departments with a price greater than or equal to $10.00, as shown in the following illustration.

✓	Item #	Description	Department	Cost	Price	
1	1004749	Artist brush set	Art	$4.95	$10.50	
2	1008726	Canvas 12" by 14" white	Art	$5.75	$12.25	
3	1003194	Canvas 8" by 10" white	Art	$5.25	$10.75	
9	1003361	Clear plastic 30 yard roll	Fabric	$21.67	$44.99	
11	1008041	Colored plastic 30 yard roll	Fabric	$22.67	$46.99	
12	1002302	Cotton fabric prints 20 yard roll	Fabric	$18.65	$34.99	
13	1002979	Cotton fabric solid colors 20 yard roll	Fabric	$17.65	$32.99	
17	1002517	Oil paint palette	Art	$5.75	$12.25	
20	1006282	Pastel crayon 50 pack assortment	Art	$6.87	$12.95	
21	1007580	Polyester fabric solid colors 20 yard roll	Fabric	$18.65	$34.99	
22	1002247	Satin fabric solid colors 20 yard roll	Fabric	$26.87	$59.99	
34						

12 Save and then close Product Inventory.

Creating the Inventory Information Memo

Some out-of-stock items in your store are acceptable, but others are not. You need to tell your employees which products are critical to have in stock. In the following exercises, you'll use a TaskWizard to create a memo that informs your employees about products that must always be in stock.

Start the TaskWizard

1   In the Works Task Launcher dialog box, click the TaskWizards tab if it is not the displayed tab.

2   On the list of TaskWizards, click Correspondence.

3   Under the Correspondence category, double-click Memo.

     A secondary Works Task Launcher dialog box appears.

4   Click Yes, Run The TaskWizard.

     The Memo TaskWizard appears.

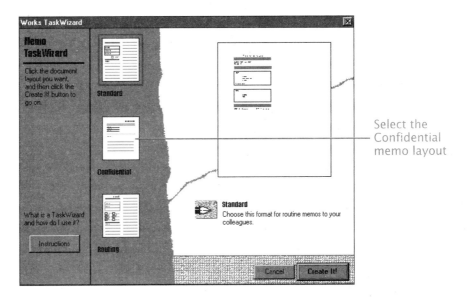

Select the Confidential memo layout

5   Click the Confidential memo layout, and then click the Create It! button.

     The TaskWizard creates the document, as shown in the next illustration.

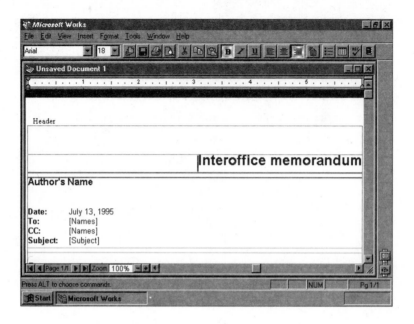

Type the memo text

1 Maximize the document, highlight the text *Author's Name*, and then type your name.

2 In the *To:* memo line, highlight the text *[Names]* and then type **All Employees**

3 Highlight the text *CC: [Names]* and the blank space after the bracket ( ]), and then press DELETE to delete the text.

4 In the *Subject:* memo line, highlight the text *[Subject],* and then type **Out of Stock**

5 Select the text *Type your memo text here,* and then type the following paragraph.

Recently, certain items that are critical to our success have been out of stock. While this may be acceptable for some items, we should never be out of stock of the products listed below. Please be vigilant in your departments and order ahead. If there is a problem with the supplier, let me know immediately so I can help solve the problem. Thank you.

6 Press ENTER twice.

Your document should appear similar to the following illustration.

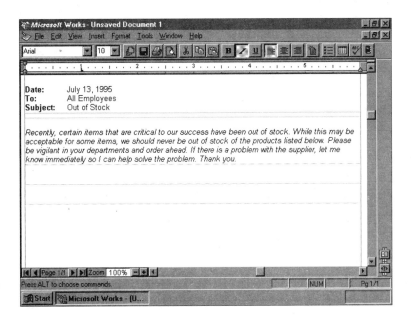

7 Save the document as Out Of Stock Memo in the Works SBS Practice folder.

Displaying the Records You Want to Add

Now that you have created your memo, you can add the list of products that employees need to keep in stock. You'll get this information from the Product Inventory database and then copy it into the Out of Stock memo. But first you'll need to open the database and display the records you want to copy.

Open the Database

▶ Open the Product Inventory database in the Works SBS Practice folder, and then maximize the database window if it isn't already maximized.

Use an existing filter

The critical items you need to keep in stock are products in the Art and Fabrics departments with a price of $10.00 or more. Since the Low Stock filter you created earlier in this lesson specifies the criteria for those items, you can use it again to display the records you need for the memo quickly and easily.

Filters

1 Click the Filters button on the toolbar to open the Filter dialog box.

2 Click the arrow to the right of the Filter Name list box, and then click Low Stock.

The defined criteria for the Low Stock filter appears in the Filter Definition section of the dialog box. The Filter dialog box should match the following illustration.

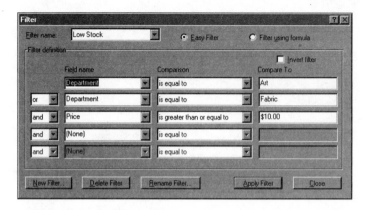

3 Click the Apply Filter button.

Works displays the records with a price of $10.00 or more in the Art and Fabric departments.

☑		Item #	Description	Department	Cost	Price	
☐	1	1004749	Artist brush set	Art	$4.95	$10.50	
☐	2	1008726	Canvas 12" by 14" white	Art	$5.75	$12.25	
☐	3	1003194	Canvas 8" by 10" white	Art	$5.25	$10.75	
☐	9	1003361	Clear plastic 30 yard roll	Fabric	$21.67	$44.99	
☐	11	1008041	Colored plastic 30 yard roll	Fabric	$22.67	$46.99	
☐	12	1002302	Cotton fabric prints 20 yard roll	Fabric	$18.65	$34.99	
☐	13	1002979	Cotton fabric solid colors 20 yard roll	Fabric	$17.65	$32.99	
☐	17	1002517	Oil paint palette	Art	$5.75	$12.25	
☐	20	1006282	Pastel crayon 50 pack assortment	Art	$6.87	$12.95	
☐	21	1007580	Polyester fabric solid colors 20 yard roll	Fabric	$18.65	$34.99	
☐	22	1002247	Satin fabric solid colors 20 yard roll	Fabric	$26.87	$59.99	
☐	34						

Copy the records to the memo

Now that you have the records you want, you can copy them to the Out Of Stock Memo document.

1 Highlight the Description field for the displayed rows, as shown in the following illustration.

☑		Item #	Description	Department	Cost	Price	
☐	1	1004749	Artist brush set	Art	$4.95	$10.50	
☐	2	1008726	Canvas 12" by 14" white	Art	$5.75	$12.25	
☐	3	1003194	Canvas 8" by 10" white	Art	$5.25	$10.75	
☐	9	1003361	Clear plastic 30 yard roll	Fabric	$21.67	$44.99	
☐	11	1008041	Colored plastic 30 yard roll	Fabric	$22.67	$46.99	
☐	12	1002302	Cotton fabric prints 20 yard roll	Fabric	$18.65	$34.99	
☐	13	1002979	Cotton fabric solid colors 20 yard roll	Fabric	$17.65	$32.99	
☐	17	1002517	Oil paint palette	Art	$5.75	$12.25	
☐	20	1006282	Pastel crayon 50 pack assortment	Art	$6.87	$12.95	
☐	21	1007580	Polyester fabric solid colors 20 yard roll	Fabric	$18.65	$34.99	
☐	22	1002247	Satin fabric solid colors 20 yard roll	Fabric	$26.87	$59.99	
☐	34						

Copy

2 Click the Copy button on the toolbar.

3 On the Window menu, click 1 Out Of Stock Memo.

TIP Make sure the insertion point is positioned at the left margin of the document so the data columns will be aligned correctly when you paste the records in the memo.

Paste

4 Click the Paste button on the toolbar.

The database fields are pasted into the memo.

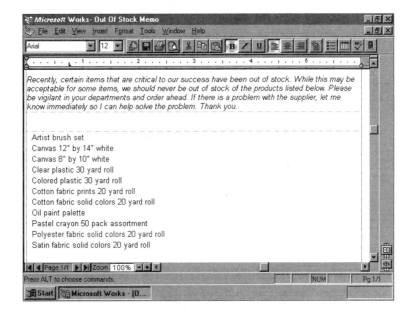

NOTE Depending on the format of the data you copy, you may have to reformat the text in the Word Processor document to make it line up properly.

5 Save and then close Out Of Stock Memo.

Converting the Data Into a Spreadsheet

Adding calculations to a database is easy, but it's not as versatile as creating calculations in a spreadsheet. You can save your database as text and then open the data in the Spreadsheet and add calculations. In the next exercises, you'll save the Product Inventory database as text and then open the data in a spreadsheet.

Save the file in a new format

1 On the Record menu, point to Show, and then click 1 All Records.

2 Click anywhere in the database.

The selected records are deselected.

3 On the File menu, click Save As.

The Save As dialog box appears.

4 Click the arrow to the right of the Save As Type list box, and then select Text & Commas.

The Text & Commas format keeps database and spreadsheet data in its column and row format when you copy or move it into another Works tool.

5 Highlight the text in the File Name text box, and then type **Inventory Text**

The Save As dialog box should now appear as shown in the following illustration.

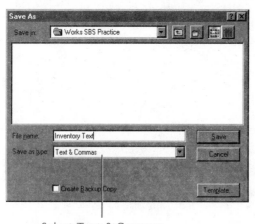

Select Text & Commas

6 Click the Save button.

A message box appears asking if it is OK to save without formatting.

7 Click the OK button.

The data is saved as text with separating commas.

8 Save Product Inventory.

Open the file in a spreadsheet

1 On the File menu, click Open.

The Open dialog box appears.

2   Click the arrow to the right of the Files Of Type list box and then select
All Files (*.*).

All file types now appear in the Works SBS Practice folder.

3   Double-click Inventory Text.csv.

The Open File As dialog box appears.

Click here to open the
text as a spreadsheet

Spreadsheet

4   Click the Spreadsheet button.

The data is opened in a spreadsheet.

5   Double-click the Column B indicator to achieve the best fit, and then click in
cell A1.

The spreadsheet should now appear as shown in the following illustration.

	A	B	C	D	E
1	1004749	Artist brush set	Art	$4.95	$10.50
2	1008726	Canvas 12" by 14" white	Art	$5.75	$12.25
3	1003194	Canvas 8" by 10" white	Art	$5.25	$10.75
4	1008727	Ceramic bud vase painted	Floral	$1.75	$4.55
5	1004748	Ceramic bud vase unpainted	Floral	$1.25	$3.55
6	2001514	Ceramic paint 10 color assortment	Art	$3.99	$7.55
7	1005883	Ceramic paint 2 oz. individual colors	Art	$0.79	$1.25
8	1008740	Charcoal pencils 5 pack	Art	$1.35	$2.99
9	1003361	Clear plastic 30 yard roll	Fabric	$21.67	$44.99
10	1007304	Colored pencils 10 pack	Art	$1.24	$2.76
11	1008041	Colored plastic 30 yard roll	Fabric	$22.67	$46.99
12	1002302	Cotton fabric prints 20 yard roll	Fabric	$18.65	$34.99
13	1002979	Cotton fabric solid colors 20 yard roll	Fabric	$17.65	$32.99
14	1006825	Easel	Art	$3.49	$7.99
15	2005975	Enamel paint 10 color assortment	Art	$2.99	$6.55
16	2001419	Hot glue dispenser	Fabric	$1.79	$3.95
17	1002517	Oil paint palette	Art	$5.75	$12.25
18	1007993	Paint thinner 2 oz.	Art	$0.75	$1.55

You can now perform spreadsheet calculations on the imported data.

6   Save the spreadsheet as Inventory Calculations in the Works SBS Practice folder, and then close it.

One Step Further: Selecting Records Using a Function

You can specify up to five conditional statements in the Filter dialog box. If you need to create a filter that contains more than five statements or that contains a formula, you can use the filter window. The filter window allows you to use formulas and functions that you cannot enter in the standard filter text boxes. In the next exercise, you'll use a function to list products with a price of approximately $1.00.

Select records using a function

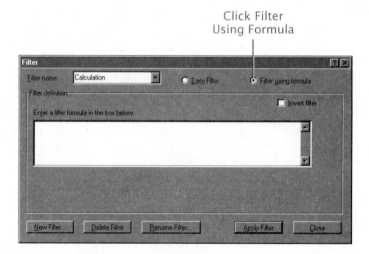

Filters

1   Click the Filters button on the toolbar.

The Filter dialog box appears.

2   Click the New Filter button.

3   Type **Calculation**, and then press ENTER.

4   Click Filter Using Formula.

A filter definition box appears.

5   Type **=round(price,0)=1**

The argument, (price,0), specifies that you want to work with entries in the Price field and that Works should round them off with no decimal places. The =1 portion of the function specifies that the records filtered by the function will be only those with an entry in the Price field that can be rounded up or down to 1. By using the round function in the filter you will display records for which the price is approximately $1.00.

The Filter dialog box should now match the following illustration.

For more information about the types of formulas or functions you can use in a filter, see the Works online Help index section on "filtering databases: formulas" and "filtering databases: functions."

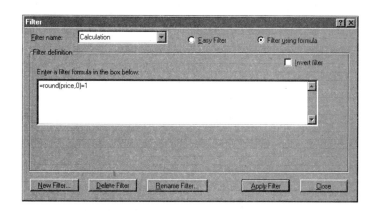

6 Click the Apply Filter button.

Works applies the filter and displays the records for which the Price field entry is approximately $1.00. Your screen should look like the following illustration.

	Item #	Description	Department	Cost	Price
7	1005883	Ceramic paint 2 oz. individual colors	Art	$0.79	$1.25
24	1002248	Silk carnation individual count	Floral	$0.68	$1.25
25	1003019	Silk leaves 5 count	Floral	$0.29	$0.99
26	2001595	Silk rose individual count	Floral	$0.78	$1.45
32	2001112	Styrofoam 5" cube green	Floral	$0.35	$0.99
33	2001562	Styrofoam 5" cube white	Floral	$0.35	$0.99
34					

7 Save your work.

If you want to continue to the next lesson

➤ Click the Close button in the Product Inventory menu bar.

☒
Close

If you want to quit Works for now

☒
Close

1 Click the Close button in the Product Inventory menu bar.

2 Click the Exit Works button in the Works Task Launcher dialog box.

Lesson Summary

To	Do this	Button
Create and apply a filter with up to five conditions	Click the Filters button on the toolbar, specify as many as five conditional statements, and then click the Apply Filter button.	
Create and apply a filter with more than five conditions	Click the Filters button on the toolbar; click Filter Using Formula; enter conditions, formulas, or functions; and then click the Apply Filter button.	
Copy database information into a document	Highlight the data to copy, click the Copy button on the toolbar, open the document that you want to receive the data, and then click the Paste button on the toolbar.	
Convert database data into a spreadsheet	Click Save As on the File menu, click Text & Commas in the Save As Type list box, type a file name, and then click the Save button. Open the document you saved as text and commas, and then click the Spreadsheet button.	

For online information about	Display the Help window, and then
Using filters	Click "Find, sort, or filter information," and then click "To create a filter to find specific text or numbers" or "To filter for records that have some contents in common"
Copying database information	Click the Index button, type **copy**, click "copying database entries," and then click the appropriate topic

Preview of the Next Lesson

In this lesson you learned how to use filters to display database information, share database information with other Works applications, and convert database records into a spreadsheet.

In the next lesson, you'll learn how to use the Database Reporting feature to create a customized database report. You'll create a standard report, modify text and report instructions to create a customized report, and format and print the report.

Lesson

12

Presenting Information Effectively

In this lesson you will learn how to:

Estimated time
30 min.

- Use the ReportCreator.
- Modify the contents of a report.
- Format a report.
- Print a report.
- Copy report data to another document.

Although you can print data directly from a database, you can use the reporting feature of the database to print your information in a more useful and readable format. *Reports* let you organize and summarize database information and provide design and content flexibility. In Works, The ReportCreator steps you through the process of generating a report so you can create a report quickly and easily.

You need to produce a customized report from the Art Products database. The report will include the description, price, and inventory value of each product, grouped by department and sorted by description within each group. You will also show a total of the inventory value for the products in each department group. The following illustration shows how your finished report will look.

283

Department —

Products grouped by — department

Inventory by Department

Product Description	Price	Inventory Value
Art		
Artist brush set	$10.50	$315.00
Canvas 12" by 14" white	$12.25	$539.00
Canvas 8" by 10" white	$10.75	$559.00
Ceramic paint 10 color assortment	$7.55	$45.30
Ceramic paint 2 oz. individual colors	$1.25	$120.00
Charcoal pencils 5 pack	$2.99	$107.64
Colored pencils 10 pack	$2.76	$151.80
Easel	'$7.99	$327.59
Enamel paint 10 color assortment	$6.55	$327.50
Oil paint palette	$12.25	$24.50
Paint thinner 2 oz.	$1.55	$32.55
Pastel crayon 20 pack assortment	$9.95	$109.45
Pastel crayon 50 pack assortment	$12.95	$64.75
Sketching pad 8" by 10" ivory	$4.35	$139.20
Sketching pad 8" by 10" white	$4.35	$26.10
Soft bristle brush 1"	$6.25	$137.50
Soft bristle brush 2"	$6.50	$175.50
Total Inventory Value:		$3,202.38
Fabric		
Clear plastic 30 yard roll	$44.99	$359.92
Colored plastic 30 yard roll	$46.99	$1,550.67
Cotton fabric assorted prints 20 yard roll	$34.99	$104.97

Inventory Value total — for the Art Department group

In this lesson, you'll work with reports to present database information effectively.

Using the ReportCreator

With the ReportCreator, you can specify which fields to include and where to place them on the report, sort and group field entries, filter the database information, and perform calculations to show statistical information about groups. You can also enhance your report by adding titles, text labels, and notes. In the next exercises, you'll use the ReportCreator to create a report.

Start the ReportCreator

1   Open Inventory Report in the Works SBS Practice folder, and then maximize the database window.

2   On the Tools menu, click ReportCreator.

The Report Name dialog box appears.

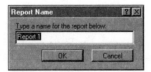

In this dialog box, you specify the report name. You can accept the name Works suggests, *Report 1*, or you can enter a new name for the report. Names can have up to 15 characters, including spaces and punctuation.

NOTE If this is the first time that you have created a report, a First-Time Help dialog box appears. Click Don't Display This Message In The Future, and then click the OK button.

3 Type **Inventory**, and then press ENTER.

The Title tab of the ReportCreator dialog box appears.

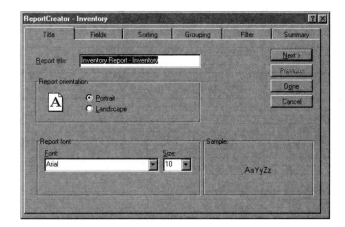

In this dialog box, you specify the report title, which will be displayed and printed at the top of the report. You can accept the name Works suggests, or you can enter a new name for the title. You can make the report title more descriptive than the report name because it can have up to 255 characters.

4 Type **Inventory by Department**

This title will appear at the top of your report.

Add fields to the report

You can display the tabs in the ReportCreator dialog box in any order by clicking the tab that contains the options you want to change.

1 Click the Next button.

The Fields tab of the ReportCreator dialog box appears. This tab displays the fields in your database in the same order as they appear in List view. You can keep or change this order in your report.

2 In the Fields Available list box, click Description, and then click the Add button.

The Description field is added to the Field Order list. The Description field will be the first field to appear in your report.

285

TIP   You can also double-click a field name to add it to the Field Order list.

3   Double-click the Price field.

The Price field will be the second field to appear in the report.

4   Add the Inventory Value field to the Field Order list.

The Fields tab of the ReportCreator dialog box should match the following illustration.

...and then click here
to add it to the report

Select a
field to
include on
the report...

Sort the report fields

1   Click the Next button.

The Sorting tab of the ReportCreator dialog box appears.

2   Click the arrow to the right of the Sort By list box, and then click Department.

Inventory items will first be sorted by the department in which they belong.

3   Click the arrow to the right of the first Then By list box, and then click Description.

The Sorting tab of the ReportCreator dialog box should match the following illustration.

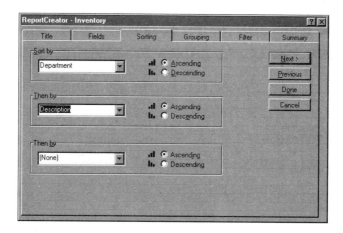

Group the fields on the report

1 Click the Next button.

The Grouping tab of the ReportCreator dialog box appears.

2 In the Group By: Department section, click the When Contents Change check box.

This option specifies that a blank line will be inserted between field entries when the field content changes. For example, Works will group all products in the Art department together, keeping them separate from the Fabric and Floral departments.

3 Click the Show Group Heading check box.

This option specifies that Art, Fabric, and Floral will all appear as group headings in your report. The Grouping tab of the ReportCreator dialog box should match the next illustration.

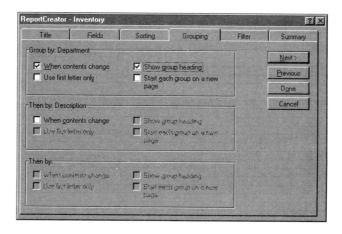

Filter the records

1 Click the Next button.

The Filter tab of the ReportCreator dialog box appears.

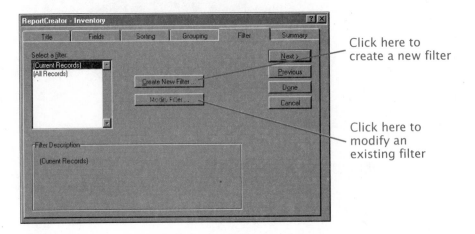

Click here to create a new filter

Click here to modify an existing filter

This tab lists all filters associated with the database. You can click a filter to use selected records to generate a report or you can click (All Records) to use all database records to generate a report.

2 In the Select A Filter list box, click (All Records).

Add summary information

1 Click the Next button.

The Summary tab of the ReportCreator dialog box appears.

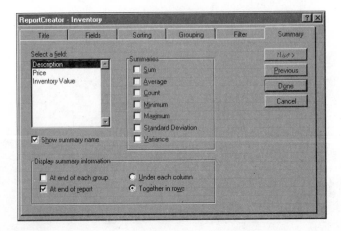

This tab lists all the fields included in your report. You can click a field if you want Works to calculate a statistical value for that field.

2 In the Select A Field list box, click Inventory Value.

Works will calculate a value for the Inventory Value field.

3 In the Summaries section, click the Sum check box.

This option specifies to add the entries in the Inventory Value field and display the total at the bottom of each section.

4 In the Display Summary Information section, click the At End Of Each Group check box.

This option specifies to print summary information at the end of each group. Notice that the At End Of Report option is also selected, indicating that a grand total of the Inventory Value entries will appear at the end of the report.

The Summary tab of the ReportCreator dialog box should appear as follows.

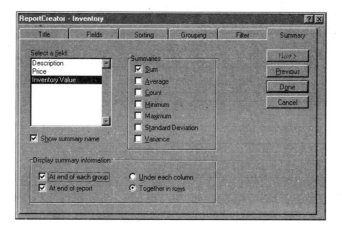

5 Click the Done button.

A ReportCreator message box appears asking if you want to preview or modify the report definition.

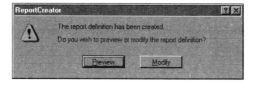

For now, you'll preview the report to see if it meets your design criteria.

6 In the ReportCreator message box, click the Preview button.

The formatted report displays in a Print Preview window, as shown in the next illustration.

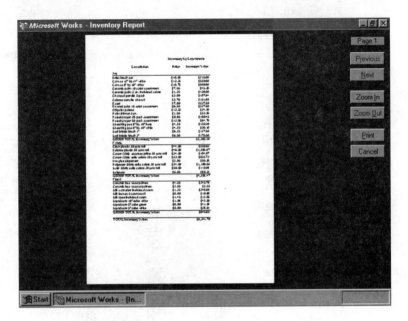

7 Click the report data twice to zoom in so you can see the numbers and report formatting.

With some additional formatting, the report can be read more easily.

8 Click the Cancel button.

The report definition appears in the database window.

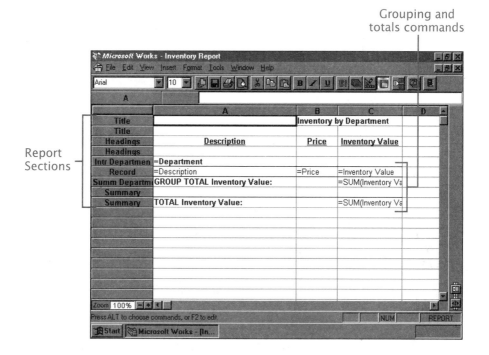

When you create a report, Works automatically creates a report definition. A *report definition* specifies the information to be included in the report and displays it in a row and column format. If you want to modify a report, you add, delete, or change the entries listed in the report definition.

Modifying the Report Content

In many cases, your report effectively presents your data. However, if the report is not exactly what you want, you can modify the report definition. In the next exercises, you'll change a heading and delete report instructions.

Change a heading

You don't have to use the field names from the database as the column headings for your report. You decide to make the first column heading more descriptive.

1   In the first Headings row, move the highlight to the *Description* heading.

2   Type **Product Description** and then press ENTER to change the group heading of the first column of data.

3   In the Summ Department row, move the highlight to column A.

4   Type **Total Inventory Value:** and then press ENTER to change the summary headings that appear at the end of each group of records.

291

Your screen should now match the following illustration.

	A	B	C	D
Title		Inventory by Department		
Title				
Headings	Product Description	Price	Inventory Value	
Headings				
Intr Departmen	=Department			
Record	=Description	=Price	=Inventory Value	
Summ Departm	Total Inventory Value:		=SUM(Inventory Va	
Summary				
Summary	TOTAL Inventory Value:		=SUM(Inventory Va	

Delete report instructions

Your report currently shows totals for each department and for the entire report. You only need to have totals for each department. The second summary row contains instructions for calculating the inventory values for the entire report, so you will delete the instructions in this row.

1 Highlight the cells in the second Summary row that span columns A, B, and C.

2 Press DELETE to delete the cell contents.

The report definition should now look like the next illustration.

	A	B	C	D
Title		Inventory by Department		
Title				
Headings	Product Description	Price	Inventory Value	
Headings				
Intr Departmen	=Department			
Record	=Description	=Price	=Inventory Value	
Summ Departm	Total Inventory Value:		=SUM(Inventory Va	
Summary				
Summary				

Print Preview

3 Click the Print Preview button on the toolbar.

The total for the end of the report is now gone.

4 Click the Cancel button to return to the report definition.

Formatting Your Report

Now that you're satisfied with the contents of your report, you can apply formatting features to make the report more attractive and easier to read. In the next exercises, you'll format your database report.

Change the font, size, and style of text

As with any Works document, you can change the font, size, and style of text in a database report.

1 Highlight the cells of the report definition as shown in the next illustration.

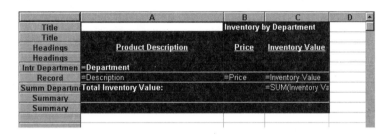

Font Name

2 Click the arrow to the right of the Font Name list box on the toolbar, and then click Times New Roman.

Font Size

3 Click the arrow to the right of the Font Size list box, and then click 12.

All the text in the report definition now appears in the Times New Roman 12-point font.

4 In the first Title row, click in column B.

The title *Inventory by Department* is now highlighted.

Font Size

5 Click the arrow to the right of the Font Size list box on the toolbar, and then click 16 to make the report title larger.

6 Click the *=Department* report instruction in column A to highlight it.

Italic

7 Click the Italic button on the toolbar.

By italicizing the report instruction, you specify that the department names at the beginning of each group in the database report will be italicized.

Your screen should now look like the following illustration.

	A	B	C	1
Title		**Inventory by Department**		
Title				
Headings	**Product Description**	Price	Inventory Value	
Headings				
Intr Departmen	*=Department*			
Record	=Description	=Price	=Inventory Value	
Summ Departmer	Total Inventory Value:		=SUM(Inventory)	
Summary				
Summary				

8 Preview the report, and then redisplay the report definition.

293

Change column widths

Your report is still difficult to read because the columns of information are too close to each other. You can change column widths to add space between the columns of your report.

1 Be sure the highlight is in column A.

2 On the Format menu, click Column Width.

The Column Width dialog box appears.

3 Type **50**, and then press ENTER.

The column width is now 50 characters.

4 Click column label B to highlight the column.

5 On the Format menu, click Column Width.

6 Type **15**, and then press ENTER to make column B 15 characters wide.

7 Change the width of column C to 18 characters.

8 Preview the report.

Your screen should now look like the following illustration.

The last column is not displayed because the columns are too wide. You will change margins in a later exercise to correct this problem.

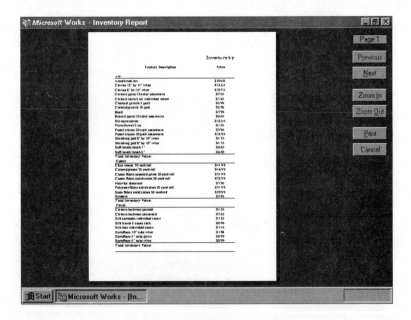

9 Click the Cancel button to redisplay the report definition in the database window.

Change the alignment of entries

You can further enhance the appearance of your report by centering the report title over the columns of information and changing the alignment of the Description heading.

Cut

Paste

1 Click the title *Inventory by Department* to highlight it.

2 Click the Cut button on the toolbar to remove the title.

3 Move the highlight to column A in the first Title row.

4 Click the Paste button on the toolbar to paste the title in the new location.

5 In the first Title row, highlight columns A through C.

6 On the Format menu, click Alignment.

   The Alignment tab of the Format dialog box appears.

7 In the Horizontal section, click Center Across Selection, and then click the OK button.

   The report title is centered across the highlighted range.

8 In the first Headings row, highlight the *Product Description* heading.

9 On the Format menu, click Alignment.

10 In the Horizontal section, click Left, and then click the OK button.

   The entries in the Product Description column will be left aligned. Your screen should look like the following illustration.

	A	B
Title	**Inventory by Department**	
Title		
Headings	Product Description	Price
Headings		
Intr Departmen	=*Department*	
Record	=Description	=Price
Summ Departmen	Total Inventory Value:	
Summary		
Summary		

11 Preview the report to view the alignment changes.

12 Close the Print Preview window.

Change margins

Since you changed column widths, the last column on the report is not displayed. You can correct this by either changing column widths again or by changing margins.

1 On the File menu, click Page Setup.

   The Page Setup dialog box appears.

2 Click the Margins tab if it isn't the displayed tab.

3 Double-click the Left Margin text box, and then type **.75**

4 Press TAB to move to the Right Margin text box, type **.75**, and then press ENTER.

5 Preview the report, and then click the Zoom In button.

The current report definition generates the report shown in the next illustration.

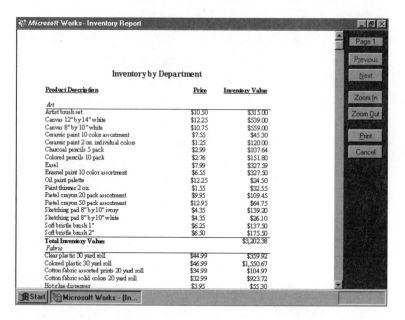

6 Close the Print Preview window.

7 Save your work.

Printing Your Report

Now that your report is formatted and organized the way you want, you can print it. But, before you print the report, you want to add a footer with the current date to the bottom of the page. In the next exercises, you'll add a footer to date the report and you'll print the report.

Add a footer

1 On the View menu, click Headers And Footers.

The View Headers And Footers dialog box appears.

2 Press TAB to move to the Footer text box, and then type **&d**

The code will place the current date at the bottom center of each page. The View Headers And Footers dialog box should look like the following.

For more information about footer and header codes, see "How to use footer and header codes" in the Works online Help Index

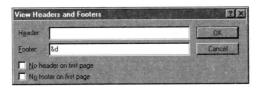

3 Press ENTER.

4 Preview the report.

The current date appears at the bottom center of the page.

5 Close the Print Preview window.

Print the report

Print

1 Click the Print button on the toolbar to print the report.

 TIP If you want to print more than one copy of a report, click Print on the File menu, and then enter a number in the Number Of Copies text box.

2 Save your work.

The report definition is saved with the database.

Copying the Report Data to Another Document

You can copy report data to another document in Works. Your accountant has found an error in the Floral department inventory and has asked you to provide the inventory information only for that department. You decide to include the report information in a letter. In this exercise, you'll filter the database to include only records from the Floral department, create a report using that data, and then copy the report data to a letter created in the Word Processor.

Filter the data

List View

1 Click the List View button on the toolbar.

Filters

2 Click the Filters button on the toolbar.

The Filter and Filter Name dialog boxes appear.

If the First-Time Help dialog box appears, click Don't Display This Message In The Future, and then click the OK button.

3 In the Filter Name dialog box, type **Floral Dept.**, and then press ENTER.

4 Click the arrow to the right of the first Field Name list box, and then click Department.

5 Click the first Compare To text box, and then type **Floral**

The Filter dialog box should match the following illustration.

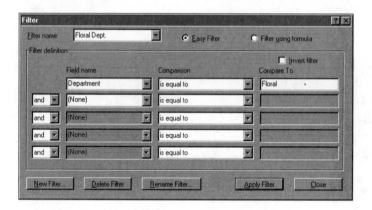

6 Click the Apply Filter button.

Works displays only the records from the Floral department, as shown in the next illustration.

	Item #	Description	Department	Cost	Price	
26	1008727	Ceramic bud vase painted	Floral	$1.75	$4.55	
27	1004748	Ceramic bud vase unpainted	Floral	$1.25	$3.55	
28	1002248	Silk carnation individual count	Floral	$0.68	$1.25	
29	1003019	Silk leaves 5 count each	Floral	$0.29	$0.99	
30	2001595	Silk rose individual count	Floral	$0.78	$1.45	
31	2001422	Styrofoam 10" cube white	Floral	$0.70	$1.98	
32	2001112	Styrofoam 5" cube green	Floral	$0.35	$0.99	
33	2001562	Styrofoam 5" cube white	Floral	$0.35	$0.99	
34						

Create the report using the ReportCreator

1   On the Tools menu, click ReportCreator.

2   In the Report Name dialog box, type **Floral** and then press ENTER.

The Title tab of the ReportCreator dialog box appears. A default title, *Inventory Report - Floral*, appears in the Report Title text box.

3   Click the Next button.

The default title is accepted and the Fields tab of the ReportCreator dialog box appears.

4   In the Fields Available list box, double-click Description to add the field name to the Field Order list box.

5   Add the Price and Inventory Value fields to the Field Order list box.

The Description, Price, and Inventory Value fields will appear in the report.

Because you need to display data from only one department and don't require a summary, you can bypass the Sorting, Grouping, Filter, and Summary tabs.

6   Click the Done button.

A ReportCreator message box appears asking if you want to preview or modify the report definition.

7   Click the Modify button.

The report definition appears.

8   Preview your report.

9   Redisplay the report definition.

Copy the report data

1   On the Edit menu, click Copy Report Output.

The report data is copied.

2   Open Inventory Letter in the Works SBS Practice folder.

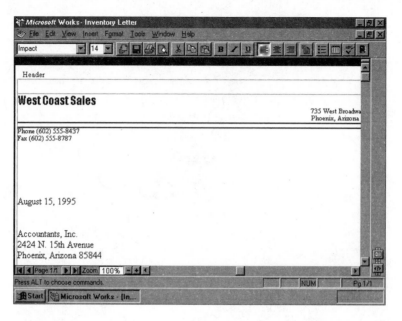

3 Position the insertion point on the second blank line above the text *YOUR NAME* at the end of the document.

4 Click the Paste button on the toolbar, and then scroll down to see the report data. The report data is pasted into the letter, as shown in the next illustration.

Paste

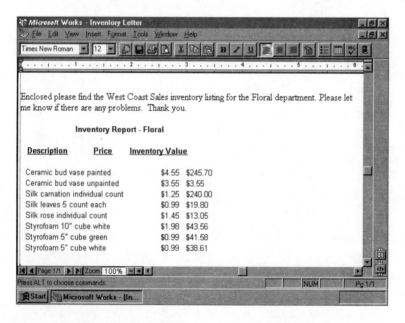

If the column headings are not centered over the data, you can adjust the tab settings in the Word Processor.

5 Insert one tab to the left of each inventory value.

6 Click anywhere in the Inventory Value heading, and then move the tab marker at the 2.5-inch mark on the ruler to the 4.0-inch mark.

7 Click anywhere in the Price heading, and then move the tab marker at the 1.5-inch mark on the ruler to the 2.75-inch mark.

Your screen should now match the following illustration.

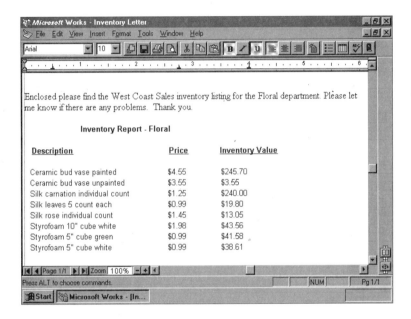

8 Print Inventory Letter.

9 Save and then close Inventory Letter.

One Step Further: Filtering a Report

If the information you need for another report already is in an existing report, you can save time by modifying the existing report to create the new one. One way you can do this is to filter the records of the existing report to extract the records you need for the new report.

Your accountant has asked for a report that includes only the records for the products in the Art department. In the next exercise, you'll filter the records of the Inventory report to create a new report.

Create a new report by filtering an existing report

1 On the View menu, click Report.

The View Report dialog box appears.

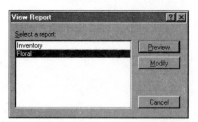

2 In the Select A Report list box, click Inventory, and then click the Modify button.

The Inventory Report definition appears.

3 On the Tools menu, click Report Filter.

The Filter tab of the Report Settings dialog box appears.

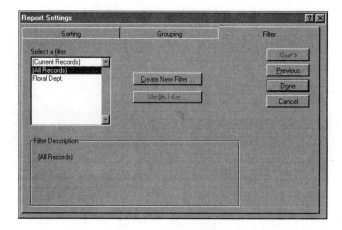

4 Click the Create New Filter button.

The Filter Name dialog box appears.

5 In the Filter Name dialog box, type **Art Department**, and then press ENTER.

The Filter dialog box appears. This dialog box is the same one that appears when you are filtering database records.

6 Click the arrow to the right of the first Field Name list box, and then click Department.

7　Click the first Compare To text box, and then type **Art**

The filter will display only database records of the products in the Art department.

8　Click the OK button.

The Report Settings dialog box reappears.

9　Click the Done button to apply the filter and return to the report definition.

10　Click the Print Preview button on the toolbar, and click the Zoom In button once.

The report is modified to include only the records for products in the Art department, as shown in the following illustration.

Print Preview

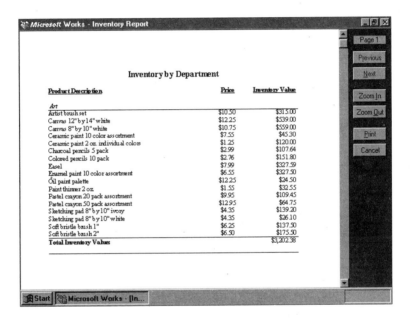

11　Click the Cancel button to close the Print Preview window.

12　Save your work.

If you want to continue to the next lesson

▶　Click the Close button in the Inventory Report menu bar.

Close

If you want to quit Works for now

1　Click the Close button in the Inventory Report menu bar.

2　Click the Exit Works button in the Works Task Launcher dialog box.

Close

Lesson Summary

To	Do this	Button
Create a report using the ReportCreator	On the Tools menu, click ReportCreator, type a name for the report, and then press ENTER. Enter options for the report title, fields to include, sorting, grouping, filter, and summary by clicking the appropriate tab or the Next button. Click the Done button from the Summary tab to create the report definition.	
Delete a report instruction	Highlight the instruction and then press DELETE.	
Change the font of text	Highlight the entries you want to change, click the arrow to the right of the Font Name list box on the toolbar, and then click a new font.	Arial
Change the font size of text	Highlight the entries you want to change, click the arrow to the right of the Font Size list box on the toolbar, and then click a new font size.	12
Change the font style of text	Highlight the entries you want to change, and then click the Bold, Italic, or Underline button on the toolbar.	**B** / **U**
Change a column width	Highlight the column you want to change, click Column Width on the Format menu, type a new width, and then press ENTER.	
Change the alignment of entries	Highlight the entries you want to change, click Alignment on the Format menu, click a new alignment, and then click the OK button.	

To	Do this	Button
Change margins	On the File menu, click Page Setup, click the Margins tab, enter new margin settings, and then press ENTER.	
Add a footer	On the View menu, click Headers And Footers, type text and codes in the Footer text box, and then press ENTER.	
Preview a report	Click the Print Preview button on the toolbar.	
Print a report	Click the Print button on the toolbar.	
Copy report data to another document	In the report definition window, click Copy Report Output on the Edit menu, open the document to which you want to copy the data, position the insertion point, and then click the Paste button on the toolbar.	

For online information about	Display the Help window, and then
Creating a report	Click "Create reports from database information," and then click "To create a report"
Changing report grouping	Click "Create reports from database information," and then click "To change how a report is grouped"
Changing report sorting	Click "Create reports from database information," and then click "To change how a report is sorted"
Modify a database report	Click "Create reports from database information," and then click "To modify a report"
Copying report data to another document	Click "Create reports from database information," and then click "To copy report information to another document"
Printing a database report	Click "Preview and print your database," and then click "To print your document or report"

Review & Practice

In the lessons in Part 4, "Keeping Track of Information," you learned how to format, find, sort, and filter database information and use the ReportCreator to create customized reports. If you want to practice these skills and test your understanding, you can work through the Review & Practice section following this lesson.

Review & Practice

Estimated time
45 min.

You will review and practice how to:

- Manipulate database information.
- Format a database.
- Modify a database.
- Use a filter.
- Work with database reports.
- Print database reports.
- Copy report data to another document.

In this Review & Practice, you have an opportunity to fine tune the skills you learned in the lessons in Part 4 of this book. You'll use what you have learned about finding and replacing text, sorting records, changing the format of text, locating and copying database information, and creating database reports to set up a database for your new Mail Order department.

Scenario

Because of your great marketing skills, along with the professional looking documents you created with Works, you have convinced investors to finance your expansion plans. Your first idea is to set up a mail order department within your store. You decide to create a separate inventory for the Mail Order department so you can track that part of the business separately. You have started a new database to track the inventory of the Mail Order department. You now need to modify, format, manipulate, and create database reports for the new department to present to your accountant.

Step 1: Manipulate Database Information

1 Open Mail Order Inventory in the Works SBS Practice folder and then maximize the database window if it isn't already maximized.

2 Use the Edit Find command to display records with *Sewing Supplies* in the Category field.

3 Display all the records in the database.

4 Highlight the Category field, and then use the Edit Replace command to replace all occurrences of *Floral* with *Florist Supplies*.

5 Open the Sort Records dialog box.

6 Sort the records in ascending order by Category and then by Description.

Your database should match the following illustration.

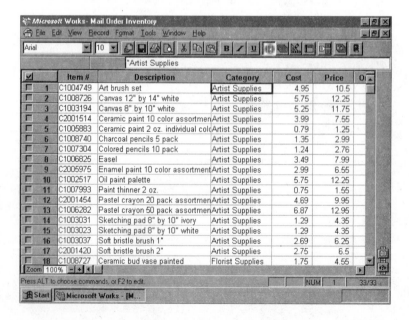

For more information on	See
Finding and replacing data	Lesson 10
Sorting database records	Lesson 10

Step 2: *Format a Database*

1 Switch to Form Design, and then highlight all of the field names, fields, and labels on the database form.

2 Change the font to Arial and the font size to 10.

3 Highlight the *Mail Order Art & Craft Supplies* label.

4 Change the font size to 20 and the font style to Bold.

5 Highlight all of the field names on the database form, and then change the font style to Bold Italic.

6 Use the Field tab of the Format dialog box to change the format of the Cost and Price fields to Currency with two decimal places.

7 Use the Alignment tab of the Format dialog box to center the field entries for the Item #, Category, and On Hand fields.

8 Add a thin outline border to the Description field.

9 Change to Form view.

Your database form should now match the following illustration.

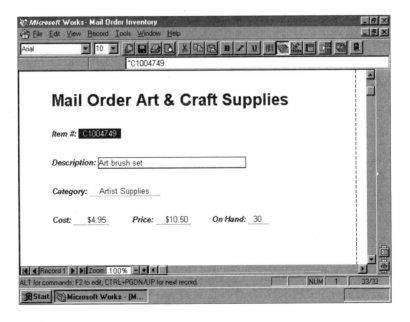

For more information on	See
Changing the font, style, and size of text	Lesson 10
Changing number formats	Lesson 10
Changing alignment of entries	Lesson 10
Adding borders and shading	Lesson 10

Step 3: Add Graphics to a Form

1 Change to Form Design.
2 Position the insertion point at X1.83" Y1.08".
3 Start Microsoft Draw.
4 Maximize the Microsoft Draw window.
5 Create the drawing shown in the following illustration using the oval, rounded rectangle, and text tools.

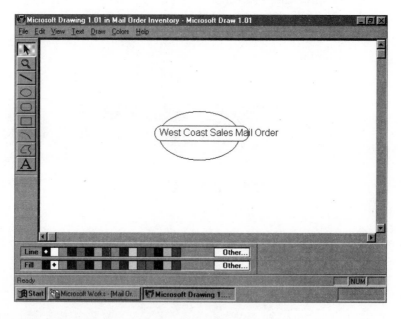

6 Change the fill of the oval to charcoal gray.
7 Change the text to Bold Italic 8-point.

8 Exit Microsoft Draw and return to the database form, saving the drawing.
Your form appears as shown in the following illustration.

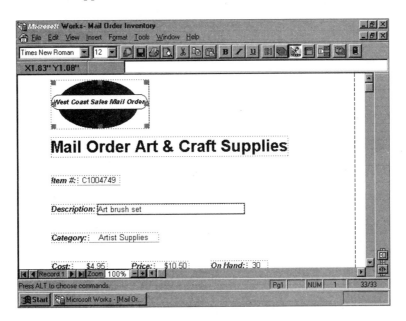

For more information on	See
Starting Microsoft Draw	Lesson 10
Drawing objects	Lesson 10
Inserting drawings into forms	Lesson 10

Step 4: Create a Calculated Field and Print the Inventory List

1 Position the insertion point at X1.83" Y4.75".

2 Use the Insert Field dialog box to add an Inventory Cost field with a Currency format and two decimal places.

3 Change the font of the field label to Arial, 10-point Bold Italic.

4 Change to Form View.

5 Enter a formula in the Inventory Cost field that multiples the Cost field by the On Hand field.

Your form should now appear as shown in the following illustration.

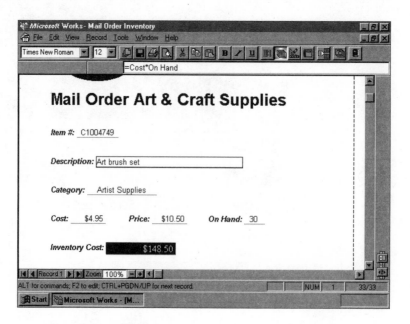

6   Change to List View, and then use the Hide Record command to display only the records that contain *Artist Supplies* in the Category field.

7   Print the displayed records.

8   Display all database records.

For more information on	See
Using calculations in fields	Lesson 10
Printing database records	Lesson 10

Step 5:   Use a Database Filter

1   Create and apply a filter, named *Cost*, to select records with a Cost field entry greater than $15.00.

2   Copy the Item #, Description, Category, and Costs fields of the displayed records.

3   Open Mail Order Letter, and then paste the database information two lines above the paragraph that begins *So whether you....*

4   Insert tabs before the text *Sewing Supplies* on each line of the pasted text so the memo appears as shown in the following illustration.

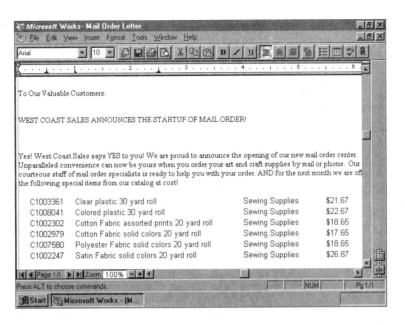

5 Save and then close Mail Order Letter.

6 Save the records in a file named *Mail Order Items* in the text and comma format.

7 Open the File Open dialog box, display all files in the Files of Type list box, and then open the Mail Order Items document as a spreadsheet.

8 Save and then close the spreadsheet.

For more information on	See
Using database filters	Lesson 11
Copying filter results to another document	Lesson 11
Converting database data to a spreadsheet	Lesson 11

Step 6:   Create a Database Report

1 Display all the records in the database.

2 Start the ReportCreator.

3 Specify *Inventory* as the report name.

4 Specify *Mail Order Inventory* as the report title.

5 Add the Description, Cost, and On Hand fields to the report.

6 Sort the report first by the Category field and then by the Description field.

7 Group the report by Category when the contents change and specify to show a group heading.

8 Create a summary that includes the sum of the Cost field at the end of each group and at the end of the report.

9 Create and then preview the report.

Your report in the Print Preview window should match the following illustration.

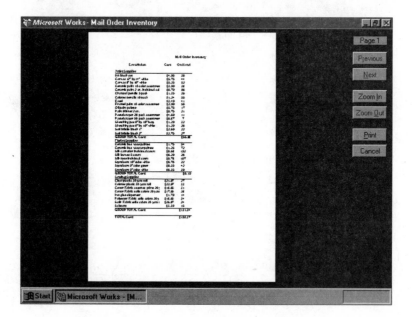

10 Close the Print Preview window.

For more information on	See
Using the ReportCreator	Lesson 12

Step 7: *Modify a Database Report*

1 Change the text *Description* in column A of the first Headings row to *Product*.

2 Delete the contents of the second summary row.

3 Change the font of all the text in the report to Times New Roman 12-point.

4 Change the point size of the *Mail Order Inventory* title to 18-point.

5 Change the width of column A to 45 characters.

6 Change the width of column B to 8 characters and the width of column C to 15 characters.

7 Highlight the Mail Order Inventory title and move it to column A in the first Title row.

8 Center the Mail Order Inventory title across columns A, B, and C.

9 Change the left and right margins for the report to 1".

The report definition should now match the following illustration.

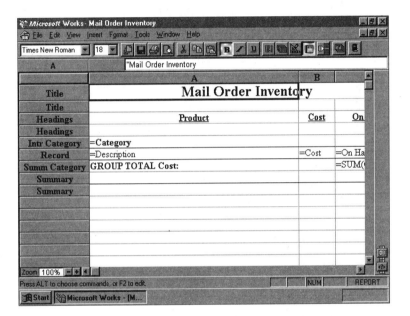

For more information on	See
Changing headings	Lesson 12
Deleting report instructions	Lesson 12
Changing the font, size, and style of text	Lesson 12
Changing column widths	Lesson 12
Changing the alignment of entries	Lesson 12
Changing margins	Lesson 12

Step 8: Print a Database Report

1   Display the View Headers And Footers dialog box.
2   Enter the code **&l&d&r&t** to create a footer that prints the current date, left-aligned, and the current time, right-aligned.
3   Print the report.
4   Save and close Mail Order Inventory.

For more information on	See
Adding a footer	Lesson 12
Printing a report	Lesson 12

If you want to quit Works for now

▶   Click the Exit Works button in the Works Task Launcher dialog box.

Appendix

Matching the Exercises

There are settings within Microsoft Works for Windows 95 that change how some screens appear and how some features operate. If these settings have been changed, your screens or features may look different than those presented in the exercises, and you may not be able to produce the same results shown in this book. You can refer to this appendix to find out how to change your computer settings to match the exercises used in this book.

Using the Practice Files

In the lessons, you open files or sample documents from the Practice Files disk. These files should be installed into a subfolder named Works SBS Practice located in the C:\Program Files\MSWorks\Documents folder. The instructions for installing the exercise files are in the "Getting Ready" section at the beginning of this book.

Matching Your Screen Display

The settings used in this book are, primarily, the defaults that were preset when you installed Microsoft Works for Windows 95. Within each of the Works tools, you can change the appearance of your screen by turning different options on or off. The following sections describe steps that you can complete for each of the tools to match your screen display to the illustrations in the book.

Display the default toolbar

If your toolbar does not appear on the screen, you should turn it on and make sure ToolTips are enabled. When ToolTips are enabled, a descriptive label appears whenever you position the pointer over a toolbar button.

Word Processor

1   In the Works Task Launcher dialog box, click the Works Tools tab, and then click the Word Processor button.

2   On the View menu, click the Toolbar option to activate it if it isn't already activated.

NOTE   When a menu command is activated, a check mark appears to the left of the command name. A command that does not have a check mark next to it is not activated. You activate or deactivate a command by clicking it.

3   On the Tools menu, click Customize Toolbar.

The Customize Works Toolbar dialog box appears.

4   Click the Reset button.

5   Click the Enable ToolTips check box if it is not already turned on, and then click the OK button.

Set display options

The following display options should also be in effect before you begin the lessons: Enable Drag-And-Drop Editing, Show Status Bar, and Show Pointer Names. The Enable Drag-And-Drop Editing option enables you to use the drag-and-drop feature. The Show Status Bar option makes the status bar visible on your screen. The Show Pointer Names option lets you see the names of the various mouse pointers as you use them.

1   On the Tools menu, click Options.

The Options dialog box appears.

2   Click the General tab, and then click Enable Drag-And-Drop Editing if the check box isn't already turned on.

3   Click the View tab and make sure the Show Status Bar and Show Pointer Names check boxes are turned on.

The View tab of the Options dialog box should match the following illustration.

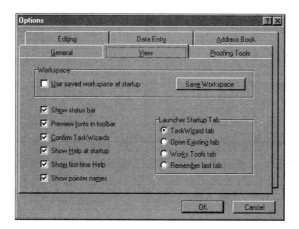

4 Click the OK button.

Use the default page setup

Most of the exercises within this book use the default page margin, size, and orientation settings. If your settings do not match the default settings, you can reset them.

1 On the File menu, click Page Setup.

2 Click the Margins tab, and then click the Reset button.

Your screen should match the following illustration.

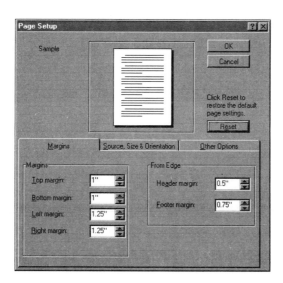

3 Click the Source, Size & Orientation tab, and then click the Reset button.

Your screen should match the following illustration.

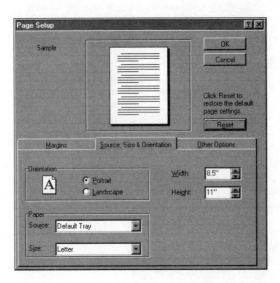

4 Click the Other Options tab, and then click the Reset button.
Your screen should match the following illustration.

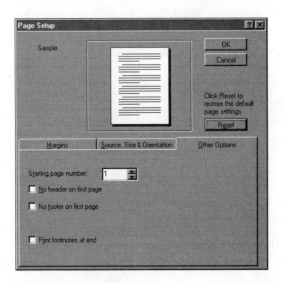

5 Click the OK button.

Matching the Word Processor Options

In order to successfully complete the exercises in the Word Processor lessons, the following options need to be in effect.

Match the character display

Works can display symbols or codes for all of the characters in a document, such as paragraph symbols at the end of each paragraph. To make the screens more readable, you should make sure this option is turned off.

 On the View menu, deactivate the All Characters option.

Set spelling options

If the Always Suggest option is in effect, Works will automatically display suggestions for words it doesn't recognize during a spelling check. For the exercises in this book, the Always Suggest option is used.

1 Type **teh**, and then click Spelling on the Tools menu.

The Spelling dialog box appears.

2 Make sure the Always Suggest check box is turned on.

3 Click the Cancel button to close the Spelling dialog box.

4 On the File menu, click Close. Do not save the changes to the Word Processor document.

The Works Task Launcher dialog box should now appear.

Matching the Spreadsheet Options

In order to complete the exercises in the Spreadsheet lessons, the following options need to be in effect.

Show the gridlines

By default, Works displays gridlines between each row and column in the spreadsheet window. You can turn off the gridlines to improve the appearance of a spreadsheet on screen. Turning the gridlines on or off does not affect how the spreadsheet will print. In the Spreadsheet lessons, the gridlines are turned on.

Spreadsheet

1 In the Works Task Launcher dialog box, click the Spreadsheet button.

2 On the View menu, activate the Gridlines option.

Use the default page setup

Although you reset the page setup options for the Word Processor, you must reset the Other Options settings again for the Spreadsheet.

1 On the File menu, click Page Setup.

2 Click the Other Options tab, and then click the Reset button.

Your screen should match the following illustration.

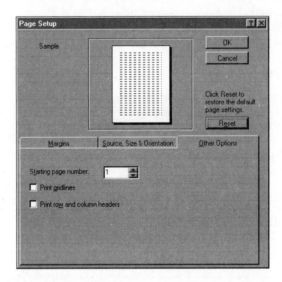

3 Click the OK button.

4 On the File menu, click Close. Do not save changes to the spreadsheet document.

Matching the Database Options

In order to complete the exercises in the Database lessons, the following options need to be in effect.

Show the gridlines

By default, Works displays lines between each row and column in the database window. You can turn off the gridlines to improve the appearance of a database on screen. Turning the gridlines on or off does not affect how the database will print. In the database lessons, the gridlines are turned on.

Database

1 In the Works Task Launcher dialog box, click the Database button.

The Create Database dialog box appears. You must enter a field before you can move beyond this dialog box.

2   Click the Add button to add a field to the database.

3   Click the Done button to close the Create Database dialog box.

4   On the View menu, activate the Gridlines option.

Use the default page setup

Although you reset the page setup options for the Word Processor and the Spreadsheet, you must reset the Other Options settings again for the Database.

1   On the File menu, click Page Setup.

2   Click the Other Options tab, and then click the Reset button.

Your screen should match the following illustration.

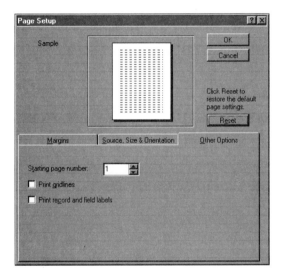

3   Click the OK button.

4   On the File menu, click Close. Do not save changes to the database document.

Glossary

This glossary includes definitions of the terms, acronyms, and other buzzwords used in the lessons.

active   An application window or document that you are currently using or working on. You can have several application windows and documents open at the same time, but only one of them can be active at any one time.

alignment   In a Word Processor document, the horizontal position of text between the left and right margins. In a Spreadsheet or Database document, alignment refers to the horizontal position of information within cells or fields.

application window   A window that contains the application components. The application window provides space in which the Works tools are displayed. It also displays the menu bar and the toolbar.

autoformats   Predefined table styles.

best fit   A Works feature that automatically adjusts the size of a spreadsheet column or database field to accommodate the width of the longest entry.

borders   Lines and boxes that you place around paragraphs, cells, fields, or drawing objects. You can use borders to draw attention to important information or to separate sections of a document.

bulletin board   An electronic communications system that you can use to exchange information about a specific subject. When you connect to a bulletin board system (BBS), you can communicate with other users, upload information from your computer to the BBS, and view and download information from the BBS to your computer.

button   An on-screen symbol that represents a Works operation or command. You click a button to execute its corresponding command.

category labels   Text that identifies each category on the X-series in a chart.

cell   The area formed by the intersection of a column and a row in a spreadsheet.

cell protection   A feature that prevents you from changing or deleting the contents of locked cells in a spreadsheet.

cell reference   The location of a cell in a spreadsheet, identified by the column label and row number. For example, the intersection of the second column and the fifth row is cell B5.

chart   A visual representation of spreadsheet data.

click   To position the pointer over an object on the screen and quickly press and release a mouse button.

clip art   Ready-made graphics that you can insert in documents. You use the ClipArt Gallery to view and select clip art.

close   To exit an application or document and remove its window from the screen.

column labels   The letters that appear at the top of each column in a spreadsheet.

conditions   Components of a filter that specify the parameters for the filter.

connect   To establish communication with another computer.

controls   Components of a dialog box—such as tabs, option buttons, or check boxes—you use to supply the information needed to execute a command.

cursor   *See* insertion point.

database   An organized collection of information.

database form   A view that you use to enter information into a database.

data labels   Text or numbers that display the spreadsheet values that a series represents in a chart.

dialog box   A pop-up window of options that appears when you choose a menu command followed by an ellipsis (...).

disconnect   To end a communication connection with another computer.

destination file   The file in which you paste linked information.

document window   A window within an application window in which you create or modify a document.

double-click   To click the left mouse button twice in rapid succession. You double-click to perform tasks such as opening a document or selecting text.

download   To receive a file or other information from another computer user, an information service, or a bulletin board system.

drag   To hold down the left mouse button, move the mouse to a different position, and then release the mouse button. You drag when you want to highlight information or move an object or window.

drag-and-drop   A technique used to move or copy highlighted information with the mouse. To move, drag the highlighted information to a new position. To copy, hold down CTRL and drag the highlighted information to a new position.

easy formats   A feature that you can use to apply existing formatting to other text in a document.

easy text   A Works feature you can use to automate the entry of long text such as disclaimers, addresses, or standard company information.

editing   Making changes to document text.

entry bar   In a Spreadsheet or Database document, the area below the toolbar that displays the contents of the highlighted cell or field. You can use the entry bar to edit cell and field entries.

field   A category of information in a database, such as description or price.

file   A collection of information stored on a disk under an identifying name. A file can contain an application, such as Works, or a document, such as a letter.

fill palette   In Microsoft Draw, the area at the bottom of the drawing window that contains color boxes you can click to change the interior color of an object.

filter   A question you ask about the information stored in a database, such as "which products are over $10.00 in price?" When you apply a filter, Works displays all of the records that match the correct answer to your question.

folder   A separate area on a disk in which you store a group of files. For example, you might store all of the Word Processor and Spreadsheet files you use to create management reports in a folder named Reports To Management.

font   A set of characters with a specific design and a similar appearance. Each font has its own name, such as Arial or Times New Roman.

font size   The size of the characters in a font. Font size is usually measured in points, with one point equal to approximately 1/72 inch.

font style   The appearance of the characters in a font. You can apply font styles such as bold, underline, and italic.

footer   Information that prints at the bottom of every page. You can use footers to add page numbers, dates, and other repetitive information to documents.

form letters   Multiple copies of the same document with personalized information, such as names and addresses, inserted into each copy of the document.

formatting   Attributes that affect the appearance of a document, such as margins, fonts, or headers and footers.

formula   An entry in a spreadsheet cell or database field that performs a calculation using existing values in other spreadsheet cells or database fields.

form design   The database view in which you create and modify database forms.

form view   The database view in which records appear on a database form. You can view only one record at a time in form view.

function   A predefined formula that performs complex calculations in a spreadsheet or database.

gridlines In a spreadsheet or database, horizontal and vertical lines between rows and columns. In a chart, the lines between categories or intervals on an axis.

header Information that prints at the top of every page. You can use headers to add page numbers, report titles, dates, and other repetitive information to documents.

Help window A window that appears to the right of the document and contains on-line information about the Works tool in use.

highlight To mark text, cells, or fields that you want to modify, move, or copy. When you highlight information, it appears in reverse video (light text on a dark background) on the screen. When you highlight a single spreadsheet cell or database field, a dark border appears around the cell or field.

icon An on-screen symbol that represents a disk drive, folder, application, document, or other object that you can select and open.

indent The distance between a paragraph and the left and right margins in a Word Processor document.

insertion point A blinking vertical bar that shows you where text or objects appear on the screen as you type or where an action, such as searching for text in a document, will begin. Also known as a cursor.

justified alignment A document style in which text aligns evenly between the left and right margins.

label Descriptive text that appears in every record on a database form.

landscape A horizontal page orientation in which a document is printed across the wider dimension of a sheet of paper.

legend labels Text and symbols that identify the markers, colors, and patterns that represent Y-series values in a chart.

line chart A graph that shows numerical data over a period of time illustrated by one or more lines.

line palette In Microsoft Draw, the area at the bottom of the drawing window that contains color boxes you can click to change the line color of an object.

line spacing The amount of space between each line in a paragraph.

link An electronic connection you create between files when you copy and paste information from one Works tool to another. *See also* source file; destination file.

list view The database view in which you can see several records at one time. The records appear as a grid of columns and rows, like a spreadsheet.

lock An action that prevents you from altering or deleting the contents of spreadsheet cells.

menu   A list of commands that you can execute with a keystroke or by clicking the mouse.

menu bar   The horizontal bar near the top of an application window that contains the names of menus.

modem   An acronym for MOdulator DEModulator. A device that a computer uses to send and receive information over telephone lines.

number format   A setting that specifies how numbers will appear in spreadsheet cells or database fields. You can display numbers as percentages, with currency symbols, or with commas.

object   Any piece of data in a document, such as a graphic image or text selection.

on-line information service   An electronic communications system that you can connect to for news, sports, medical, legal, or other information.

open   To start an application, display the contents of a document in a window, or enlarge a minimized window.

orientation   The position of a document on the page. Orientation can be portrait (vertical) or landscape (horizontal).

palette   *See* fill palette; line palette.

paragraph alignment   A document style which determines how paragraphs are positioned between the left and right margins.

paragraph spacing   The amount of space above and below a paragraph.

pie chart   A chart with a circle divided into slices. Each slice represents a single value in an X-series.

point   A unit of measure used to specify the size of a font. One point is equal to 1/72 inch.

pointer   An on-screen symbol that indicates where an action will occur in your document.

portrait   A vertical page orientation in which a document is printed across the narrower dimension of a sheet of paper.

range   A block of cells in a spreadsheet. A range can be as small as a single cell or as large as an entire spreadsheet.

record   A collection of related information in a database about a person, a place, an item, or an event.

ReportCreator   A Works feature that helps you automate the task of creating a report. The ReportCreator takes you step-by-step through the process of creating the report.

report definition The database view in which you specify how Works summarizes and prints database information.

row numbers The numbers that appear at the beginning of each row in a spreadsheet.

ruler A reference tool that is displayed at the top of a Word Processor document. You can use the ruler to change the indents and tab settings for the current paragraph or the entire document.

save To store the contents of a document in a file on a disk.

script A recorded sequence of keystrokes and commands that automates a communication task.

scroll bars The bars located at the right and bottom edges of a window, which you can use to scroll through the window using a mouse. Each bar contains scroll arrows, which you can click to scroll one line, column, or row at a time.

search characters Letters, numbers, or symbols that specify the text of an entry you want to locate using the find feature.

series A range of spreadsheet information displayed in a chart. A Y-series is a range of numbers displayed as lines or bars; an X-series is a range of text entries used to identify groups or categories of data.

settings A set of parameters that two computers use when communicating. When you send and receive files, both computers must use the same settings.

shortcut key combinations Keys you can press to execute commands without using the menu system.

shortcuts Icons on your desktop you can double-click to start applications.

sign off To type the information required to disconnect from an information service or bulletin board system.

sign on To complete a connection to an information service or bulletin board system by typing a user ID, password, or other required information.

sign-on script A recorded sequence of keystrokes and commands that automates the procedure to connect to another computer, an on-line service, or a bulletin board.

sizing handles Small squares on the borders of a highlighted field or other object. You can drag a handle to resize the field or object.

sort To arrange data in a specified order. For example, you might sort a list of names and addresses into alphabetical order by last name.

source file The file from which you copy linked information.

spreadsheet A grid of 256 columns and 16,384 rows in which you enter text, numbers, and formulas.

synonym A different word with the same or similar meaning as another word. You can use the thesaurus in the word processor to find synonyms for words in your documents.

tables Formatted blocks of text that are organized in cells like a spreadsheet.

taskbar An element located on the desktop in Windows 95. You can click the taskbar to open menus to select programs.

TaskWizard An automated process for creating documents and forms. When you use a TaskWizard, you answer questions about the document or form you want to create and the TaskWizard performs the steps according to your instructions.

template A predesigned document with the basic layout, formatting, and sample text already in place. You can use a template to create new documents.

toolbar A row of buttons in an application window you can click to execute commands.

toolbox In Microsoft Draw, a set of tools on the left side of the drawing window that you can use to draw shapes and lines, add text, and view different parts of a drawing.

upload To send information to another computer user, an information service, or a bulletin board system.

wildcard character A single character that you use to take the place of a character or a group of characters when you search for text or filter a database.

window A rectangular area on the screen in which you can display and work with documents in an application.

WordArt A feature you can use to create text objects with special effects.

word wrap A feature that automatically begins a new line of text when the current line reaches the right margin.

X-series A group of related data plotted along the vertical edge of a chart.

Y-series The data plotted along the horizontal line at the bottom of a chart.

Index

IMPORTANT — READ CAREFULLY BEFORE OPENING SOFTWARE PACKET(S).

By opening the sealed packet(s) containing the software, you indicate your acceptance of the following Microsoft License Agreement.

Microsoft License Agreement

MICROSOFT LICENSE AGREEMENT
(Single User Products)

This is a legal agreement between you (either an individual or an entity) and Microsoft Corporation. By opening the sealed software packet(s) you are agreeing to be bound by the terms of this agreement. If you do not agree to the terms of this agreement, promptly return the book, including the unopened software packet(s), to the place you obtained it for a full refund.

MICROSOFT SOFTWARE LICENSE

1. GRANT OF LICENSE. Microsoft grants to you the right to use one copy of the Microsoft software program included with this book (the "SOFTWARE") on a single terminal connected to a single computer. The SOFTWARE is in "use" on a computer when it is loaded into temporary memory (i.e., RAM) or installed into permanent memory (e.g., hard disk, CD-ROM, or other storage device) of that computer. You may not network the SOFTWARE or otherwise use it on more than one computer or computer terminal at the same time.

2. COPYRIGHT. The SOFTWARE is owned by Microsoft or its suppliers and is protected by United States copyright laws and international treaty provisions. Therefore, you must treat the SOFTWARE like any other copyrighted material (e.g., a book or musical recording) except that you may either (a) make one copy of the SOFTWARE solely for backup or archival purposes, or (b) transfer the SOFTWARE to a single hard disk provided you keep the original solely for backup or archival purposes. You may not copy the written materials accompanying the SOFTWARE.

3. OTHER RESTRICTIONS. You may not rent or lease the SOFTWARE, but you may transfer the SOFTWARE and accompanying written materials on a permanent basis provided you retain no copies and the recipient agrees to the terms of this Agreement. You may not reverse engineer, decompile, or disassemble the SOFTWARE. If the SOFTWARE is an update or has been updated, any transfer must include the most recent update and all prior versions.

4. DUAL MEDIA SOFTWARE. If the SOFTWARE package contains both 3.5" and 5.25" disks, then you may use only the disks appropriate for your single-user computer. You may not use the other disks on another computer or loan, rent, lease, or transfer them to another user except as part of the permanent transfer (as provided above) of all SOFTWARE and written materials.

5. LANGUAGE SOFTWARE. If the SOFTWARE is a Microsoft language product, then you have a royalty-free right to reproduce and distribute executable files created using the SOFTWARE. If the language product is a Basic or COBOL product, then Microsoft grants you a royalty-free right to reproduce and distribute the run-time modules of the SOFTWARE provided that you: (a) distribute the run-time modules only in conjunction with and as a part of your software product; (b) do not use Microsoft's name, logo, or trademarks to market your software product; (c) include a valid copyright notice on your software product; and (d) agree to indemnify, hold harmless, and defend Microsoft and its suppliers from and against any claims or lawsuits, including attorneys' fees, that arise or result from the use or distribution of your software product. The "run-time modules" are those files in the SOFTWARE that are identified in the accompanying written materials as required during execution of your software program. The run-time modules are limited to run-time files, install files, and ISAM and REBUILD files. If required in the SOFTWARE documentation, you agree to display the designated patent notices on the packaging and in the README file of your software product.

LIMITED WARRANTY

LIMITED WARRANTY. Microsoft warrants that (a) the SOFTWARE will perform substantially in accordance with the accompanying written materials for a period of ninety (90) days from the date of receipt, and (b) any hardware accompanying the SOFTWARE will be free from defects in materials and workmanship under normal use and service for a period of one (1) year from the date of receipt. Any implied warranties on the SOFTWARE and hardware are limited to ninety (90) days and one (1) year, respectively. Some states/countries do not allow limitations on duration of an implied warranty, so the above limitation may not apply to you.

CUSTOMER REMEDIES. Microsoft's and its suppliers' entire liability and your exclusive remedy shall be, at Microsoft's option, either (a) return of the price paid, or (b) repair or replacement of the SOFTWARE or hardware that does not meet Microsoft's Limited Warranty and which is returned to Microsoft with a copy of your receipt. This Limited Warranty is void if failure of the SOFTWARE or hardware has resulted from accident, abuse, or misapplication. Any replacement SOFTWARE or hardware will be warranted for the remainder of the original warranty period or thirty (30) days, whichever is longer. Outside the United States, these remedies are not available without proof of purchase from an authorized non-U.S. source.

NO OTHER WARRANTIES. Microsoft and its suppliers disclaim all other warranties, either express or implied, including, but not limited to implied warranties of merchantability and fitness for a particular purpose, with regard to the SOFTWARE, the accompanying written materials, and any accompanying hardware. This limited warranty gives you specific legal rights. You may have others which vary from state/country to state/country.

NO LIABILITY FOR CONSEQUENTIAL DAMAGES. In no event shall Microsoft or its suppliers be liable for any damages whatsoever (including without limitation, damages for loss of business profits, business interruption, loss of business information, or any other pecuniary loss) arising out of the use of or inability to use this Microsoft product, even if Microsoft has been advised of the possibility of such damages. Because some states/countries do not allow the exclusion or limitation of liability for consequential or incidental damages, the above limitation may not apply to you.

U.S. GOVERNMENT RESTRICTED RIGHTS

The SOFTWARE and documentation are provided with RESTRICTED RIGHTS. Use, duplication, or disclosure by the Government is subject to restrictions as set forth in subparagraph (c)(1)(ii) of The Rights in Technical Data and Computer Software clause at DFARS 252.227-7013 or subparagraphs (c)(1) and (2) of the Commercial Computer Software — Restricted Rights 48 CFR 52.227-19, as applicable. Manufacturer is Microsoft Corporation, One Microsoft Way, Redmond, WA 98052-6399.

This Agreement is governed by the laws of the State of Washington.

Should you have any questions concerning this Agreement, or if you desire to contact Microsoft for any reason, please write: Microsoft Sales and Service, One Microsoft Way, Redmond, WA 98052-6399.

CORPORATE ORDERS

If you're placing a large-volume corporate order for additional copies of this *Step by Step* title, or for any other Microsoft Press book, you may be eligible for our corporate discount.

Call **1-800-888-3303, ext. 62669,** for details.

The Step by Step Practice Files Disk

The enclosed 3.5-inch disk contains timesaving, ready-to-use practice files that complement the lessons in this book. To use the practice files, you'll need the Windows 95 operating system and Works version 4 for Windows 95.

Each *Step by Step* lesson uses practice files from the disk. Before you begin the *Step by Step* lessons, read the "Getting Ready" section of the book for easy instructions telling how to install the files on your computer's hard disk. As you work through each lesson, be sure to follow the instructions for renaming the practice files so that you can go through a lesson more than once if you need to.

Please take a few moments to read the License Agreement on the previous page before using the enclosed disk.